T0375200

Financial Valuation of Employee Stock Ownership Plan Shares

Larry R. Cook
CPA, ABV, CBA, CDFA

WILEY

John Wiley & Sons, Inc.

For general information on our other products and services or for technical support, please contact our Customer Care Department within the United States at (800) 762-2974, from outside the United States at (317) 572-3993, or fax (317) 572-4002.

Wiley also publishes its books in a variety of electronic formats. Some content that appears in print may not be available in electronic books. For more information about Wiley products, visit our website at www.wiley.com.

ISBN-13 978-0-471-67847-2
ISBN-10 0-471-67847-3

10 9 8 7 6 5 4 3 2 1

From the Author

Most who know me know that I am passionate about some things in life. The pursuit of broad-based equitable equity sharing is one of them. Rather than rehearse the sheepskins hanging on the wall, I feel compelled to share a brief glimpse of my background in reference to this work.

My parents owned and worked in a small printing business in Houston, Texas, Northside Printing. My brother, Ken, and I experienced firsthand the long work hours, hardships, sacrifices, joys, and business cycles during the family's 20 years of private business ownership. Unknowingly, we both inherited the spirit of freedom and satisfaction that comes from a job well done and the pride of ownership we felt when we told others "our parents own their own business." I am forever grateful to my dad, Rudy, and mom, Ruth, for their encouragement, integrity, endurance, and unwavering support. Thanks, Mom and Ken (and wish you were here to see this, Dad)!

My first career job following graduation from college was with an industrial electrical contractor in Houston, Texas, Wolfenson Electric, Inc. As I recall, when I started there, we employed about 90 employees. When I left, that total was about 400. Little did I know that over my 10 years' employment tenure there, I would become a member of management, an officer of the company, an administrator of two employee retirement plans and a welfare medical insurance trust, an employee owner through management offerings of direct shares of common stock, and fully vested as an employee participant in an Employee Stock Ownership Plan and Profit Sharing Plan.

Knowing what I know now, it took extraordinary forward thinking and trust to accept recommendations from a young and aggressive "college kid" on the part of the owner, Sid Wolfenson. This company afforded me the opportunity to learn the importance of evenhandedness and doing the right thing by the company's employees from the President, Elbert Scribner Jr., in those years immediately following the implementation of ERISA. These experiences led me to the profession of business valuation and the co-authoring of one valuation book and the authoring of this work.

Sid, I will never forget my foundation of business understanding and your making me "pack my powder" before bringing ideas to you, and Junior, your word and handshake were bonds that made the company an inspirational place for those seeking not only a career but a positive work atmosphere. Thanks, Sid and Junior!

In the 23-plus years that have followed, my professional course has been filled with many experiences and people. During several years working in valuation and practice sales, Mike Hill and Roger Hill of the then–Business & Professional Associates not only mentored me but also were fun fellows with whom to work and be associated. Thanks, Mike and Roger!

Working with my public accounting partner, Ernest "Rocky" Revia, III for nine years honed skill sets in accounting, auditing, tax controversy representation, negotiation, income, gift and estate tax, acquisition of other firms, admissions, and divestitures of partners. I worked with a diverse mix of business owners on a variety of issues. Rocky, I shall never forget the meager practice beginnings, lessons learned, and the good times in our friendship and partnership. Thanks, Rocky!

The contributing authors cited in the next few pages are individuals that have my utmost respect and admiration. Over my career, I've had the joy of meeting and working with many bright, well-versed, talented, and energetic people. Some I have known through career pursuits, others their entire lives, but all are made of the right stuff. Thanks, Susan, Judy, Don, Tony, Carey, Tom, and James for your contribution to this work!

To Michelle "Shell" Bobo, for your "head to the grindstone" in that small office compiling extensive research of a topic you initially knew nothing about but assisted in coordinating, corralling, writing, and pulling it all together. To Delores Trapani, thanks for keeping me focused, diverting phone calls and staying late to get this work out. Mega thanks, Dee and Shell!

To Louisa Brown, Eva Lang, Susan Parmlee, and Judy Lee for their edit comments. To Jim Hitchner for allowing me to participate in coauthoring *Financial Valuation Applications and Models* that started this process. To Don Drisdale and Chris Best for their counsel and discussions on ESOP topics.

Thanks to my daughter, Dallas, for your positive attitude and understanding why dad spent some time away from home on weekends and late nights the last summer before your freshman year at Pepperdine to get this book completed. You'll always be my "Red Princess."

When I consider all the education, training, people, lectures, seminars, conventions, lessons, and experiences of life, far and away the most enduring, consistent, supportive and unwavering, has been my wife, consultant, and best friend, Nancy. There are no words that can adequately describe what you have meant and do mean to me! You're my real hero in life! I love you and thank you!

Contents

Preface

What can be expected from this book? Is it worth the price of admission? Who will be best served by spending the time reading its contents, cover to cover? Is this another how-to book? Is it a publish-or-perish text? Will it meet the expectations of being informative and relevant?

There are many fine texts and authors that cover numerous topics in the financial valuation of private businesses. This book will focus on giving the business appraiser, a financial advisor to the plan trustee, the underlying logic, theory, laws, and rules. Its aim is to be useful, complete, and practical. Hopefully, this will fulfill its objective specific to the financial valuation of private equity shares owned by an Employee Stock Ownership Plan.

FORMULA FOR AN EMPLOYEE STOCK OWNERSHIP PLAN

Is there a formula for an Employee Stock Ownership Plan? **Yes**, there is, and it's best to put this up front and from the beginning!

> *ESOP = an equity investment(s) in a private company packaged in an ERISA wrapper!*

Algebraically expressed:

$$ESOP = (EQ \pm INV + PVT + CO) \times ERISA$$

ESOP = Employee stock ownership plan
Equity (EQ) = Common or preferred stock
Investment (INV) = Possibility of loss/Optimism of gain
Private (PVT) = Closely held business
Company (CO) = Plan sponsoring corporation
ERISA = Employee Retirement Income Security Act

(This is for ESOPs holding equity shares of private companies, those for public companies with active markets sip from a different cup.) Please hang on to this formula throughout the book. It is the bedrock for those using this text as a guide in the financial valuation of private company ESOP shares.

SUITABILITY AND THE ESOP

What differentiates this retirement investment strategy from conventional investment portfolio management theory? In a word: *suitability*. Suitability is defined in *The American Heritage Dictionary of the English Language* as "appropriate to the purpose or an occasion." It stems from the investment community's fiduciary duty to provide recommendations that are appropriate in the circumstances to that individual customer.

In most ESOPs, there is no portfolio, no asset diversification, no income or growth choice, no portfolio rebalancing or asset allocations, no sector rotation, no control by the employee over trading in their best interests, no "good until cancel orders," no stop losses or limit orders, no options or warrants or hedges, no straddles, or buy or sell signals or market timing, no equity remedy from capital markets, no primary or secondary offerings, little or no immediate liquidity—it's a private company equity incentive stock awards plan designed entirely for all (eligible) employees.

In other words, an ESOP is all about one company called the sponsor and its management, operations, culture, employees, market share, customers, profitability, and longevity. Sponsor company shares held as an investment by an ESOP in this environment are subject to market and value pressures and swings.

EMPLOYEE CULTURE AND THE ESOP

Who in the world would make such an investment? The answer: Welcome to capitalism and private business ownership. Private business ownership is what makes capitalism and the United States of America the most unique and powerful economic force in the world. Can private business ownership be shared through an ERISA plan ESOP? You bet!

Entrepreneurial ownership is the incubation of independent thought with the challenge of competing for a better way of doing things in order to achieve extraordinary returns and a better life. Entrepreneurs have some semblance of control over their career and future earnings. It's down, it's clean, and it's very true. Is it misunderstood? Yes. Is it worth the risk to consider implementing an ESOP? Absolutely.

How in the world could such an investment strategy so uncertain, so seemingly frail, find its place in a qualified retirement plan, be governed by ERISA, and be laced with tax incentives? And how did it find its way to and get through Congress in the first place? What a novel idea—employees actually having the opportunity to be enriched through a beneficial ownership of equity in the very company in which they work.

We will cover this, and much more, in this complete guide to *Financial Valuation of Employee Stock Ownership Plan Shares*.

About the Editor and Author

L arry R. Cook, CPA, ABV, CBA, CDFA, is the owner of Larry R. Cook & Associates, PC, a financial services firm located in Houston, Texas. His practice focus is on business valuation, collaborative law acting as a financial neutral, financial advisor, and succession planning, which includes wealth management, asset protection, and related services to the private business owner. He has 32 years of experience in business valuation and related fields while in industry and private practice.

Larry is a certified public accountant (CPA), and is accredited in business valuation (ABV) by the American Institute of Certified Public Accountants. He earned the designation of certified business appraiser (CBA) in 1985 from The Institute of Business Appraisers. He holds a Series 7, 63, and 65 securities license, and Group 1 and 4 insurance licenses. He is also a registered investment advisor actively engaged in wealth management. Larry is a certified divorce financial analyst (CDFA) and has completed advanced family mediation training (alternative dispute resolution) and collaborative law training.

Larry graduated with a BBA from Sam Houston State University, Huntsville, Texas, in 1972, and was a member of the first graduating class of accounting majors from the university. Larry has served in a number of capacities and committees for national, state, and local professional organizations. He is founder and director of The Texas Association of Collaborative Financial Practitioners. He is currently a member of the International Academy of Collaborative Professional (IACP) and the AICPA Business Valuation Litigation Service Executive Committee. He previously served as the president of the Financial Consulting Group, chairman of the ABV Credential Committee for the AICPA, a past board of director member of the Texas Society of CPAs, as regional governor and on the Business Valuation Standards for Professional Practice Committee of the Institute of Business Appraisers, and on the advisory board of the North Harris Montgomery Community College-Accounting Advisory.

He has been recognized for his service to the profession, which include being awarded the AICPA "Business Valuation Hall of Fame" award, the "Distinguished Service to the Profession" award by the Houston Chapter of CPAs, "Lone Star Path Finders" award by the Texas Society of CPAs, and "Outstanding Committee xiv | About the Editor and Author

Chairman" award by the Houston Chapter of CPAs. Larry coauthored the *Financial Valuation, Applications and Models,* by James R. Hitchner (published by John Wiley & Sons).

He has provided expert testimony in U.S. Tax Court, on valuations of private entities, on marketability and minority interest discounting, on purchase price allocation of intangibles, noncompetition agreements and common stock value, and in civil courts on divorce matters and factoring and usury contract damages. He has been engaged in numerous valuations, estate, and income tax disputes representing taxpayers before the Internal Revenue Service at the appeals and district counsel level. He has obtained a private letter ruling from the Internal Revenue Service, specific to community property state valuations of intangibles and decedent estates. Larry is frequently retained for valuation issues resulting in depositions, mediations, arbitrations, damage and losses, and private settlements in valuation and related financial interests. He has been engaged and assisted clients in the sale, merger and acquisition of businesses and business interests, provided fire and business interruption studies and negotiations, and worked with decedent estates, asset protection, succession, wealth management, and wealth transfer plans.

He has participated as an instructor for courses on a wide range of subjects for a number of audiences such as the AICPA, TSCPA, IBA, and FCG. Some of the topics covered were "Collaborative Law Training for the Financial Advisor," "Financial Forecasting," "Financial Analysis," "How to Value an Accounting Practice," "Stretch IRA Plans—Getting the Most Out of Your Benefit Plan," "Employee Stock Ownership Plans," "Justification of Purchase—Testing Your Valuation," "Discounts," "Family Limited Partnerships," and "So You Want to Be a Business Appraiser" (game show) "Business Succession Planning." He also served on several panels for various question and answer sessions at national conferences and as a panelist for three closed-circuit television programs specific to business valuation.

About the Contributing Authors

Michelle Bobo, J.D., is an attorney licensed to practice in Texas. She is a graduate from Texas A&M University and received her law degree from Washburn University School of Law. She practiced employment and labor and has had extensive experience in research and writing.

James Coleman is president of The Woodlands, Texas branch of the First National Bank of Edinburg, Texas. James has many years in the banking industry as a senior loan officer and commercial lender. He is a graduate from Baylor University.

Thomas L. "Tom" Corley, CPA/ABV, CBA, CFE, is manager of valuation services at Pattillo, Brown & Hill, LLP, of Waco, Texas. Tom actively serves as trustee for a number of small to medium-sized Employee Stock Ownership Plans throughout the continental United States and Hawaii. He holds a B.S. in Accounting and an M.S. in Business Administration from Louisiana State University.

Judy R. Lee, CPA, CDFA, is a financial analyst and consultant with Larry R. Cook & Associates, PC, Houston, Texas. She has provided tax planning, structuring, representation and business analysis, and valuation services. Judy received a bachelor of business administration in Accounting from the University of Houston, and is mediation trained.

Carey W. Lindsey, QKA, APA, is the Director of Business Development for the Loren D. Stark Company, Inc., a third-party administration firm in Houston, Texas. He provides design, implementation and administration of qualified plans, specifically Employee Stock Ownership, Defined Benefit, and 401(k) plans. Carey holds a B.S. in Finance from the University of New Orleans.

Susan D. Parmlee, CDFA, is a financial analyst and consultant with Larry R. Cook & Associates, PC, Houston, Texas. She has assisted in numerous valuation, employee benefit, tax planning, structuring, and settlement services. Susan is a graduate of Texas A&M University with a B.S. degree in Food Science and Technology, has completed courses in accounting at the University of Houston, and is mediation trained.

Anthony B. Smith (Tony), CPA, is president and CFO for Custom Forest Products, San Antonio, Texas. He has spent a career in finance and management and works in positive leadership encouragement and team building. Tony graduated from Brescia University in Owensboro, Kentucky, with a B.S. degree in Accounting.

Donald D. Stark, J.D., is president of the Loren D. Stark Company, Inc. specializing in estate analysis, pension, profit sharing, and life insurance. He is the senior attorney in the law firm of Donald D. Stark of Houston, Texas. Mr. Stark received a B.S. degree with a major in Insurance from the University of Pennsylvania, Wharton School of Business and his J.D. from South Texas College of Law.

1

Introduction to ERISA and ERISA Plans*

The employee stock ownership plan, or "ESOP," has emerged as a special qualified retirement plan that offers not only the benefits of employee ownership but additional benefits beyond what Congress ever imagined during the infancy stages of creation. Esops have, for the most part, proven to be a mechanism for creating not only increased wealth among employees and liquidity for private shareholders, but also the means for increased improvements of company production and growth, and, in many cases, stability and perpetuity.

A qualified retirement plan, such as an ESOP, in the context of this text means a retirement plan sponsored by an employer who may contribute to the plan on a tax-deductible basis as an ordinary and necessary business expense. The plan itself is a tax-exempt entity, and the beneficiaries pay no tax until the actual receipt of the deferred benefit—a unique subsidized system of wealth accumulation for retirement purposes.

HISTORY OF THE QUALIFIED RETIREMENT PLAN

Pre-ERISA

Several qualified retirement plans evolved prior to the Employee Retirement Income Security Act of 1974 (ERISA) as the result of previous tax legislation. The Revenue Act of 1921 exempted the income from a trust from current tax, the Revenue Act of 1928 permitted funding of past service liabilities, and an amendment in 1942 to the Internal Revenue Code (IRC) was designed to prevent discrimination and restrict deductions for retirement plan funding. Nevertheless, since the Internal Revenue Service (IRS) regulated retirement plans on a district-by-district basis, much inconsistency prevailed. ERISA put an end to this nonconformity, and qualified plans gained their greatest advantage.

---

*This chapter was contributed by Don Stark.

Post-ERISA

The legislation passed subsequent to ERISA contained provisions reducing the benefits of qualified plans: the Tax Equity and Fiscal Responsibility Act of 1982 (TEFRA), the Deficit Reduction Tax Act of 1984 (DEFRA), the Retirement Equity Act of 1984 (REA), the Tax Reform Act of 1986 (TRA '86), the Omnibus Budget Reconciliation Act of 1987 (OBRA '87), the Technical and Miscellaneous Revenue Act of 1988 (TAMRA), the Revenue Reconciliation Act of 1989, the Omnibus Budget Reconciliation Act of 1990, and the Unemployment Tax Act of 1992. Contrarily, most of the legislation passed subsequent to ERISA has had a positive effect on ESOPs.

Between 1955 and 1970, the IRS approved only thirty (30) plans to invest principally in employer stock, called *stock bonus plans*. During the same period, the IRS approved 93,000 profit sharing plans. It is not possible to guess how many of those profit sharing plans invested in employer stock because no guidelines existed during this time. For example, pre-ERISA profit sharing plans could purchase equipment needed by the employer and lease the equipment to the employer and receive tax-deferred income, or purchase a stockpile of raw material needed by the employer and sell it to the employer. These investment options were not permissible post-ERISA, but the ownership of employer stock became well codified by ERISA.

ERISA CODIFIES THE ESOP

ERISA first created a new concept referred to as a *party of interest*.[1] All individuals and entities who are associated in some way with the plan causing a conflict of interest are parties of interest. The concept is far reaching, but obviously, the sponsor[2] of the plan (i.e., the corporate employer), the stockholders, board of directors, employees, and plan trustee are parties of interest. ERISA also established the concept of the *prohibited transaction*,[3] which prohibits a plan from conducting any transaction with a party of interest, and the Internal Revenue Code (the Code) imposes a tax on prohibited transactions.[4]

If there were no exception to this rule, ESOPs would not be possible.

However, ERISA provides an exception to the acquisition and sale of "qualifying employer securities"[5] if done by an "eligible individual account plan"[6] for adequate consideration and no commission charged.[7]

An eligible individual account plan is a profit sharing plan, or an ESOP, merely because such a plan "explicitly provides for acquisition and holding of qualifying employer securities"[8] which is "a security issued by an employer for employees covered by the plan."[9] Therefore, if the purpose of the plan with regard to company stock is only to buy and sell such stock, the plan need only be an eligible individual account plan, thereby avoiding many of the complex and high-maintenance rules applicable to ESOPs.

There are five principal reasons why an individual account plan that is not an ESOP may not be appropriate.

1. ERISA defines an ESOP as an individual account plan that is designed to invest primarily in qualifying employer securities and meets such other requirements of IRS regulations.[10]

   What "primarily" means has not been well established, but by virtue of this aspect, it should generally be prudent for an ESOP to purchase employer stock.

2. Only a loan to an ESOP is exempt from the prohibited transaction rules.[11]

3. The nonrecognition of gain upon the sale of employer stock under IRC Sec. 1042 is available only to an ESOP.

4. Tax-deductible dividends are available to a C corporation only in conjunction with an ESOP.[12]

5. Although the Small Business Job Protection Act (1996) amended IRC Sec. 1361(c) to permit a qualified plan to be a stockholder of an S corporation, such an asset is treated as an unrelated trade or business, thereby producing a tax liability for the plan (unrelated business taxable income, or UBTI). In 1997, the code was amended exempting ESOPs from the UBTI.[13]

ERISA exempts all eligible individual account plans from ERISA diversification requirement, but such exemption would seem more applicable to ESOPs.[14] The fiduciary duties mandated by ERISA undoubtedly make the purchase of qualifying employer securities a risky proposition for an eligible individual account plan that is not an ESOP by participants who are not also principals.

USES OF AN ESOP

An ESOP has many potential uses, some of which include the following:

- Selling the company to its employees as an exit strategy for the majority owner
- Setting up a business continuation plan
- Purchasing a competitor
- Retiring a minority interest
- Raising tax-deductible working capital
- Retiring debt principal on a tax-deductible basis

No matter what the objective, benefiting from the magic of an ESOP requires only the right fact situation and compliance with certain rules.

2

Business Owner/Management Perspective*

L earning about ESOPs and their impact on employee culture and productivity
is a concept rather than a forgone conclusion to the business owner. Motivations to implement these complex plans, coupled with the learning curve and the cost, require the hardest of management deliberations. However, providing a viable alternative to sensitive and difficult ownership transfers—while at the same time affording management and other employees the opportunity to participate in a nondiscriminatory retirement plan—has real merit. It assists those equity holders interested in providing a career home within a stable work environment and an equity stake in the long-range outcome of the company.

OBSERVATION

Most business owners and management draw on their learned life experiences in managing and motivating a work force. Management styles have positively changed over the years to work in a more creative and participatory environment. Attracting and keeping quality personnel is an utmost priority for those companies that continually pursue expanding business and a healthy work environment. For the employee seeking challenge, work experiences gained from different work and compensation environments provide the reward of finding that better place, spending years in a profession with a vision, and making a mark in corporate America.

What most involved employees desire is the opportunity to participate in the capital system by ownership in their company. Many work long hours, perhaps traveling all over the world, making considerable personal sacrifices to maintain a good standard of living. They tend to associate their own self worth with that

---

*This chapter was contributed by Tony Smith.

5

of their impact on their company. It isn't surprising that most personnel know that their financial net worth can be enhanced if they participate in the value growth of their company in addition to compensation gained from their salaries. The equity owners that build successful businesses have the capability of creating enormous net worth for their families and enjoy the added privilege of social and business prestige. These same folks make up the bulk of the new money by leveraging others' energies and keeping the wealth generated by their efforts.

The potentially key employee constantly looks for that special company which wants to grow rapidly and is interested in the employee's personal financial goals for the future. The constant search for a corporate association that provides a mechanism to offer the employee an equity stake with the chance to build significant net worth helps set in motion the formula for a long-term career. An ESOP provides that anchoring basis.

Learning about ESOPs is not a course taken in school, but instead is learned because of circumstances unique to handling ownership alternatives in a succession plan for equity owners. Awareness of an ESOP as an alternative begins when a situation arises, such as a buyout of an equity shareholder, and when other shareholders and management subscribe to an employee culture of "work and think like owners."

Attending seminars or reading books on the topic can be overwhelming because plans are very complex. Learning that a quality business valuation is a key ingredient to the success of implementing a plan, together with knowledgeable financial advisors and plan administrators, cannot be overemphasized. When assessing the positives and negatives of an ESOP, several come to mind that bear summation:

- Valuations are far too complex and the implications of being wrong are too serious for amateurs.

- At first blush, the concept of using an ESOP to buy out shareholders appears to be too good to be true.

- Immediately intriguing, ESOPs require the development of financial models for implementing and visualizing how to work within a tax-free environment.

- Then comes the realization that the company could gain competitive advantage by having an ESOP.

- Additonally, an ESOP satisfies the need for the buyout of an existing shareholder while offering a like kind exchange to the selling shareholder with deferral of personal taxes to future years.

Part of the interest in working with an ESOP is that the existing shareholders create a market for their shares by implementing an ESOP. This possibility offers them a place to sell their shares and an alternative that isn't available for most private companies, barring an outright sale to another company, which may not be in their best interest. Bargaining in good faith with existing shareholders and having the ability to borrow money in a qualified plan narrows the decision for future expectations of earnings and when to anticipate the shareholders' sale of their shares.

For some companies one of the alternatives available for buying out the shareholders is to take the company public. The realities and requirements associated with the cost and energy can be daunting. Any careful deliberation about going public will likely bring a definite conclusion: "not feasible." When consultants are brought in to make suggestions about meeting the requirements of a shareholder buyout, a suitable question is, "Does this company fit the profile of a good ESOP candidate?"

A PERSONAL STORY

After more than 20 years of business experience in the financial area and practicing as a CPA with a large accounting firm and with one publicly traded company, my skills in tax and consulting were directed toward compiling financial statements and preparing tax returns, primarily for small businesses. The first 15 years of my career found me working long hours and traveling all over the world, making considerable personal sacrifice, and while I gained much in the way of valuable experience, I wanted something different.

During my second job interview for a newly created CFO role with a multistate, U.S. private-health-sector corporation seeking aggressive growth, the CEO abruptly cut me off from further selling myself, told me that he had already decided to make me an offer, and wanted to talk about my personal financial goals for the future.

From all of my earlier career experiences, I knew that I needed to participate in the equity of a company to ever have the chance to build a significant personal net worth. My introduction to ESOPs came shortly after accepting the CFO role. I had asked for what I considered a modest 3 percent of the company's common stock as part of my employment package. A few weeks later, the CEO and I settled on 2 percent, but considering my portion of the ultimately active ESOP, I would end up owning the desired 3 percent.

The day I started at the company, it had approximately 100 full-time employees in a few states, a modest infrastructure, and little in the way of debt capacity and financing. The common stock, with no viable market for its shares, was like most private companies' worth, far less than that of their big brother public companies. A year into the job our business was growing rapidly.

In the four ensuing years of my tenure there, the company was valued for ESOP shares substantially higher than any previous period or the early years' buy/sell arrangements. During that same four-year period, the company grew in revenues and margins over 2000 percent and had 1,300 full-time employees in a number of states with very significant annual revenues, elevated margins, and the prospect for continued dynamic growth in revenues and profits into the future.

I've been very blessed, and credit much of my financial wealth building to an ESOP.

My First Steps into ESOPs

How did I find my way to ESOPs? It wasn't in the CPA firm. In fact, I don't recall learning anything more in college about ESOPs than knowing it was a form of retirement plan that wouldn't likely be on the CPA exam, so I didn't waste any further time on the topic. My awareness of ESOPs didn't start until the fall of 1999, when our CEO asked me to value our company's stock. He wanted to buy out his dad and several employees who together owned about 45 percent of the stock.

I attended a business valuation conference in hopes of learning how to value our stock. Following one of the best presentations at the seminar, I introduced myself to the panel asking who they would recommend to perform a valuation in our area. The panel suggested that I call a valuator with known experience in valuations and employee stock ownership plans.

Although I was out of town at the seminar, our CEO met with his dad to discuss buying out his stock, thinking that we'd soon know the fair market value and thinking that his dad would finance the sale. What our CEO learned was that his dad wouldn't consider selling out to his son. He had plenty of financial security and was willing to take the company public and/or sell his stock to the employees.

Shortly after returning from the valuation seminar, our CEO felt the best solution for buying out the shareholders would be to take the company public. Within a few days, I replaced our small local CPA firm with one of the most highly recognized CPA firms for public companies in our regional area. The firm called for a strategic planning meeting. The CEO and I were very excited, and we were anticipating considerable discussion around the process of going public.

What we heard in the meeting came to both of us as a shock. As already noted, my primary reason for replacing our current CPA firm with this big firm was to prepare for going public. The first thing the CPAs recommended was that we remove from consideration any thoughts of going public. What they recommended was that we buy out the current shareholders through an ESOP and increase our CEO's compensation.

We held numerous discussions regarding the firm's advice and eventually agreed to proceed with an ESOP. It would be my responsibility for negotiating the purchase of the CEO's father's stock. As for the then-employees holding shares subject to stock buy-back restrictions, they really didn't have an alternative. Under the terms of their stock grant, they were obligated to transact.

I told the firm to proceed with whatever it took to bring an ESOP to life and told the CEO that I thought I could form the ESOP for about $50,000. When I again met with the CPA firm, I learned the amount would be substantially more than anticipated, over twice my anticipated budget in fees to form the ESOP. By including legal fees, the CPA firm estimated implementation of the plan would cost over three times the initial budget. It further estimated that it would take several months of work before the ESOP would be viable. I was too embarrassed to tell the CEO how much the new estimated amount would be. As a defensive measure and to save face, I called the financial advisor-appraiser whom I felt would be more reasonably priced.

The decision to call the financial advisor probably saved my job. The financial advisor, understanding that I was value conscious and realizing the long-term potential of our account, made an interesting proposal. He suggested that we could team up with an ESOP administrator, who also happened to be an attorney with whom he had done several deals before. The approach was to keep the ESOP simple; as he explained, it is always possible to add benefits to an ESOP, but it is harder to take them away. The financial advisor and the ESOP administrator agreed to start up our ESOP, including legal fees, for what were much more reasonable fees and timing, and we early retired the other firm.

With the ESOP documents being drafted and the plan in the works, I began the task of negotiating the stock purchase with the CEO's dad. His dad could be a very tough businessman, who had once asked me to coach all—several hundred—of our local employees on their facial expressions. He expected people to smile in public. Like his son, he was an engineer. They both loved detail and were notorious for asking a million questions. They liked dealing with people who could answer questions on the fly.

This is where the choice to use the financial advisor paid off. During what turned out to be the last of a series of meetings where the CEO's dad agreed to sell his stock, the financial advisor was able to answer all the hardball questions that were posed to him. I learned an invaluable lesson from that experience, that as much as the technical side was important, so too were the personalities involved. I went into the meeting thinking we could buy his stock for about the same per share price paid to those shareholders with shares subject to a purchase agreement. It did not work out exactly as I planned. These issues were considered in the negotiation:

- Years ago, the CEO had agreed to a minimum price for a certain block of shares. It was documented in the corporate minutes. When taking this into consideration, it resulted in the CEO's dad, with no share restrictions, receiving more per share while the employees were being offered and received according to their share agreement. I was faced with the reality of how to explain this event to the work force.

- The bank involved as the financier was willing to amortize the ESOP's stock purchase note over five years. The CEO's dad insisted in the negotiation that he should be paid off in no more than four years. Three years into the deal, the CEO's dad reminded the bank that he only had one more year to be paid off. Another experience lesson: When dealing with ESOPs, I strongly recommend that all promises and/or changes be placed in writing. This situation caused considerable grief for more than three years, although it was eventually satisfactorily resolved.

- Going into the negotiation, the CEO asked that I buy enough of his father's shares that his post-transaction residual ownership interest would be less than 4.99 percent of the company because regulations of the industry sector we participated in required that all shareholders with 5 percent or more ownership interest be fingerprinted every time we opened a new location. With our rapid expansion plans, the CEO's dad was being fingerprinted frequently.

- The introduction of the tax-deferred benefit of IRC § 1042 sealed the deal, as the qualified replacement property options, with their extended holding period to maintain deferred status, was the kicker needed to close the deal.

After a few hours working through the details with the financial advisor's assistance, I settled with the CEO's dad. He agreed to sell about 32 percent of the company in a single leveraged buyout with the ESOP. By design, our ESOP was to borrow the funds from a bank. To entice the bank to lend the money, the CEO's dad, who was required by the provisions of the like kind exchange rules under § 1042 to invest all of the proceeds in marketable securities, would then be pledged to the bank as collateral. The deal went together, and at this point it looked as though we were all winners. The bank note was amortized to pay down the bank note quarterly. Each quarter as I paid down the principal, the bank agreed to release an equal amount of the seller's pledged securities. It worked, at least for a while.

After the close of the deal, I was celebrating its success, for which I believe the financial advisor deserved most of the credit. The CEO's dad had a substantial sum sitting in a virtually no-risk fund, returning about 1 percent. Pursuant to the code section, the seller had up to one year to invest the funds in qualified securities. The bank provided the CEO's dad with a listing of high-quality rated stocks that were acceptable to the bank as collateral. I was not involved in the stock selection. That was a personal choice to which I was not privy. What I did learn was that I and the public stock quickly fell from their previously elevated status.

Within a couple of months, the CEO called me into his office. He was quite disturbed by the fact that his dad's publicly traded, quality stock investment portfolio had already lost 20 percent of its value. As CFO of the company and trustee of the ESOP, action was required. The impact of such a large decline in value triggered a breach in a loan covenant that required the company to make corrections. By contract with the bank, the company was in a position to advance the equivalent of a prepayment of a full year of note payments because the portfolio value (collateral) had fallen below the debt margin requirement.

Within a year, the seller's value of the shares had fallen another 20 percent. Once again, a prepayment was made of another year of note payments to meet the bank's requirement. Over the next year the investment portfolio remained constant. From inception of the ESOP to three years later, the seller had lost 40 percent of his investment portfolio while the ESOP's portfolio increased substantially. The 4.99 percent that the seller retained continued to grow in value. I suppose he found consolation in the fact that he so generously spread wealth to the employees, as I don't recall him ever expressing regret for having sold his stock.

With the significant growth of our company came significant bonuses. At that time, all of the company executives owned stock options that were starting to vest. We were a young leadership team, a few of whom still owned starter homes. We were all growing restless with what to do with our new riches. The youngest member of our executive team started construction on a new home. He was a very conservative type who was risk evasive. While our stock was increasing rapidly, he was of the opinion that a bird in the hand is worth much more than two in the bush. He asked the CEO if he could cash in his vested options. Our CEO was committed to keeping the benefits and compensation fair across the team. He was faced with an interesting issue. Do I buy the stock now at today's per-share value, or next year at what would likely be a significantly higher price—or in a few years more at an even potentially higher price?

Included in the options plan were terms that allowed the executives to sell to outsiders. The company, of course, had the first right of refusal. Outsiders were interested in the stock, and the CEO had to do something. The ESOP was in a good cash position because the company had been converted to an S corporation the year following the transaction with the selling shareholder, and dividends were primarily paid for income tax considerations of the other outside shareholders as they had been paid into the plan and resided in the form of cash.

ESOPs by design invest primarily in company stock. It made perfect sense to buy a number of shares from treasury, making funds available to exercise the options held by the executives who started working for the company when the stock was worth much less. Two years before, six executives had reported to the CEO. They were all more or less at the same level in the options plan. Three of us were holding a significant number of options, while the other three were held fewer shares. The CEO wanted all of us to be in at about the same number of shares.

The CEO had to decide the market price to exercise the options. At the time, I was trustee and had to resign immediately because of the obvious conflict of interest. The CEO replaced me as trustee. After resigning, I then provided financial modeling under certain assumptions to assist in arriving at a reasonable per share value. A few months earlier, the CEO's dad had been interested in selling a portion of his 4.99 percent to the ESOP. At that time, the financial advisor had advised me to discount the already discounted minority price by an additional amount since the ESOP was not obligated to make such an acquisition. He stated that the ESOP share valuation was based on circumstances, such as the put right, which were part of the adequate consideration provisions of the Department of Labor.

As trustee, I was to negotiate, again in good faith and for the benefit of the employees, to obtain a favorable price to the plan. Although we didn't do a transaction with the CEO's dad at that time, the discount logic stuck. As for price, the financial advisor had just recently issued an estimate as part of the annual ESOP stock valuation for the fiscal period ended. As for the options, we were not scheduled to receive the funds for several months from the ESOP value at year end. By then, our stock would likely substantially increase because we were growing so rapidly. In any case, we more or less accepted a discounted price, and the options were exercised.

The CEO asked me to tell him how many shares the young executive who was building the house would need to sell in order to pay for his new home in cash. I had to find out how much he was paying for the house and estimate his federal income tax rate. Under this scenario, he would need to exercise a significant amount of his options. Like the other executives, he did not have enough vested shares at that time to make it work and was unable to buy the house. To be fair, the CEO exercised his power to accelerate the option vesting for all proportionately.

Four years into this business, after growing from 100 to 1,300 employees, the CEO and I agreed to go our separate ways. I had wanted more input into the operations of the company and wanted the ESOP to begin to diversify its now mounting holdings and use its cash as leverage to buy other businesses. The CEO wanted another direction. Fortunately, we arrived at an amicable separation and have maintained our friendship. The stock optioned cash distribution was sufficient for me to move forward.

Upon my departure, I wasn't sure what I would do. The one thing I was certain of was that I wanted to be in charge of another ESOP, but this time, I wanted the ESOP to own 100 percent of the stock, to grow internally, and/or to buy other businesses. A CPA friend introduced me to a partner in his firm who worked on ESOPs, who then introduced me to a client of his who was considering selling to an ESOP. He hired me under a consulting contract to create a 30 percent owned ESOP. I was excited about putting the deal together, but wasn't planning on working long-term because I wanted to be a part of a 100 percent ESOP.

After the first month of my engagement, I pointed out that the existing CFO was not a good fit for the company. The CEO then hired me full time as CFO, with the understanding that I implement a purchase of the company over some reasonable period of time through an ESOP. Within what felt like a few days, he asked me to put the ESOP on hold and focus on cleaning up whatever problems needed to be fixed. Six weeks into the job, I found myself working much longer hours than I had intended.

After a few months as the new CFO, I fell ill for some time, but within a day of my return, the CEO openly discussed with me his desire to sell the company. He was approaching a mature business age and wanted to do some other things in his life. He promised to take care of me if the new owners didn't want me to stay on board. He then asked me what I'd do if I were in his shoes. I dug down to the deepest levels of my heart and shared with him my honest feelings. I told him that, given the culture of the company and his commitment to the employees, I would sell out to an ESOP. Asking why, I explained to him that through the experience of my recent illness, I had realized that the material things in my life meant nothing compared to the people. I expressed to him that whether he sold to an ESOP or to an outsider, he'd still receive his money. I went on further to explain that an outsider would likely break up the company and terminate several employees. In addition, I explained that it didn't feel to me that he was ready to walk away from the company, at least not immediately.

I suggested that by selling to the ESOP, he could help with customer relations, about which he was very passionate. He asked me how much I would sell. I said 100 percent. He then looked me in the eyes and asked if it could be done by fiscal year-end, which was only five weeks away. I said, yes, I could make it happen. He then stated that that is what he wanted to do—to sell 100 percent to an ESOP, and that he would act as the bank and that the ESOP could make the payments to him.

I immediately called into action the ESOP team—the financial advisor-appraiser, the plan administrator for the ESOP, the trustee counsel, and plan design counsel. We did pull off the transaction in time, but we had to overcome some interesting hurdles in doing so.

Several weeks prior to fiscal year-end I had agreed with the CEO on a price range for the business. Two weeks before the closing, I hired our CPA firm to start due diligence work on our most significant asset, inventory. We performed a physical inventory at the close of business on the last day of the fiscal year. It took a few weeks of work to wrap up the numbers. Inventory and certain balance sheet accounts were overstated. Some months later, we were able to resolve the inventory issue and the valuation of the company. Although we did experience a problem with the assets, we made strategic moves that would assure earnings would soon be on track with projections and exceed our original expectations. Monthly sales continued to push to new levels, ahead of what was planned for in year three.

KEY POINTS

As you can see from my experiences, ESOPs can be very challenging, yet rewarding. This chapter concludes with several lessons that I've learned over the past five years of focusing my time and efforts on S Corp ESOPs:

Valuable Lessons

- *Make use of the psychology of the deal.* The personalities involved in negotiating the sale transaction are more important than having added technical knowledge.

- *Don't be intimidated by ESOP startup times.* It doesn't take a year, as many people believe. The legal work can be done from start to finish in less than two months.

- *Orderly books are important.* The cleaner your financial books and records, the quicker you can finish the due diligence and the valuation.

- *ESOPs are a mid-market product.* The large accounting firms are not as well versed on ESOPs. Money was expended that was not necessary in training firms. Get competent people with knowledge and experience in ESOP transactions, from the initial feasibility studies to completion.

- *The term "employee participant" is referred to frequently with ESOPs.* It means all plan eligible personnel. In a nutshell, you can make just about any decision or change to your plan document as long as it benefits the employee participant.

Communication

- *Documents that I felt were simple to understand were still voted too complex.* As a finance professional, I've been advised to stop drafting documents for lower-level personnel.

- *Create a Web site on your intranet to store your plan document, plan summary, annual audit report, and any other pertinent data.* You're required to report this data. It will save time and money by reporting electronically.

- *Statement presentation is important.* Work hard to help employees understand their annual statement. Use arrows with boxes of text, explaining in simple terms what each number means.

- *Do not promise a specific value.* In my first ESOP, the CEO regularly communicated to employees that their stock could be worth a substantial amount per share in time. Don't play games with the work force. They can't be fooled with hype and overzealous talk.

- *Explain death benefits.* I did a poor job of communicating death benefits in my first ESOP. Two employees died in the first year. Under our plan, vesting was accelerated to 100 percent immediately upon death. The beneficiaries had no idea that their loved one had any death benefits, so initially, the families did not realize that they had financial protection. The two cases paid out substantial sums, and it was rewarding to see them receive this as part of a plan.

- *I highly recommend keeping detailed minutes.* Years into a deal, someone will recall something he or she thinks the trustee communicated. I recommend documenting the logic supporting why the trustee agreed to take particular action on any ESOP topic.

- *Allocation accuracy—triple-check your work.* It's 500 times harder to fix an ESOP allocation inaccuracy after the fact. Spend some time seriously thinking of the best method of reallocating shares of terminated employees. You don't have to allocate in the same way as regular shares which are released for allocation, based on paying down ESOP debt.

- *Your trustee and/or a delegate from your company should attend at least one or more ESOP-related seminars per year.* ESOPs are highly regulated and the penalties for errors are severe. Don't buy the valuation software offered for sale at the valuation seminars. I found that I never had the time to figure out how to really use this software. Let your valuation financial advisor keep up with and develop that.

Valuations

- *Nearly every appraiser I meet wants to do my valuation.* I believe they enjoy preparing valuations much more than tax or other financial work. Be prepared to say no.

- *Plan for the valuation to take considerable time.* It's a lot of work, expect it to take at least one month or two beyond your year-end closing or financial audit completion date.

- *Make the executives write the executive portion of the company profile.* In the valuation or other assessment of the company profile with the appraiser's interview with management, a most important section is a write-up or organizational chart, if included, about the executives. I solved this by making our executives write that piece. You can't satisfy them with whatever you say. If they don't write it, be sure to let them at least proofread what you say about them before finalizing.

- *Valuation professionals are great ESOP consultants.* The financial advisor consultants earned more money answering various questions throughout the year than by doing the valuation.

- *Preparing valuations more frequently than annually are often impractical.* Our company was growing so fast that we asked the appraiser to give us a price on daily valuations. We wanted the employees to feel as though they were on the trading floor on Wall Street. After considerable planning by the appraiser, we found that the cost was absurdly high.

- *Make sure the CEO understands the purpose of the valuation.* The CEO of my first ESOP never believed that the valuation was anything more than preparing a forecast and then plugging several numbers into a valuation model. Appraisers should make it a point to be available and present, if requested, to explain to the executive team the basis of what can be done to further enhance the value of their company (another great benefit of the ESOP and usage of the appraiser as a financial advisor to the trustee).

- *Know your limits.* As trustee, I wanted more frequent valuations but was afraid to do them myself for fear of having too much of an adjustment between my estimate and that of the appraiser.

- *You need to learn about the valuation term "adequate consideration," discussed further in Chapter 13 of this book.* The appraiser uses this term often.

SUMMARY

ESOPs require a commitment in time, money, and energies. There is no better plan for the company that has the culture and with which the plan is suitable. Much goes into the preparation, deal making, transaction, transition, documentation, and postadministration and detail of the plan. Decisions are made quickly, and the deal typically comes down to a few days.

Most business owners will experience the impact of an ESOP only once in their career. Positive and negative experiences are a fact of any businessperson's life. What is paramount is a thorough understanding of the process and the realities of adding owners who are your employees to the mix. If that makes sense, then there is a basis for tremendous rewards. If that is not the case and the deal goes forward, the odds may shift away from ideal.

The ESOP can make perfectly good financial sense and not fit the culture, or vice versa. There is only one way to know for sure. A careful and thorough analysis of management and employee culture should include input not only from shareholders and management but from human resource personnel in assessing if an ESOP is right for the subject company. Planning and timing are very important aspects of the feasibility and implementation of a plan.

3

Who Is a Good Candidate for an ESOP, and Why?

It has been estimated that within the next 10 years, Baby-Boomer business owners will transact a whopping $6 trillion in business interest transfers. Which of these companies are candidates for an ESOP? Not surprisingly, an ESOP is on the radar for many owners, with the acceptance of qualifying S corporation shareholdings in ESOPs, a favorable and reasonable lending environment, and a favorable tax impact to the outside shareholder and employee participant. With the rise in popularity of ESOPs, more companies now consider whether it would be beneficial to set up an ESOP. Helpful research has been conducted since the emergence of ESOPs in an attempt to facilitate outside shareholder owners in making an informed determination.

THE BENEFITS

The first step is for a company to consider the benefits of creating an ESOP. Although differing circumstances—such as the market, industry, and the plan for the future unique to each individual company—will determine the focal benefit(s), the following are some of the most commonly cited benefits among business owners:

- *Contributions to the ESOP are tax deductible.* Like most other qualified retirement plans, company contributions to an ESOP, as well as contributions within certain limits to repay the loan, are tax deductible. Unlike other loans, where only the interest is tax deductible, within an ESOP a company can also deduct the principal.

- *ESOPs provide shareholder and/or corporate liquidity.* Pretax dollars become available to finance company growth and/or to create ownership liquidity at the time of individual employee retirement. Because the sponsor

19

company can take a tax deduction for stock or cash contributions made to an ESOP, there is a viable mechanism to provide needed funds on a tax enhanced/deductible basis to accomplish improvements in needed cash flow and working capital. Additionally, an ESOP can provide enhanced liquidity for acquisitions.

- *Rollover of gains.* Internal Revenue Code (IRC) § 1042 allows an ESOP that acquires at least 30 percent of stock to defer capital gains tax as long as the proceeds are reinvested in "qualified replacement property" within a 15-month window, 3 months leading up to the transaction and 12 months after the date of sale.

- *If the company is an S corporation, the ESOP's share of earnings from the S corporation is not subject to federal or, in many states, state corporate taxation, nor is it considered "unrelated business income taxable."* This is true as long as certain anti-abuse provisions are not violated. If an S corporation is wholly owned by an ESOP, the company's earnings are completely nontaxable to the plan.

- *Increased owner control of business identity and business continuity.* When an owner is prepared to sell a personal stake in the company, an ESOP provides a vehicle whereby the company can literally be turned over to known and trusted employees, rather than lose its identity through a merger or acquisition.

- *Defense against hostile takeovers.* Although this use has been under intense scrutiny and receives a heavy dose of regulation, if a takeover is imminent, an ESOP can buy the company and thus circumvent job losses and the difficulties inherent in acquisition.

- *Vehicle for gifting.* Owners can make gifts of their outside shareholding to charities in conjunction with the plan's ability to continue to invest in employer securities.

- *Improved morale.* Studies have shown that offering employee ownership in most cases results in increases in production and morale.

GOOD ESOP CANDIDATE INDICATORS

Although there are differing views on what exactly makes a good ESOP candidate, a number of characteristics reveal themselves as essential qualifiers. Following is a list, although not exclusive, that can be used as a guideline for determining whether a company is a good ESOP candidate:

- The candidate company is a corporation taxed as an S or C corporation under IRS regulations. The company cannot be another type of entity; it must have the corporate characteristic.

- The candidate company is private or publicly traded, with significant ownership generally held by a few individuals.

- The candidate company reasonably expects to have continuing revenues, cash flows, and payroll expenditures sufficient to sustain ESOP plan contribution levels to meet its obligations and primarily invest in employer securities.

- The candidate company has a sturdy earnings or cash flow history over an appropriate time period.

- The candidate company expects to pay significant federal income taxes into the future.

- The candidate company has paid significant federal income taxes in the past.

- The candidate company has outside stockholders with current and/or contemplated future interests in selling some or all of their stock.

- The candidate company has within its current employ, or can reasonably obtain, replacement management should the selling outside shareholder be a principal executive within the company.

- The candidate company has customarily made contributions to another qualified employee retirement plan that could be available to an ESOP.

- The candidate company has an ESOP culture.

Although there are no mandatory candidate company criteria, general economic thresholds follow operational characteristics that the sponsoring company must consider prudent in the formation of an ESOP. These economic thresholds often track as a minimum of 25 employees, an annual compensation coverage payroll is $1 million or more, the sponsoring company has been in business at least 5 years, the shareholders are predominantly older, and business valuation in the aggregate of the company is at least $3 million. In addition, the company has a plan for capable succession management, has the ability to grow the business — including growth through mergers or acquisitions, has a sensible earnings history, and can secure arm's-length third-party financing. Moreover, outside shareholders are psychologically prepared to share or transfer ownership with their employees.[1]

FEASIBILITY STUDY

Once a company appears preliminarily to be a viable candidate for an ESOP, it is often suggested that a feasibility study be conducted. The feasibility study is discussed in greater detail in another chapter as related to the responsibilities of the plan fiduciary/trustee. A feasibility study will help company owners to further consider, at a more in-depth level, the efficiency and practicality of an ESOP. There are typically four portions of a feasibility study: (1) preliminary appraisal (indication of value), (2) design study, (3) financial analysis, and (4) repurchase liability study.[2]

In a feasibility study, a preliminary indication of value generally involves providing the anticipated plan trustee, outside shareholders, company management, lender, the plan designer, legal counsel, and financial analysts a broad-brush approximation of what may be considered in the context of ERISA as adequate consideration, or—more typically defined—as the fair market value of the company's common equity stock.

This preliminary indication of value is often displayed in writing and in the form of an approximate range of equity value indications and is by and large prepared in advance of a contemplated transaction. Accordingly, it is important for the appraiser to clearly indicate from the onset the purpose and intended use of the valuation computations as that of feasibility.

The design study should analyze applicability of entity structure, any shareholder or share restrictions, stock bonus, options, or warrants. Additionally, the study must ensure that any ESOP transaction can meet the covered compensation issues for plan contributions that the sponsoring company is able to secure borrowing, if applicable, and the plan covers all employees. Participant allocations must be transparent, the corporate minutes and shareholder records books must be in order, and the question must be answered whether other sponsor-company qualified plans will be adjusted or joined with the ESOP. Further considerations include participant vesting schedules, plan termination, hardship, retirement, and similar plan directives.

As an example of what might affect an ESOP valuation, if one or more shareholders elect a like kind exchange to defer tax consequences to a future period under IRC § 1042, the rollover provision, when transacted with an ESOP, impacts them in the way they participate as a post transaction plan participant. Other 25 percent-plus shareholders and their immediate family members are limited or precluded from receiving participant allocations until the stock that generated the favorable tax treatment is allocated to the plan. In some instances, sponsoring companies reduce the depressive impact of ERISA to this group of individuals by providing additional benefit to them after an ESOP transaction. In this regard, the additional future financial impacts to the company operations on a post–ESOP transaction basis, should be considered in the valuation of the shares on a pretransaction basis in order to meet adequate consideration provisions of ERISA. See further details in Chapter 10.

In the financial analysis of the feasibility of implementing an ESOP, an assessment is made using the sponsoring company's historic financial data and provides forward-looking financial modeling to assess possible effects that the ESOP might have on the operations of the company, including the equity stock value. These generally follow a probability analysis that projects future benefits to employees, operational benefits, contribution levels needed, anticipation of impact of debt to the company, anticipated stock appreciation, stagnation or decline, and a candid analysis of the cash flows to the company and that available to satisfy the required needs of the ESOP.

A repurchase liability study brings a forward-looking financial model that is designed to forecast what the ESOP and sponsoring company may reasonably expect over a long-term business or ESOP timeline, assessing the liquidity provided by converting ESOP shares into cash by departing participants. A repurchase liability study quantifies the question of, "How much cash is needed and when?" so that a funding program can be implemented to insure that needed cash will be available.[3]

Once a feasibility study is complete, the company should have the requisite information to make a reasonably informed decision of the feasibility of implementing an ESOP. A feasibility study is not, however, a substitute for owners, shareholders, managers, and employees getting involved in their own learning and understanding of the intricacies of an ESOP. As of this writing, many resources offer assistance in the assessment, implementation, and management of an ESOP.

COMPENSATION LIMITATIONS

One of the more common questions among business owners is whether their company is too small for an ESOP. Although there is no particular size requirement for an ESOP to be effective, there are certain guidelines that The National Center for Employee Ownership (NCEO) have compiled as assistance in answering this question.[4] The two main issues to consider are calculating the cost and analyzing cost versus benefit.

The following items should be evaluated in calculating cost:

- The fees associated with preparing plan documents and government filings depend on lawyer drafting fees, legal costs for time, and owner knowledge of ESOP issues.

- If valuation has already taken place for other purposes, obtaining an annual update valuation will be less costly.

- The cost of administration must be evaluated. In the case of a leveraged ESOP, companies must consider loan commitment fees, legal fees for the lender's counsel and loan documents, and possible financial consulting for structuring the transaction. This cost depends on the number of company employees. As an example, administering an ESOP for 20 employees costs approximately $2,000/year. A leveraged ESOP will cost more, including the possible cost of a financial advisor and the increased difficulty of obtaining a loan, and/or an increased number of sources of financing.

Several questions are offered as pivotal in determining cost versus benefits:

- What are the alternatives?
- What is the effective tax rate involved?
- How will annual costs compare to annual contributions?
- Is your payroll adequate?[5]
- Will the company valuation meet the expectations of selling shareholders?

As a private company with concerns of how size may relate to the effectiveness of an ESOP, it would be helpful to research other private companies that decided to make an ESOP work and consider their experiences. *The Employee Ownership Report* is a publication by NCEO that contains ESOP case studies. In the November/December 2003 issue, there was an ESOP case study involving Union Fish Company, which created an ESOP with only five employees. Such an article might be helpful to the small company preoccupied with the decision as to whether their company not only fits the profile of an ESOP culture but also the economics for its formation.

SUMMARY

Once the issues particular to a company and those discussed in this chapter are addressed, a company should possess a reasonably clear understanding of whether it would be beneficial to create an ESOP. Additional help in this determination is in the multitude of available case studies of ESOPs, and the variety of reputable and recognized resources available to companies today.

4

Trustee Duties
in ESOPs*

Fiduciaries are either named in the ESOP plan or they are identified pursuant to a procedure spelled out in the plan. ERISA Section 3(21) defines a fiduciary as anyone who:

- Exercises any discretionary authority or control regarding the management or disposition of plan assets
- Renders investment advice for a fee with respect to any money or property of the plan, or
- Has any discretion or responsibility in plan administration.

Some examples of named fiduciaries are the trustees, the investment manager, and possibly the plan administrator.

The term *fiduciary* is derived from Roman law and means (as a noun) a person holding the character of a trustee, or a character analogous to that of a trustee, in respect to the trust and confidence involved in it and the scrupulous good faith and candor that it requires.[1] As is suggested by the definition, a person who undertakes such duties has committed to act for another's benefit in regard to a specific activity. To apply the definition to an ESOP enterprise, the trustee is (or should be) committed to performing his or her duties solely for the benefit of plan participants and beneficiaries.

> Trustees who fail to perform in accordance with this commitment may find themselves personally liable to the plan participants and beneficiaries for damages.

---

*This chapter was contributed by Tom Corley.

> ERISA requires every ESOP plan to have one or more trustees who are named in the plan or appointed by another named fiduciary.

The trustee must have exclusive authority and discretion over management and control of the assets of the plan, except where the trustee is subject to the proper direction of another named fiduciary in accordance with the terms of the plan or delegation to another fiduciary (such as an investment manager) has been effected to manage, acquire, and dispose of assets.

A trustee may also be identified as a *directed trustee* or an *independent trustee*. The difference is simply that a directed trustee is one who is subject to the directions of another named fiduciary, such as the plan administrator, the plan sponsor, an investment manager, or even the participants of the plan.

STANDARD OF CARE

> The standard of care for fiduciaries and trustees operating ESOP plans is the Prudent Person Standard of Care. To satisfy the standard, a fiduciary must act "with the care, skill, prudence, and diligence under the circumstances then prevailing that a prudent man acting in a like capacity and familiar with such matters would use in the conduct of an enterprise of a like character and with like aims" (ERISA Sec. 404(a)(D).

On the surface, the requirement does not appear extremely difficult to meet in most circumstances. After all, if a fiduciary/trustee is diligent and cautious and their actions are always in the best interest of plan participants, how can they fail the prudent person standard of care? Unfortunately, the courts have measured against the standard with differing results, and some of the results have been difficult to understand. For example, hiring and obtaining opinion of independent counsel by itself does not satisfy the rule. The fiduciary/trustee must make his or her own investigation of the assumptions and premises forming the advice of independent counsel. Furthermore, the claim or defense of *good faith* does not satisfy the rule. The courts have said that it is no excuse where a fiduciary acted "with a pure heart and an empty head."

PRELIMINARY FEASIBILITY STUDY

A precursor to all successful ESOP transactions is a thorough feasibility study. This is the first step to the project and requires an in-depth review of the financial capabilities of the company both before and after the proposed transaction.

Although the study does not require a complete valuation of the company stock, it should include enough valuation insight to provide a preliminary indication of value and the likely price of shares to be sold within a fairly tight range. This is, of course, necessary in order to produce projected financials that are meaningful and that contain predictive and useful insight into likely cash flows after the transaction is complete. A thorough study can help eliminate costly mistakes (including the initial decision to become an ESOP company). A thorough study can also prepare and develop management expectations for post-ESOP operations.

Should the trustee be involved in the feasibility study? More often than not, the trustee is not hired (or even identified) until the feasibility study is complete. This may not be the best approach because an experienced trustee can provide valuable insight into how the feasibility study should be prepared and what is needed in the way of information to support a valid conclusion that an ESOP is feasible. Furthermore, a trustee involved in the feasibility study will have a better understanding of the transaction and can assist in avoiding common problem areas.

THE INITIAL DUTY OF VALUATION

One of the first duties that a trustee should perform is to select an appraiser to value the shares of the proposed ESOP company. In a perfect world, the trustee should be given full authority to make the selection of appraiser and should make the selection based on qualifications, prior experience, and the trustee's ability to communicate issues and concerns with the appraiser or the appraisal firm.

The trustee may, on occasion, be called on to approve management's selection of an appraiser. This is, certainly, less than the ideal situation, and the trustee should grant such approval with a great deal of caution and only after a careful review of valuator skills and qualifications, coupled with a background review to assure that the valuator is truly independent of company management and all other parties to the transaction. Ultimate responsibility for the outcome of the appraisal still resides with the trustee.

In the case of *Reich vs. Valley National Bank of Arizona* (known as the Kroy case), the court criticized the trustee for a number of reasons, including the fact the trustee was engaged only a few days prior to the ESOP closing and did not engage or approve selection of the valuation firm.

> The court found that the trustee accepted the value of the capital stock being purchased by the ESOP without a thorough review of the valuation report or the valuation principles used and did not participate in the valuation process. The court stated that "passive acceptance of reports does not relieve ERISA fiduciaries from liability."[2]

In looking behind the court's criticism, it seems the court believes the trustee should be held accountable for the correctness of the valuation and that trustees should be active participants in the valuation process.

The *"Dairy Fresh"* case[3] is another example of the court finding that the trustee violated his duty of loyalty and prudence. In this case, the participant shareholders of the ESOP borrowed money to purchase company shares. Due to an incorrect calculation of debt by the appraiser, the ESOP ended up owning 80 percent of the outstanding shares. When the mistake was discovered several years later, and a lawsuit was filed, the court found that the trustee had violated his duty of loyalty and prudence, even though he had relied on the appraiser's independent evaluation.

Although the trustee certainly need not be a qualified valuator, the trustee should participate in the process and should question the validity and/or assumptions behind projected financial statements, capitalization rates, and cash flows. It goes without saying that a trustee should have mastered the mechanics of financial statements and cash flows, what they mean, and how they are used in the valuation process.

DUTY TO NEGOTIATE THE PURCHASE PRICE

> Once the valuation is complete, the trustee has a duty to negotiate the purchase price of the shares of stock being purchased for the ESOP. IRS Code § 401(a)(28)(C) requires that an ESOP purchase stock at its fair market value (FMV), as determined by an independent appraiser using "adequate consideration" and "fairness" standards.[4]

An interesting aspect to DOL requirements is that the purchase price should be the fair value at the time of purchase. The *time of purchase* requirement usually provides a "chicken and egg" exercise at closing because the closing can't take place prior to receipt of the valuation information, and the valuation is usually performed several days after the end of an accounting cycle. Valuators are usually called upon to provide a *fairness opinion letter* as of the date of closing, which is likely to be several days (perhaps weeks) after the end of the accounting cycle upon which the appraisal was based. The usual solution is for the valuator and/or the trustee to ask management for a *comfort letter* (sometimes described as a *take-out letter* or a *bring-down letter*), indicating no material changes have taken place after end of the accounting cycle upon which the valuation was based, up to and including the date of closing. Other valuators see the need to issue a separate limited appraisal to supplement the first and to opine on the interim period. Either solution is viable, although issue of a limited appraisal is a bit more cumbersome.

Once fair market value is determined, the trustee should negotiate a transaction price with the seller. The adequate consideration standard requires that purchase price be no more than fair market value but does not preclude paying less than fair market value. Many times a seller is willing to discount the shares in recognition of employee loyalty and service to the company. A seller that is willing to discount the shares can assist in improving the probable success of the ESOP. Whether the seller is willing or not, the trustee should ask for the best deal that he or she can convince the seller to make, simply because a lower debt and lower debt service commitments (to the seller or to a financial institution) will also improve the probability of success. Negotiations with the seller should not only include the share price but also the terms of repayment if the transaction is seller-financed.

PLAN DOCUMENTS

The plan documents control the actions and activities of the plan, the trustees, and the plan administrators. It is important that plan documents be prepared by a qualified ERISA attorney thoroughly familiar with the intricacies of ESOPs. If properly drawn and updated, the documents will comply with the latest IRS and DOL requirements, thereby precluding delays in getting a favorable determination letter from the IRS.

Documents can be customized for the particular ESOP client or they may be drafted from a plan provider service, which allows the attorney to choose plan provisions that are appropriate and allows the plan to be tailored to the case at hand. Usually plans that are prepared from plan provider services are designed to meet IRS and DOL requirements, and red flags will be raised by the plan provider service for any portion of the plan that is in question or outside the parameters of the IRS Code and DOL regulations. Choices will be given to the client regarding such decisions as participation requirements, retirement age, and vesting schedules. A trustee familiar with the pros and cons of these decisions can be helpful to the client by explaining the advantages and disadvantages of each alternative.

Trustees should also be thoroughly familiar with the documents simply because of their responsibility as adjudicator for questions and decisions that will almost always arise in the course of administering the plan. As always, if there are questions that are material enough to warrant legal opinion, a trustee should not hesitate to seek legal counsel.

The following documents are essential to all plans:

- *Employees' Stock Ownership Plan.* This document is the most important of the group and should be carefully drafted because it provides the basic instructions as to operation of the plan. It will include critical definitions, participation rules and details of qualification, contributions and forfeitures, allocations of employer contributions, participant vesting, termination of service, time and method of payment of benefits, and a myriad of administrative provisions.

- *Employees' Stock Ownership Trust.* The trust document is the instrument that describes the legal status of the entity and provides the plan with qualification as a tax-exempt entity under IRC § 501(a). The document will normally describe the management and control of the trust funds and name the responsible parties (i.e., an ESOP committee) to carry out the functions intended by the plan. The document will also spell out the trustees' duties and describe the general powers allocated to them. Additional instruction may also be provided regarding valuation of the fund and changing of trustees.

- *Summary Plan Description.* A summary plan description (SPD) is included with the plan documents to be given to the plan participants. The SPD is designed to remove the legalese and provide a more readable document highlighting only the major elements of the plan. This document, if carefully prepared, will answer a large number of the questions that are common with most plan participants. The SPD can also be useful as a quick reference to answer routine questions without combing through the details of the full plan document.

There will be additional documents necessary to complete corporate governance requirements, provide indemnification, and complete fairness opinion requirements. Some examples are:

- *Resolution by the Board of Directors.* This document is the instrument that records action by the board of directors to adopt the plan. It will usually spell out the shares to be sold to the ESOP and the price at which the shares are to be sold. The resolution will also provide authorization for borrowing (if the ESOP is leveraged or if a loan is involved) and perhaps some of the details of the terms. The resolution may also appoint trustees and delegate needed authority to the ESOP committee.

- *Additional resolutions.* Some boards of directors will follow the adoption of the basic plan with an additional resolution spelling out recognition of repurchase liability and will detail the mechanics of how the company will meet those responsibilities (e.g., sinking fund, key man insurance, etc.).

- *Indemnification agreements.* The employer/owner should be asked and should agree to indemnify both the ESOP committee members and trustees. These documents spell out the employer/owner's agreement to hold harmless the individual committee members and trustees (subject to the relevant provisions of ERISA) from costs and expenses, including legal fees for actions and/or causes relating to performance of duties.

- *Fairness opinion letter.* As a part of the engagement of an independent valuator, trustees should require the valuator to provide a fairness opinion regarding the transaction. Valuation guidelines contained in DOL Proposed Regulation 29 CFR, Part 2510.3-18 are to be considered by the valuator in preparing the letter, which should be effective on the date of the transaction.

Documents that relate to purchase of shares by ESOPs can vary, depending on the specifics of the transaction. Although these documents are equally important to those just discussed, they will almost always be more closely related to commercial transactions than to ESOPs, and for that reason will not be reviewed here. Nevertheless, trustees should carefully review them for inconsistencies with basis plan documents and with corporate governance documents. Some examples of documents relating to purchase of shares by the ESOP are as follows:

- *Stock purchase agreement*—Between the owners and the ESOP trust
- *Credit agreement*—Between the lender (company/employer) and the trust
- *Nonrecourse promissory note*—Between the trust and company/employer
- *A stock certificate*—Issued to the ESOP Trust
- *A pledge agreement*—From the ESOP trust (pledgor) and the company/ employer (pledgee)
- *Promissory note*—From the company/employer to the lender (bank, or if seller-financed, the stockholder)
- *Security agreement*—From the company/employer to the lender

Every ESOP transaction is unique and has its own specific document needs. A skilled ERISA attorney is an absolute must in all transactions. A trustee, however, should carefully review and question any and all documents for inconsistencies, conflicts, and overall propriety. Future administration of the plan can be severely hampered by poor documentation at inception.

PLAN OPERATIONS AND ADMINISTRATION

After the closing and when the plan is fully operational, the trustee should hire (or assist the ESOP committee in the hire of) a third-party administrator to perform the ministerial duties normally associated with qualified retirement plans. For example, a census of the workforce (to include name, age, date of hire, etc.) will be needed to determine qualified plan participants. The census is normally maintained in a database program and will be used as a basis for computing allocations of benefits, vesting, forfeitures, breaks in service, and related matters necessary to comply with the intricate set of rules found in all qualified retirement plans. The third-party administrator is also the preparer of recurring reports required by the IRS and DOL, such as the annual Form 5500, individual participant statements, and the annual report.

The trustee's duty relative to plan administration is similar to his duties regarding valuation. Although trustees need not be a qualified plan administrator, they must have an overall understanding of the rules relating to operation of qualified retirement plans because, again, they are ultimately responsible for performance of the function. Although the rules for plan administration are quite extensive and sometimes difficult to understand, trustees are often the adjudicators for questions that will arise in regard to eligibility for participation, eligibility for benefits, payment of benefits, disputes regarding account balances, and similar issues. Some of the questions and issues can be very complex, and trustees may need to seek legal advice and counsel to settle the matters with fairness while remaining in compliance with plan documents and IRS/DOL regulations.

THE ESOP COMMITTEE

In many cases, trustees are employed by and report to the ESOP committee (rather than the board of directors). Regardless of a trustee's reporting responsibility, the ESOP committee is an integral part of the ESOP and can be a very positive influence in its success. ESOP committees usually perform best when guidelines are adopted and in place to instruct the committee regarding the mechanics of appointment, resignation, or removal, and to specifically spell out the powers and duties of the ESOP committee. The usual list of powers and duties includes some or all of the following:

- To call meetings and provide recommendations to the trustee on all plan matters
- To review the annual valuation for accuracy, completeness, and timeliness
- To complete a performance evaluation of the trustee and recommend to the board to directors either continuance or removal
- To review the annual plan administration documents for accuracy, completeness, and timeliness
- To enforce the terms of the plan and the plan rules along with the policies and regulations the committee adopts (All such decisions of the ESOP committee may be deemed final, subject to ERISA, the IRS Code, DOL regulations, and any other federal or state laws.)
- To communicate with plan participants on all matters relating to the plan (This responsibility would include answering questions, clarifying issues, and, as best possible, ensuring that plan participants are well informed of their rights under the plan.)

The board of directors appoints the committee, and it is usually composed of members that form a cross-section of the company. The design and composition of the committee should be such that all employee-participants have representation and, more importantly, feel comfortable in expressing their views to one or more of the committee members. A free flow of information between employee-participants and management is healthy and necessary for a successful plan.

The first point of communication between employee-participants and management, and/or the trustee, is the committee. Many routine questions that arise can be dealt with at the committee level and should be the first contact for employee-participants with questions, grievances, or issues relating to plan participation.

The ESOP committee is frequently used as the source for communication of annual results and for distribution of annual plan participant statements. Some committees provide extensive review of results and make comprehensive projections of values for participants upon retirement. Although such projections may be useful as motivation tools, they are definitely in the realm of speculation, and for that reason the committee should use them with caution.

PROBLEM AREAS FOR TRUSTEES

The Exclusive Purpose Rule sums up the general duties of a trustee as outlined in ERISA § 404(a)(1) which speaks to all fiduciaries. Simply stated, there is an overall requirement for a fiduciary/trustee to discharge duties solely in the interest of the plan participants and "for the exclusive purpose of providing benefits to participants and beneficiaries and for defraying reasonable expenses of administering the plan." This is straightforward in that retirement benefits are the sole focus and concern of the trustee. The DOL has consistently refused to extend the trustee's concern and responsibilities to include such matters as the participants' concern for keeping their jobs.

The Exclusive Purpose Rule when viewed in conjunction with the Prudent Man Rule as previously discussed, makes it quite clear that a trustee must at all times avoid areas where there are conflicts of interest (or even perceived areas of conflict of interest) and must focus solely on protecting the financial interest of participants and beneficiaries regarding their future retirement benefits from the plan.

If a trustee is faced with a conflict of interest or is unsure of a decision that needs to be made, the trustee should either resign and/or secure independent legal or investment counsel for advice. The trustee should also conduct a thorough review of the facts in order to avoid the potential for breach of ERISA rules.

To fail in this regard may subject the trustee to personal liability for losses to the plan and possibly other equitable relief the courts deem appropriate.

If there is a single area that seems to cause more problems for trustees and causes more instances of breach of duties, it is *self-dealing,* which is a form of conflict of interest. Although it is common in small plans for former or current owners or members of management to take on the added responsibility of trustee of the ESOP, it is not good practice. To do so places the trustee in conflict almost from inception. One cannot serve two masters.

The beneficial interest of the participants and the beneficial interest of owners/ members of management is opposite by nature. For example, a former owner/ president who is paying himself compensation above the norm for his position is at odds with his duty as trustee to be responsible for the financial benefits of plan participants and beneficiaries. This problem was well illustrated in *Delta Star v. Patton.* In this case, the president and chairman of the board of Delta Star was also a member of the board of trustees. Over a period of several years, he had increased salary and bonus payments to himself unilaterally and well beyond reasonable levels, despite rather dismal earnings on the part of the company. In ruling against the president, the court noted that although ERISA does not expressly bar a trustee from serving as a director or officer of the company, ERISA "does not sanction any derogation of duty from the strict fiduciary requirements imposed upon the trustee."[5]

A similar conflict of interest and set of related problems exists when officers/directors attempt to transact the sale of shares to the ESOP plan in their dual capacity as officers/directors and as trustees of the plan. Again, the transaction is, on the surface, suspect because of the inherent inability to serve two masters, each with competing spheres of interest. Although it is possible for an officer of a corporation to serve in both roles and not violate their duties as fiduciaries, the person serving dual roles has a duty to act with extreme caution, and their decisions must always be made with consideration of the interest of the participants and beneficiaries.

TRUSTEE DUTIES RELATING TO REPURCHASE LIABILITY PROGRAMS

The Achille's heel of ESOPs is repurchase liability and the tendency of management to ignore the company's looming responsibility at some point in the future to pay participants and beneficiaries for the fair market value of shares allocated to their accounts. Although most companies understand that beneficiaries will require payment, only the more judicious will correctly plan and prepare for this responsibility.

The first step in dealing with the problem is to understand the size and timing of the responsibility. (*Note:* Under GAAP, the liability for repurchase of shares from plan participants is not required to be booked and thus will not show up on financial statements). In order to reach such understanding, it is necessary to prepare (or hire a professional to prepare) a repurchase liability study. Such studies take into account all of the variables such as age and years of service of the employees, combined with actuarial studies of death and disability and coupled with projected values of the ESOP company to predict, as best possible, the probable amounts and points in time that payments will be required for death, disability, and retirement. Such studies can be quite complex, and, of course, the accuracy of the input will determine the reliability of the finished product, which is a schedule of estimated payments by year into the future.

After preparation of the study, what should follow is the decision as to how the company will make the payments. A number of possibilities exist, including ignoring the matter and meeting the commitment with a pay-as-you-go approach. However, this method is unlikely to satisfy the requirement of adequate security imposed by the IRS and DOL.

Although the term *adequate security* is not defined in the regulations, Revenue Ruling 80-69 does indicate that the security must be pledged, tangible, and accessible.[6] Furthermore, it must be saleable or foreclosable, and the security must not be subject to any unreasonable loss of principal or interest. This makes for a rather high standard in order to meet requirements of adequate security.

Methods that could be considered would include the following:[7]

- *A sinking fund*—Funds are kept in a savings account for the specific purpose of repurchasing shares as participants retire.

- *S corporation method*—An S Corporation ESOP could accumulate cash in a repurchase account inside the ESOP to pay participants upon retirement.

- *Recycling method*—The company continues to make cash contributions to the ESOP for the purpose of purchasing some or all of the shares from retired employees.

- *Corporate-owned life insurance method*—Life insurance is purchased on key personnel, and the cash build-up in the policies is borrowed to purchase shares as participants retire.

THE TRUSTEE IN A POST-ENRON ENVIRONMENT

The Enron debacle has provided a number of valuable lessons for ESOP trustees in addition to pointing out new ways to fail in carrying out duties on matters that have already been decided. It is likely that litigation specific to the breach of fiduciary duties will extend over the next several years.

The Enron ESOP provided retirement benefits to 7,600 employees, beneficiaries, retirees, and their beneficiaries.[8] As such, the ESOP was one of the largest investors in Enron company stock, with approximately $1,000,000,000 in total assets at the beginning of 2001.

Among the allegations by plaintiffs was that Enron officials, the administrative committee, and Northern Trust (a directed trustee) breached fiduciary duties because they continued to invest in Enron securities beyond the time they knew or should have known that Enron's financial position was declining, and Enron's stock price was falling rapidly. The plaintiffs argued that fiduciaries did not act prudently and solely in the interest of the plan participants as required under section 404 of ERISA and did nothing to protect from huge losses, even though the fiduciaries knew or should have known they were paying too much for Enron stock.[9]

Defendants in a prior case, *Moench v. Robinson,* countered with the argument that ESOP plan documents required them to invest in shares of the company.[10] This defense has previously failed and is likely to fail again, as the courts have already held ESOP fiduciaries liable under ERISA where trustees continued to knowingly invest in shares of a failing company. More specifically, the courts held that fiduciaries are obligated to operate the ESOP in accordance with its mandate as set forth in the ESOP document to invest in capital stock of the sponsor company, unless the fiduciary determines that such investment is contrary to its ERISA obligation to act in the exclusive interest of the participants and beneficiaries of the ESOP.[11]

Litigation of all the matters that relate to the Enron retirement plans is likely to be lengthy, expensive, and time consuming. It also appears that much of the thrust of the plaintiff's actions will relate to issues that have surfaced in earlier case law. However, new issues appear to be emerging. For example, there may be no corporate shield for fiduciaries who are also officers of the company.[12] Because officers of Enron were exercising discretionary authority over the plans, the courts have ruled they were in fact fiduciaries and could be held personally liable. This issue will continue to evolve.

SUMMARY

An ESOP trustee is subject to the "Prudent Person Standard of Care." By the standard, a fiduciary must act "with the care, skill, prudence, and diligence under circumstances then prevailing that a prudent man acting in a like capacity and familiar with such matters would use in the conduct of an enterprise of like character and with like aims.[13]

The ESOP trustee should be involved as an active participant in the initial valuation process. Although the trustee is not required to be a qualified valuator, the ultimate responsibility for accuracy of outcome rests with the trustee. The valuation is the basis for negotiation of the purchase price, which can be no more than fair market value as determined by an independent appraisal using adequate consideration and fairness standards.

ERISA is very clear that ESOP trustees have an overall requirement to discharge their duties for the exclusive purpose of providing benefits to participants and beneficiaries and for defraying reasonable expenses of administering the plan. This rule (described as the *Exclusive Purpose Rule*) is the reason that an ESOP trustee should avoid all self-dealing, conflicts of interest, and even perceived conflicts of interest.

5

Beneficial Interests, Rights of Participants, and Vesting*

There are several limitations with regard to ESOP contributions and allocations that should be explained in order to illustrate the process by which shares are allocated to employees.

BENEFICIAL INTERESTS

An ESOP must be designated to invest primarily in employer securities (IRC § 4975(e)(7)(A)). The contributions to an ESOP may be in the form of the employer's own stock or through cash contributions. When cash contributions are made, the trustee or fiduciaries of the plan usually invest those contributions primarily in employer stock.

Contribution and Annual Addition Limits

The limitations on deductible contributions generally allow employers to deduct up to 25 percent of the aggregate eligible compensation of plan participants. The 25 percent limit on an exempt loan under IRC § 4975(d)(3) is subject to a special deduction limit under IRC § 404(a)(9). Leveraged ESOPs may apply the 25 percent limit to the principal portion of the loan and may deduct all of the interest income that is paid. ESOP payments deducted under this special limit are not subject to the normal 25 percent deduction limit under IRC § 404(a)(3). Eligible payroll is essentially all compensation paid or accrued to the participants during the employer's taxable year. The maximum compensation that may be considered for any employee for taxable years beginning in 2004 is $205,000 (indexed for inflation) (IRC § 401(a)(17)). This special deduction limit is not available to S corporations.

There are also limitations as to the maximum allocation that any single participant may receive in an ESOP. The contribution attributable to principal payments

---

*This chapter was contributed by Carey Lindsey.

for any single participant is limited to the lesser of 100 percent of compensation or $41,000 (2004) indexed for inflation. All qualified plans must be considered in this limitation, including employee deferrals in a 401(k) plan maintained by the employer or controlled group member.

In addition, no more than one-third of the employer contributions that are used to repay an exempt loan deductible under IRC § 404(a)(9) may be allocated to highly compensated employees (HCEs) for the interest to be excluded from the individual limit (IRC § 415(c)(6)). If this condition is not satisfied, forfeitures of employer securities, which were acquired with the proceeds of the exempt loan, are also treated as annual additions in calculating the individual limit. Interest is not deductible if the company sponsoring the ESOP is an S corporation.

Employers may also deduct "reasonable" dividends paid on C corporation ESOP shares under IRC § 404(k). There are four ways that a dividend may be paid in order to be deductible. The first is cash paid from the employer directly to the participants. The second is cash paid through the plan *pass-through dividends,* where within 90 days after the close of the plan year, the dividends are distributed to participants. Another option is to allow the participant to elect between a cash dividend and reinvestment in qualifying employer securities within the plan. The final option is a dividend paid to the plan used to repay an exempt loan under IRC § 4975(d)(3).

Allocations to Employees

An ESOP is a qualified plan under ERISA and is subject to most of the same eligibility and allocation rules as other qualified plans. The maximum length of employment that may be required for eligibility is one year of service and entry dates no later than six months after completing the eligibility requirements. The plan may require two years of service to participate, but participants must become fully vested immediately on participation. In the initial year of an ESOP, the plan may, but is not required to, exclude service prior to the effective date of the plan. In addition, the plan may require that an employee be over age 21 to participate in the plan.

A year of service is generally measured during a 12-month period beginning from the first hour of service performed by the employee. The plan may continue to use the 12-month initial eligibility period; however, many plans elect to shift the eligibility period to coincide with the plan year and vesting computation period. The plan may not require more than 1,000 hours in the initial or subsequent eligibility periods. Hours may be counted using actual hours for which an employee is paid or based on one of the approved equitable methods.

An ESOP is also subject to the coverage requirements of IRC § 410(b), which require benefits to be provided on a nondiscriminatory basis. To meet this requirement, an ESOP must cover a percentage of non–highly compensated employees who have met the eligibility requirements equal to at least 70 percent of the percentage of highly compensated employees who have met the eligibility requirements that are covered by the plan. For example, a plan that covers 50 percent of the highly compensated employees eligible under the plan would have to cover 35 percent of the non–highly compensated employees (70 percent × 50 percent).

Allocations of employer contributions are typically made using a pro-rata approach that allocates shares on each employee's compensation relative to the total eligible compensation already discussed. The plan may also permit matching contributions based on employee 401(k) deferrals. There are additional allocation formulas that may be used, such as a point's allocation; however, this formula would not meet one of the safe-harbor allocations and would require additional testing to assure that the ESOP is in compliance with the nondiscriminatory contribution requirements of the Internal Revenue Code. Permitted disparity formulas, which take into account social security contributions made by the employer, are not available to ESOPs.

Shares that were purchased with an exempt loan and have not been allocated are held in a suspense account and are generally held as collateral for the loan. This occurs when an ESOP borrows money in order to acquire employer stock. The ESOP may borrow the money from a commercial lender such as a bank or directly from the corporation sponsoring the ESOP. The latter is usually accomplished through a "mirror" loan between the corporation and a bank. As cash contributions are made from the corporation to the ESOP, shares are released from the collateral suspense account and allocated to participants' accounts, generally in proportion to each participant's relative compensation. The shares may be

---

Illustration

On January 15, 2003, the XYZ Company ESOP borrowed $1,000,000 from ABC Bank and used the proceeds from the loan to purchase 20,000 shares of the XYZ Company outstanding stock at $50 per share. The 20,000 shares purchased will be held as collateralized shares within a suspense account. XYZ Company made cash contributions to the ESOP for the plan year ending December 31, 2003, which totaled $200,000. The ESOP, in turn, uses these funds to pay principal and interest on the outstanding loan to ABC Bank. The principal and interest based on the terms of the loan were $175,000 and $25,000, respectively. The plan would reflect this by releasing 3,500 shares ($175,000/$50) using the principal-only method of releasing shares. The amount used in determining if the company is within the deduction and annual addition limits would be the principal paid on the note; $175,000. The value of each participant's account on December 31, 2003, will be based on the stock valuation determined by an independent appraiser at the time they are allocated.

released using the principal only method, or the principal and interest method. If the term of the loan is more than 10 years, the principal and interest method must be used.

Participants for which shares have been allocated will be entitled to a beneficial interest in the number of shares allocated on their behalf. The ESOP shares are held in a trust and are legally owned by the plan's trustee. The trustee is generally appointed by the board of directors and may be directed by an ESOP administrative committee.

RIGHTS OF PARTICIPANTS

ESOPs are subject to the same nondiscriminatory requirements as all qualified plans with regard to benefits, rights and features. However, there are additional requirements that must be made available to participants of an ESOP.

Asset Diversification Requirements

Employees who have reached age 55 and have 10 years of participation in an ESOP have the right to diversify a portion of their stock over a 6-year period. During the first five years of the six-year period, the employee has the right to diversify up to a total of 25 percent of company stock acquired by the ESOP after December 31, 1986. During the sixth year, the employee may diversify up to a total of 50 percent, less any previously diversified shares. There are two methods that an ESOP may use to satisfy the diversification requirements. The first option is for the ESOP to offer at least three alternative investment options within the ESOP or another plan maintained by the employer. The ESOP may also satisfy the diversification requirement by distributing cash or company stock to the participants.

The election period for which a participant must have the right to diversify is 90 days following the end of each eligible plan year. The plan administrator or fiduciary responsible must execute the participant's direction within 90 days after the 90-day election period. The plan may also meet the diversification requirements by transferring the amount to another plan that allows the investment options for diversification.

Voting Stock

IRC § 409(e) sets forth the voting rights that apply to all ESOPs. (Voting rights are further expanded upon in Chapter 14). The trustee of the ESOP is responsible for voting the ESOP shares. In a privately held company, the trustee may make voting decisions independently or take direction from an ESOP administrative committee. However, voting rights must be passed through to participants, based on their allocated shares for any corporate matter that involves a merger or consolidation, recapitalization, liquidation, sale of substantially all assets of a trade or business or similar transaction that would affect the structure of the company. In public corporations, all voting rights pass through to participants.

Distribution Rights (Put Option)

ESOPs are generally required to give participants the right to sell stock that has been distributed back to the company at its current fair market value. The put option must be made available for at least 60 days following the distribution; and if not exercised, for another 60 days during the next plan year. There is an exception for corporations whose bylaws restrict ownership to active participants and for S corporations.

The payment of distributions from an ESOP under IRC § 409(o) requires that a distribution in the event of disability, death, or normal retirement age, be made available no later than one year after the close of the plan year in which the participant separates from service. If the participant separates from service for any other reason, distributions must be made available no later than one year after the fifth plan year following the plan year in which the participant separates from service. IRC § 409(h)(5) allows the payments to cover the repurchase of shares put back to the company to be spread over a period of up to five years. The five-year period may be extended by one year for account balances over certain indexed dollar amounts.

VESTING

A participant's vested percentage will determine the amount of the participant's account balance that he or she will be entitled to on termination of employment. Generally, a participant is credited with a year of service for vesting in any year in which they are credited with 1,000 hours or more. ESOP shares that have been allocated are subject to statutory vesting requirements. The plan's vesting schedule must satisfy at all levels one of the minimum schedules:

- *Five-year cliff vesting.* Under five-year cliff vesting, an employee must be 100 percent vested after completing five years of service.
- *Seven-year graded vesting.* Under seven-year graded vesting, an employee must be 100 percent vested after completing seven years of service. Since this option allows the employer to delay 100 percent vesting for a longer period, there are minimum percentages that apply to earlier years:
  - □ 3 years of service—20 percent vesting
  - □ 4 years of service—40 percent vesting

□ 5 years of service—60 percent vesting

□ 6 years of service—80 percent vesting

If the contributions are used as employer matching contributions to employee 401(k) deferrals, the minimum vesting schedules are accelerated to three years for *cliff vesting* and graded vesting must begin after two years and be completed after six years.

A top-heavy plan is required to satisfy the vesting requirements under either a three-year cliff vesting schedule, or a six-year graded schedule. The term cliff vesting is used because the employee will leap from no vesting to 100% vesting upon completing the third year of service. A plan is generally considered top-heavy when more that 60 percent of the total fair market value of the plan's benefits are attributable to key employees, as defined in IRC § 416.

The plan may also be written to exclude service prior to the plan's effective date and/or the attainment of age 18 in calculating an employee's years of service for vesting purposes.

Example 1

John was hired on January 1, 1995, by XYZ Company at the age of 21 and terminated employment December 31, 2004. XYZ Company established an ESOP on January 1, 2002. The plan's vesting schedule is a five-year cliff schedule and excludes service prior to the effective date of the plan. Since John terminated prior to completing five years of service with XYZ Company, he has not vested interest in any allocation that he may have received for the years in which he was a participant in the XYZ Company ESOP.

Example 2

Consider the same fact as in Example 1, except that the XYZ Company plan has a seven-year graded schedule and service prior to the effective date of the plan is counted for calculating vested percentages. The plan is not top heavy. Since John terminated employment with greater than seven years of service, he is 100 percent vested.

The nonvested portion of a participant's account is generally forfeited and reallocated to other participants. The forfeiture may also be used to offset future employer contributions. The guidelines for allocating forfeitures are determined by the plan documents.

Terminated participants that are rehired prior to 5 one-year breaks in service must receive credit for prior service. The participants' full account balances must also be restored if they received no prior distribution. In the case of a partial distribution, a participant may repay the amount of the distribution to the plan within five years of rehire. After 5 one-year breaks in service, the participant's account balance is not required to be restored.

SUMMARY

Participants in an ESOP share in the investment of employer securities held within the plan as beneficial equity owners. A beneficial interest owner differs from that of a direct owner in a equity investment as the ability to *at-will* transact in their own interest is barred or controlled until triggering events as noted in this chapter are at hand as promulgated through ERISA and the plan design documents. In all material respects this translates to a restriction on the vesting, allocation of shares to the participant accounts, timing, and conversion of ESOP shares by the participant to other alternative investments, or cash.

In a private company environment with no public or active market, the shares held by the ESOP are the only shares that are available for ERISA mandated put rights. These rights may be best described as an opportunity to keep or transact the shares with either the plan or the company or both.

These details, together with other chapters in this text, provide a basis for the limited market environment for the ESOP shares and considerations for liquidity adjustments in the valuation of the shares and their comparison to those shares that are transacted in an active market.

6

Employee Benefit Perspective

"Ownership is a risk, but it carries with it rewards that are worth the risk, as proven by the overwhelmingly positive track record of employee ownership in this country,"[1] as stated by Michael Keeling, president of the ESOP Association. The concept of *think-like owners* captured in this quote provides a compelling reason for consideration of an ESOP.

BENEFITS OF ESOP TO EMPLOYEE

The benefits of an Employee Stock Ownership Plan to the employee have been researched and documented in many different studies. Invariably, there will exist differing beliefs on the subject; however, the overall results have shown that ESOPs have a positive impact on their outside shareholders, the companies, and their employees. There are an estimated 9,000+ ESOPs and a total of 8.2 million ESOP participants in the United States, representing 7.7 percent of private-sector employees.[2] Since their inception in 1974, the number of ESOPs being formed has been growing, especially with the new tax benefits of ESOP plans being allowed as S corporation shareholders (which is discussed at length in Chapter 15). It is important to note that ESOP companies, on average, outperform non–ESOP companies by approximately 2.3 percent on a number of measures, such as sales and employment growth.[3]

BENEFITS OF OWNERSHIP

The following are some of the specific attributes to the employee participant and the company:

- *Improvement of productivity.* Productivity improves by an extra 4 to 5 percent, on average, in the year an ESOP is adopted, and the higher productivity level is maintained in subsequent years. This one-time jump is more than twice the average annual productivity growth of the U.S. economy over the past 20 years.[4]

- *Sales increases.* Adoption of an ESOP is associated with an average increase of 2.3 percent in sales per employee.[5]

- *Retirement assets.* Initial results indicate that, on average, ESOP participants have 2.5 times more retirement assets than non-ESOP participants.[6]

- *Higher firm survival.* ESOP companies file bankruptcy less often than non-ESOP companies. One study tracking U.S. public companies from 1983 found that those with substantial employee ownership stakes were 20 percent more likely than their industry counterparts to survive through 1995.[7] Similarly, a study tracking all privately held companies with ESOPs in 1988 found they had higher survival rates than similar firms without ESOPs.[8]

> From a logical standpoint, this think-like-owners concept of beneficial ownership makes sense, given human nature is to take better care of the things that are yours.

OWNERSHIP CULTURE

To understand the psychology behind what makes employee ownership important, one needs to be familiar with the term *ownership culture.*

> Ownership culture is defined as the extent to which members of an organization think and act like owners.

Psychologists studying ownership suggest that the things we own are intimately tied to our sense of self, and that when employees care about their companies and the community of people who work there, their motivation is far more profound than their own financial well-being.[9] Surprisingly, however, data from the General Social Survey from the National Opinion Research Center shows that 32.1 percent of employees with stock or stock options in their company say they are more satisfied with their financial condition, compared to 23.1 percent of those without company stock.[10]

> Simply put, a strong ownership culture correlates directly to the success of the ESOP and sponsoring company.

The type of industry an employee is in can greatly affect their attitude as it relates to employee ownership. Case in point; the travel industry: With the increase in Internet usage, and the 1990s airlines capping commissions to such agencies, the travel industry had been cut in half from 1995 to 2002. Travel and Transport, Inc., is one example of a travel company preserved through employee ownership and the forming of an ESOP.[11] Travel and Transport, Inc., is a full-service travel management company. As of 2002, the company had 700 employees in 30 states, and the Omaha-based company was the ninth-largest travel management company in the United States and 74th largest majority employee-owned company. It was founded in 1946, but in 1991 two of the six owners, owning approximately one third of the company, were ready to sell. The board agreed that the best exit strategy was formation of an ESOP to buy out the owners. The employees were given the option on a voluntary basis to move money from their profit sharing plan into an ESOP. At least 90 percent was needed to raise the goal of $1 million; they got 98 percent. The ESOP, via a bank loan, acquired 30 percent of the shares. Then in 2000, the ESOP took out another loan to buy an additional 40 percent of the stock and converted to an S corporation (the first year this was available). In 2002, the ESOP bought the remaining 30 percent.

Although much of the right culture was in place at the outset, management has taken additional steps since the formation of the ESOP. Company financial information is shared in two principal ways. All employees are invited to an annual shareholder's meeting where the year's progress is reviewed in detail. Alternatively, employees can keep up to date with monthly staff meetings where managers provide updates on key numbers, trends, and challenges. These staff meetings also provide a forum for open discussions. In 2002, a Pride Committee was established to facilitate discussion of issues between management and employees on a regular basis.

The previous case study is an example of the concepts central to a successful ESOP—employee pride through ownership, job stability, management communication, sharing financial information with ESOP participants, and so on.

In examining the psychology of ownership, two researchers report that a sense of ownership has three primary determinants:

1. *Means of acquisition.* People need to understand the mechanism by which they became owners and to accept that mechanism as legitimate. This implies an understanding of the ESOP and the extent to which it gives them the legal status of owners

2. *Attachment.* As used in their research, attachment means intimate knowing. It entails a high degree of knowledge about the company and its operations.

3. *Control.* In this context, control does not mean absolute decision-making authority, but it does imply a degree of influence over the company and the daily work experience.[12]

Consider the retiring employee who has reached the age of 55, has participated in the ESOP for more than 10 years, and is ready to sell his stock. This employee will have the option of electing up to 25 percent of their stock account balance to be diversified into other investments. Once this employee is 60 years of age, with the 10-year minimum involvement, they are allowed to elect up to 50 percent to be diversified. This exemplifies the built-in flexibility of an ESOP to its employee participants.

THE COMPANY'S ROLE

An employee must also realize that different companies vary in their expectations of the results with an ESOP. The company expectation is important for employees to consider when an ESOP is made part of a benefits package. Certain employers simply want to provide employees with an added benefit. In these cases, the company could have minimal expectations that the ESOP will change any part of the psychology of the work force.

> In any business, the "fish" stinks from the head! Management and shareholders set the tone and expectations.

The second group of employers has expectations that being a part of ownership of a company should provide positive results. These results could be that the ESOP will provide a performance incentive. This expectation is born from the concept that if one "owns" a portion of the company, they will be inspired to perform better and work harder because the results will be personally gratifying and have a personal positive financial reward for them as owners.

In addition, an ESOP company may experience a sense of community within the ESOP participants; invoking improved attitudes, a stronger sense of family, and more involvement and communication.

> To illustrate: During my tenure as plan administrator-post ESOP, we had employee owners actually fistfight over waste and inefficiency!

Research indicates that much of the success of the ESOP is determined by how the management explains the details, company expectations, benefits and risks of forming an ESOP, the rights of participants, and the exchange of information between the company and the employees. If the details and benefits of the plan are not explained with sufficient reliability and completeness to enable the employees to understand the process and characteristics inherent in an ESOP, employees may be leery of its fascinating and empowering potential.

MANAGEMENT'S ROLE

Management plays a vital role. It is not difficult to understand the difference between employees and managers when it comes to company ownership. Inevitably, some participants may own more of the company than others, and therefore, may develop stronger feelings of the effects of ownership. However, if managers fail to address how the employees feel and a void in communication between the two levels is present, the ESOP may not reach its full potential. In one ownership culture survey, managers were asked what percentage of the work force felt like owners. They overstated the percentage of the work force who felt like owners by about 20 percent.[13]

Bridging understanding and ownership perception with participants should be a focus for management by ensuring that there exists a clear communication between the management and employees on the operation of the sponsoring company. If the risk and benefits to the employee are explained in a forthright and trustworthy manner, the employees will consider themselves more informed and will endeavor to continue to work toward the continued success of the company.

Kevin Ruble and Juli Baldwin, of The Pearl Group, in an article titled *"Help! Our Ownership Culture is Broken,"* describe the importance of motivating employee-owners to "understand, or conceive, the business the way an owner would."[14] The article comments on employee-owners embracing the spirit of doing the right thing, instead of focusing on doing things right, which results in a culture of risk avoidance and fear.[15] If you are an owner or manager in an ownership culture that is floundering, take certain steps to assure that all of the supports that can be given the employee owners are being taken.

ENRON EFFECT ON EMPLOYEE OWNERS

Events in our none-too-distant past, such as the negative impact of Enron and other shadowed corporation fallouts, have altered the landscape of certain attitudes in the stability and risk perceptions of ESOPs. Employees were financially aggrieved by deception and greed of collusion and misrepresentations of the corporate leadership and their independent accounting firm. In an effort to reduce the panic and fear instilled in employee owners, there has been an increase post-Enron to pass legislation pertaining to restricting employee ownership and requiring diversification avenues. In response, many companies now offer alternative retirement plans, or plans in addition to an ESOP.

For example, Sara Lee Corporation, "to achieve its objective of becoming "the employer of choice for highly talented people," instituted a series of broad-based stock ownership plans that would provide ownership to virtually every employee. Through a combination of stock options, ESOP participation, a 401(k) plan, and an ESPP (employee stock purchase plan), more than 50 percent of Sara Lee employees, in one form or another, are company owners."[16] The key for companies, to a certain degree, seems to be to ensure that they offer diversification options to employees in an effort to reduce the risk of total loss from only one type of investment mechanism.

SUMMARY

The benefits of ESOP participation have been studied, researched, and reported. From an employee ownership perspective, there are risks and benefits within and outside their control that must be considered. Many factors, both within the control of the employee, and not, will affect the success of the company and, through the ESOP, the employee participant's investment in its shares. Once an employee becomes an owner, history reveals that knowledge and involvement are major ingredients that play an important role in not only the improvement and benefit of the employee owner's confidence, career satisfaction, and increased financial wealth, but also for the welfare of the company, other plan participants, management, industry, economy, and the plan itself.

7

Leverage and the ESOP: A Lender's Perspective*

The purpose of this chapter is to provide a banking perspective on lending in a leveraged ESOP transaction. Many companies contemplating an ESOP are most likely familiar with the merits of this type of transaction. When structured properly, transacting shares with an ESOP is a win–win situation with significant income tax and other motivating advantages that abound if the company is a candidate and has the right employee culture for a leveraged ESOP. The shareholders and management of the company may have even discussed the subject with a lender to determine a preliminary indication of interest in financing such arrangement. Although a banker would likely find this chapter of interest, it is primarily targeted toward a borrower in an ESOP environment.

LOANS FOR OPERATIONS OR OUTSIDE SHARE PURCHASES

All things being equal, loans from commercial lenders follow an understanding that the loan proceeds will be used in the operation of a business and thus reside in some form or fashion to purchase assets, replace other debt instruments, and provide working capital or similar operational matters of the company. This is not necessarily the case with ESOP lending, as loan proceeds can be, and often are, used to acquire shares of private equity stocks from existing shareholder owners of a closely held corporation. The proceeds are not used for the production of income from the company but are handed over to the shareholder; thus, only reside as a debt obligation of the sponsoring company to be repaid from its ongoing production of income.

INFORMED ADVISORS AND EXPERIENCED BANKS

From a lender's perspective, the borrower contemplating debt in a leveraged ESOP transactional environment should engage a financial specialist who has

---

*This chapter was contributed by James Coleman.

experience in this area and who will review the various aspects of a leveraged ESOP and its associated nuances with the borrower and lender. In most cases, the borrower also will have obtained additional viewpoints that corroborate the ESOP transaction and the borrowing as appropriate and financially feasible under current conditions.

If life experience is the best teacher, a lender with a small bank or a specialty lender, such as a commercial finance company or a real estate–oriented institution, may give a blank stare when a leveraged ESOP transaction is requested for the first time. Although these types of loans are not out of the ordinary, they are comparatively complicated, and most bankers have not had an opportunity to participate first hand in this type of loan structure in the past. ESOP loan documentation is quite voluminous, and the ESOP closing transaction is almost always date sensitive. Additionally, the transaction is subject to intense scrutiny by various governmental agencies. The importance of facilitating the borrowing transaction in a timely and legally appropriate manner is obvious.

The lending institutions most likely to have expertise in this type of transaction are large commercial banks. Over the last couple of years, leveraged ESOP transactions have gone from an exotic, niche-type loan to a highly sought after transaction where larger institutions have trained staff and developed entire ESOP-related transaction departments. Moreover, the larger stock brokerage houses have developed telemarketing programs to develop leads for this type of loan, and insurance agents often introduce the idea of a leveraged ESOP when the subject company renews or proposes commercial insurance matters. There are numerous financial advisors with a specialty in this type of transaction who assist the sponsor company in obtaining financing for the stock purchases from outside shareholders or from newly issued shares. Because it is important that the sponsor company choose the source of its financing wisely, it should obtain referrals from financial advisors and lenders that have experience with these types of loans.

WHAT TO EXPECT FROM THE BANK

For those lenders that understand the ESOP transaction and its requirements, these loans are highly desirable. The banks that have an understanding of leveraged ESOPs will likely be aggressive in their desire to put them in their loan portfolio. While there is a high expense on the bank's side in booking and monitoring these loans, as well as a learning curve to surmount, these loans are typically made to companies with very solid financial basics (i.e., ideal customers from the bank's standpoint).

As an example, if an ESOP transaction involves an election under the special IRC § 1042, collateral for the debt may largely be diversified, high-quality, publicly traded (liquid) securities. In other words, these loans are extremely solid, and the terms and rate offered by the lender should be very competitive. If the

ESOP-sponsoring company is currently enjoying a relationship with a lender who understands these transactions, the existing and continuing business with them will act as an additional incentive for those relationships to continue.

Loan Specifics

Although there is not adequate space to provide a tutorial in borrowing money, there are a couple of identifiable specifics to ESOP lending. These loan specifics can be generally grouped into discussions on structure of the loan, documentation issues, and servicing, both from the borrower's standpoint and that of the lenders.

The structure of the note is fairly rigid from a maturity and payment standpoint. There is no balloon payment, and the amortization of principal and interest payments is straightforward. Term payments are typically made on a quarterly basis, because the loan liquidates over a period that will normally be determined as ideal for plan contributions to the ESOP to purchase stock and vest the employee participants. Typically, the lender takes the proceeds of the stock sold by its owners and uses it as security and takes an assignment of the company stock sold to the ESOP as collateral. This lender position is not normally subject to significant negotiation.

Where surety can get sticky is in the margin requirement that the lender expects and often requires on the security in the form of cash or publicly traded stock in the event of reinvestment under IRS like-kind provisions under IRC § 1042. Lenders normally make commercial loans on high-quality publicly traded stock, with more stock value than loan principal, to protect the surety coverage in the event of a decline in the general market or the publicly traded stock held as surety for the note. Lenders commonly look at leveraged ESOP loans as liquid secured transactions. As an example of a typical loan margin requirement, $1.25 or $1.50 in stock or other assets are pledged in relation to every $1.00 that the lender loans. This margin requirement varies, depending on the aggressiveness of the lender, its perception of the credit-worthiness of the transaction, and the surety pledged or guarantee given.

It is not unusual for a liquid or stock-secured transaction having a value to loan amount ratio of one to one at inception of the loan, primarily due to the initial ESOP transaction generating no available margin. This is often mitigated by the fact that the high-quality borrower is paying down the loan principal on a systematic, regular interval, and the lender may have other collateral secured. That being said, there is always a potential note call on the borrower, guarantor, or other responsible party if the loan margin falls below acceptable levels. It is vital to understand this issue. In the event the loan margin falls below acceptable levels, the lender most often requires other collateral in the form of cash or acceptable stocks, added to the existing portfolio pledged. Negotiations in this area are critical for the understanding of all parties to the transaction. It is not unreasonable or unusual to require the lender to release surety when the margin exceeds a prescribed amount, thereby allowing the owner of the pledged portfolio to realize liquidity prior to final maturity of the loan.

For example, a lender once made an ESOP loan to a company where the selling shareholder pledged a diversified portfolio consisting of 20 stocks. The loan committee, during approval of the loan, requested the list of public stocks being pledged, and upon review, were in general agreement that these public equity shares indeed were of the highest quality and represented a diversified portfolio. Each of the 20 stocks comprised exactly 5 percent of the portfolio at origination, and there was no concentration of any one stock or in any one specific industry sector. A margin requirement of 1:1 was negotiated. Within months of the leveraged ESOP transaction, one of the stocks was involved in one of the largest corporate failures in America. Within a year of the consummation of this loan, 18 of the 20 premium equity stocks had significantly fallen in value. The lender looked for this shortfall to be covered by the selling shareholder. The sponsoring company was in a position to advance payments and place company cash in a collateral account to cover the shortfall and maintain the margin as agreed. They were allowed to recover these funds as the loan was paid down or the portfolio went up, and the margin was ultimately restored.

Banks can be persuaded to use other collateral, both in addition to and entirely in place of publicly traded securities. Although most bankers are quite fond of liquid collateral, it is possible to use other collateral. The borrower should be made aware that negotiating substitute collateral can make an already complicated transaction more complicated and may lead to changes in other terms.

Documentation Issues

The larger the transaction and the more sophisticated the lender, the more likely there will be special clauses in the documents. On any type of loan with a lender, the borrower may not be successful in negotiating the deletion of demand and other clauses. These are provisions in the documents giving the bank the right to call the loan, even if there is no specific failure of any single clause. The borrower should request this verbiage be removed to eliminate any ambiguity in the event of a default.

Additionally, a right to cure any default clause should be included, requiring the lender to notify the borrower in the event of a default. This *right to cure* clause can be divided into monetary and nonmonetary defaults. Monetary defaults are generally straightforward; they involve a missed or past-due payment of principal and interest. It is reasonable for the borrower to request a relatively short period of time after notice to cure this type of default, such as 10 days from the date of the notice.

Nonmonetary defaults involve noncompliance with requirements other than loan payments. These types of defaults may pertain to reporting requirements or the maintenance of financial covenants related to cash flow, leverage, or liquidity of the sponsoring company or another guarantor. Certain events such as bankruptcy may trigger a note default. Although the borrower might not be able to eliminate all such covenants, it should negotiate reasonable reporting requirements, particularly if the loan is secured by liquid securities or other similar assets. An extended cure period for nonmonetary default can be requested, but will not normally be granted in excess of 30 days. Failure to cure a default in a timely manner will possibly trigger the right of set off or forced sale of any liquid securities collateralizing the transaction, as well as the potential for other unpleasant responses from the lender.

Servicing the loan from the lender's standpoint will consist primarily of keeping track of the collateral. The lender can automate this process and monitor it regularly. The lender is required to release the company stock it is holding in the ESOP's name in increments as the loan principal is paid down. The certificates of the subject company pledged should be divided into multiple certificates, and the number of certificates should correspond to the number of payments in the amortization of the loan. This tends to encourage quarterly payments of principal and interest. The lender also monitors the sponsor company's financial information on a regular basis, just as it would for any working capital loan. The customer should also automate this process so the bank does not have to ask for the information. The borrower should negotiate the provision of their financial information to prevent the burden of producing unnecessary and unusual documentation.

Additional Requirements

There is additional annual reporting required when an ESOP is originated, detailed elsewhere in this book. Be aware of these requirements. Any time a loan is over the million-dollar threshold, a financial audit is normally required by commercial lenders of the sponsor company's financial statements. If the borrower is not accustomed to having independent financial statement audits performed on an annual basis, it should include this requirement into its cost of borrowing and implementing an ESOP. First-year financial audits can be a pricey expenditure.

Loan documentation and related expenditures are generally borne by the borrower. The lender typically requires its approved attorneys to draft all the related loan documents, including those specific to the ESOP. Although this is a one-time charge, it can be significant and should be considered.

REPAYMENT OF THE LOAN USING ESOP ASSETS

A lender can seek repayment of a loan to an ESOP only out of the following plan assets:

- Assets acquired with exempt loan proceeds that are collateral for the loan
- Collateral used in a prior loan repaid with the proceeds of the current loan

- Contributions made to the ESOP by the sponsoring company to the plan
- Earnings on the collateral

Should the loan secured by the sponsoring company's securities held in the suspense account default, the lender can have the suspense account assets transferred to the extent of the remaining loan balance.

RELEASE OF STOCK FROM SUSPENSE ACCOUNT

In general, as the loan principal is repaid, the sponsoring company stock used to secure the debt is released from the suspense account. The employer shares used to secure the initial debt, including any renewal, extensions, or refinancing, are released (an ERISA requirement) from the suspense account after 10 years, thus releasing it as collateral.

IRC § 4975 (d)(3) and Regulation § 54.4975-7(b)(3) provide that an ESOP loan must be primarily for the benefit of the ESOP participants. Thus, a plan should not provide that the loan may be repaid using proceeds derived from the sale of unallocated employer securities held in the suspense account. If repayment is made by selling unallocated sponsoring company shares, those shares sold will not be available for allocation to the participant's accounts, and such activity could cause the loan not to be exempt from the prohibited transaction rules as an exempt loan.

Employer securities acquired with an ESOP loan create an obligation by the employer to make annual contributions to the plan sufficient to meet the plan's obligation of paying interest and principal on the debt.

SUMMARY

These comments provide insight for the appraiser as to the fundamental importance of debt and collateral for the loan and also provide some of the important aspects related to a lender's perspective on ESOP lending. As with any transaction of this importance, obtaining competent legal counsel from an attorney skilled in the issues relating to leveraged ESOP transactions is very important and helpful.

When considering a third-party lender, the borrower may ask for a referral to a source of financing from the financial advisor and then obtain details of related ESOP experience. It is important for the borrower to develop at least two viable lenders and require them to give a commitment letter or term sheet, detailing the terms and conditions of the lending offering. This commitment letter is regarded as an initial offer and can be further negotiated, while the term sheet will provide an apparent picture of the lenders' level of interest and capabilities.

The note structure is similar to other loans. The borrower should negotiate to obtain the best terms and interest rate available and should pay particular attention to the requirements related to the collateral value and consider where substitute collateral will come from if the portfolio underperforms or other collateral is rendered inadequate.

8

Independence, Objectivity, and Good Faith

An annual valuation of shares held in the ESOP of a sponsoring company is required in accordance with the Tax Reform Act of 1986. A valuation is also required when the ESOP makes its first acquisition of stock, if the ESOP sells out its stock position, and whenever there is a transaction with a controlling stockholder or member of a control group.

VALUATION OF SHARES

Every ESOP valuation must fulfill two government departments' regulations, those of the Internal Revenue Service (IRS) and those of the Department of Labor (DOL). The primary charge of the IRS is, not surprisingly, tax revenue generations, concentrating on deductibility, statuses of entity for tax, transactions with the ESOP, shareholder treatment on sale, transactions to and from the sponsoring company, reporting, and so on. The primary charge of the DOL regarding ESOPs is the welfare of the plan participants, providing compliance with ERISA, good faith, reasonableness, and reporting, and ensuring nondiscrimination in plan features and benefits.

WHAT CONSTITUTES INDEPENDENCE AND OBJECTIVITY

Engaging an ESOP appraiser to fulfill these valuation requirements is the responsibility of the ESOP plan trustee (a fiduciary responsibility). Among other considerations, the trustee must ensure that the appraiser is independent and objective. What constitutes the requirements *independent* and *objective* is not thoroughly understood and often not easily answered. There is a lack of qualifying literature related to the specific subject matter.

WHAT CONSTITUTES GOOD FAITH

The Department of Labor is convincingly clear that any fiduciary engaged in the development of and responsibility for the estimation of adequate consideration of ESOP shares, must meet and act in the capacity of certain good-faith criteria. The DOL also makes it clear that the fiduciary duties, which include the appraiser, must fit an elevated standard to that of routine, as the consequences are crucial to the determination of adequate consideration of the ESOP shares. An equitable result in the determination of adequate consideration hinges on the statutory exemption to the prohibited transaction rules promulgated by ERISA.

DOL DEFINITION USED FOR GUIDANCE

The DOL Code of Federal Regulations § 103(a)(3)(A) requires that the accountant retained by an employee benefit plan be "independent" for purposes of examining plan financial information and rendering an opinion on the financial statements and schedules required to be contained in the annual report filed with the DOL. The Department of Labor released an Interpretive Bulletin in reference to these regulations, providing guidelines for determining when a qualified public accountant is independent:

> Under the authority of section 103(a)(3)(A) the Department of Labor will not recognize any person as an independent qualified public accountant who is in fact not independent with respect to the employee benefit plan upon which that accountant renders an opinion in the annual report filed with the Department of Labor. For example, an accountant will not be considered independent with respect to a plan if the following three criteria hold true.
>
> (1) During the period of professional engagement to examine the financial statements being reported, at the date of the opinion, or during the period covered by the financial statements, the accountant or his or her firm or a member thereof had, or was committed to acquire, any direct financial interest or any material indirect financial interest in such plan, or the plan sponsor, as that term is defined in section 3(16)(B) of the Act.
>
> (2) During the period of professional engagement to examine the financial statements being reported, at the date of the opinion, or during the period covered by the financial statements, the accountant, his or her firm or a member thereof was connected as a promoter, underwriter, investment advisor, voting trustee, director, officer, or employee of the plan or plan sponsor, except that a firm will not be deemed independent in regard to a particular plan if a former officer or employee of such plan or plan sponsor is employed by the firm, and such individual has completely disassociated himself from the plan or plan sponsor and does not participate in auditing financial statements of the plan covering any period of his or her employment by the plan or plan sponsor. For the purpose of this bulletin, the term "member" means all partners or shareholder employees in the firm

and all professional employees participating in the audit or located in an office of the firm participating in a significant portion of the audit;

(3) An accountant or a member of an accounting firm maintains financial records for the employee benefit plan.

However, an independent, qualified public accountant may permissibly engage in or have members of his or her firm engage in certain activities which will not have the effect of removing recognition of his or her independence. For example, (1) an accountant will not fail to be recognized as independent if at or during the period of his or her professional engagement with the employee benefit plan, the accountant or his or her firm is retained or engaged on a professional basis by the plan sponsor, as that term is defined in section 3(16)(B) of the Act.

However, to retain recognition of independence under such circumstances, the accountant must not violate the prohibitions against recognition of independence established under paragraphs (1), (2) or (3) of this interpretive bulletin; (2) the rendering of services by an actuary associated with an accountant or accounting firm shall not impair the accountant's or accounting firm's independence. However, it should be noted that the rendering of services to a plan by an actuary and accountant employed by the same firm may constitute a prohibited transaction under section 406(a)(1) (C) of the Act. The rendering of such multiple services to a plan by a firm will be the subject of a later interpretive bulletin that will be issued by the Department of Labor.

In determining whether an accountant or accounting firm is not, in fact, independent with respect to a particular plan, the Department of Labor will give appropriate consideration to all relevant circumstances, including evidence bearing on all relationships between the accountant or accounting firm and that of the plan sponsor or any affiliate thereof, and will not confine itself to the relationships existing in connection with the filing of annual reports with the Department of Labor.[1]

INTERNAL REVENUE DEFINITION

The IRS, as the other relevant regulating agency, describes in IRC § 401(a)(28)(c) that an ESOP that holds employer securities that are not readily tradable on a securities market must have all valuations of those securities made by an "independent" appraiser.[2] Section 401 goes on to say that an appraiser is independent if requirements similar to those found under § (a)(1) for a "qualified appraiser" are satisfied. Unfortunately, § 170(a)(1) does not provide a clearer explanation, but rather simply restates the term *independent*.[3] For further clarification, Treasury Regulation § 1.170A–13(c)(5) provides that a qualified appraiser must declare the following on the appraisal summary:

- The appraiser holds himself/herself out to the public as an appraiser or performs appraisals on a regular basis.

- The appraiser is qualified to make appraisals of the type of property being valued; and provides a description of his/her qualifications pursuant to Reg. 1.170A–13(c)(3)(ii)(F).

- An appraiser is not independent if the appraiser is the taxpayer that maintains the ESOP (or a member of the controlled group of corporations that includes such taxpayer), the appraiser is a party to the transaction in which the ESOP acquired the property, the appraiser is employed by the taxpayer maintaining the ESOP (or any entity described in subparagraphs a. or b., above), the appraiser who regularly appraises an entity described above and who does not perform a majority of his or her appraisals for other entities.[4]

IRS Announcement 94-101 provides a definition more thorough than IRC § 401, and is akin to the definition provided in the DOL's Interpretive Bulletin. The purpose of the announcement was to provide a checklist for pension plan auditors. Under the section titled *Employee Stock Ownership Plan (ESOP) Issues,* the IRS mentions "appraisal independence" and provides a list of several examples when an appraiser would not be independent and an example of when an appraiser is independent. The IRS explains that as long as the appraiser performs a majority of appraisals for entities other than the employer maintaining the ESOP or entities related to it, the appraiser is an independent appraiser.

DEFINITION OF USPAP

The Appraisal Standards Board of The Appraisal Foundation (a congressionally authorized foundation trust and not-for-profit source for appraisal standards and appraiser qualifications), develops, publishes, interprets, and amends the Uniform Standards of Professional Appraisal Practice and Advisory Options (USPAP) on behalf of appraisers and users of appraisal services. The 2004 edition is the thirteenth annual publication of USPAP and the sections cited in this text are its most current. Although this is a living document, the areas specific to independence and objectivity are cornerstone items in the quest for pure play appraisals for all appraisal assignments. Knowing this publication is used by state and federal regulatory agencies and others in annual interpretation and amendment of current regulations is of considerable importance in this and other areas of appraisal services.

Several sections of the USPAP standards apply:

- Ethical conduct
- Performance of assignments
  - With impartiality
  - Objectivity
  - Independence
  - Without accommodation of personal interest

- Written appraisal reports contain a signed statement
- Limited only by the reported assumptions and conditions
- Personal, impartial, and unbiased analyses, and conclusion
- No present or prospective interest to the property
- No personal interest with the parties involved
- No bias with respect to the property
- No bias to the parties involved

REQUIREMENTS OF APPRAISER

An added complication in the determination of an appropriate appraiser is that there is no particular degree or license required in this field. However, it is important to realize that the industry has attempted to be self-regulating by creating organizations and associations that bestow upon professionals certain designations. These include, but are not limited to CPA, ABV, CBA, ASA, CFA, and CVA. Each will consist of similar but differing requirements for designation, depending on the organization bestowing the designation. Although these labels may seem confusing to those outside the industry, the benefit is that they may provide a starting point in the decision-making process of hiring an appraiser.

RELEVANT CASE LAW

It is important to realize that the majority of lawsuits filed regarding ESOPs involve the issues surrounding the valuation and the appraiser. The focus in a large number of these cases is on the process that was utilized in obtaining the valuation, as opposed to the actual valuation amount itself. It is no surprise, with the lack of a definitive description as to what constitutes "independence" and "competent" in relation to the appraiser, that this issue is often the focal point of debate in a lawsuit.

Although, as already stated, most ESOP cases involve valuation and appraisal issues, there has not been an abundance of case law that specifically provides much direct assistance in how independence of an appraiser should be determined. However, a review of the case *Capital City Excavating Co., Inc. v. Commissioner*[5] is helpful. In this case, the fact that the treasurer of the company, who was also a member of the board of directors, accomplished the appraisal did not preclude a favorable decision for *Capital City* by the U.S. Tax Court. In this case, the IRS contested the appraisal result as being too high and therefore representing more than adequate consideration for the shares sold to the ESOP. The court found that the methodology used and the price at which the treasurer ultimately arrived was reasonable under the circumstances. The court said, "A showing of adequate consideration requires not only that the sale price reflect fair market value, but also that the process by which the price set conform to established standards of fiduciary care." No mention was even made as to the appraiser's independence—even though the appraisal had been performed by someone who was clearly a company insider as treasurer of the company and a member of the board of directors. It is important to realize that the court focused on the process involved, and not the value determined.

The conclusion that can be drawn is that an appraisal can be independent if, first, appraisals are done for companies outside the one for which the appraisal is being provided, and, second, the firm or individual appraiser hold themselves out to the public as an appraiser, rather than just an administrator. Until further regulations or laws are established, these guiding principles from regulations and interpretations from case law are the only true guidelines to follow in defining the "independence" and "objectivity" of an appraiser.

APPRAISER'S ROLE

It is important to remember that in the context of ESOPs and independent appraisals, a distinction must be made between the role of the appraiser and that of an appraiser as *financial advisor*. The main difference lies in that the appraiser's purpose is to determine the fair market value (FMV) of the company's shares. The financial advisor evaluates the overall reasonableness within the adequate consideration requirement of the ESOP transactions and interrelated matters and communicates their observations, suggestions, and recommendations to the plan trustee on matters of the valuation.

The foundation for an ESOP trustee to obtain an impartial, objective, and independent appraiser is ERISA's mandate to give reasonable assurance that the ESOP not pay more than "adequate consideration" for the securities it acquires nor provide retirement benefits through transactions of the sponsoring company securities for less than adequate consideration. This mandate is to ensure that the ESOP beneficial ownership interest is treated equitably, and the most logical method to ensuring equitable treatment to the plan participants is for the appraiser to objectively estimate FMV of the shares of the company held by the plan. The standard set by the IRS for fair market value can be found in IRS Revenue Ruling 59-60.[6]

SUMMARY

Impartiality, objectivity, and independence are three words that are not necessarily synonymous in every context, as most valuation literature lists all three when defining the requirements for valuation of ESOP shares. Collectively, these words take on a special meaning, and it is within this shared context that we find the true essence of *professional neutrality*.

Ensuring that an appraiser is professionally neutral is one of the most important decisions the company will have to make in relation to an ESOP and its plan trustee. With the guidance of regulations, code sections, ethics, standards and case law—coupled with common sense and an effort at reasonable judgment—impartiality, objectivity, and independence should be attainable.

9

The Appraiser as a
Financial Advisor

F acilitator, guide, advisor, consultant, specialist, fiduciary, expert in ERISA — the appraiser whose job it is to act as a financial advisor (FA) to the plan trustee must wear all these hats.

ROLE OF THE FA

The fundamental role of the FA is to assist the plan trustee, or named fiduciary, in the financial assessment of evenhandedness in financial reporting and plan transactions involving the shares held by the plan and to provide a basis for the trustee to comply and act in good faith. Trustees are responsible for the valuation of the assets of the plan. If plan trustees are appropriately independent, they can decide to undertake the valuation themselves. In this instance, a trustee must possess the expertise to compose the valuation in fulfillment of the various requirements necessary to meet the prudent and sound business principles provisions of proposed DOL rules. However, in most cases, the trustee engages an FA and defines his or her specific role, which generally centers on the valuation of plan shares. The FA role may be diverse for each engagement, and in some instances there is more than one FA. Although the roles may be ill defined and interrelated, they require a working understanding of ERISA, valuation, plan design, plan administration and ability to act objectively.

As Related to the Plan Asset Valuation

The FA's role related to plan asset valuations is grounded in the *Federal Register* (DOL-Pension Welfare Benefits Administration–29 CFR Part 2510 Proposed Regulations; the full text of this regulation can be found in the *Federal Register* at *www.fdic.gov/regulations/trust/trust/secea.html*. The DOL no longer cites the proposed regulation as not being required because it was not designed as authoritative. However, it continues to be referenced and is included under FDIC guidance in their valuation of securities when there is no organized market for the shares involved.)

Good faith is a general matter established by an objective (unbiased) standard of conduct, rather than a subjective (biased) standard of conduct. The DOL establishes that two factors must be present for good-faith provisions to be met:

1. The FA must apply sound business principles of evaluation and conduct a prudent investigation of the circumstances prevailing at the time of the valuation.

2. Either the fiduciary making the valuation must be independent of all the parties to the transaction other than the plan, or the fiduciary must rely on the report of an appraiser who is independent of all the parties to the transaction other than the plan.

It appears clear that an FA can be either a firm or an individual who provides service and is responsible to the trustee. It is also clear that in order to act in the capacity of FA as appraiser, the FA must be neutral and cannot be an interested party. It is the trustee's responsibility to make all decisions that are exclusively in the best interest and benefit of the plan participants.

As an Independent Advisor

The job of the FA is that of an independent advisor, contractual with the plan and often paid for by the sponsoring company.

> Payment of fees by the sponsoring company or the plan itself does not in any way impair the independence of the FA.

The FA advises the trustee as an analyst on financial matters specific to valuation issue, timing, and structure that assist the trustee's financial negotiations with selling shareholders and other related decisions. Examples of the FA's assistance may include plan feasibility studies, share valuation, debt and cash-flow modeling, terms and conditions of loans, basic financial analysis, forecasting of various decision-tree scenarios, plan content and structure, tax status of the sponsoring company, consideration of outside investments of the plan, plan liquidity, and repurchase liability studies.

The plan trustee, however, has the ultimate responsibility for all plan decisions and directing its activities, and as such, they are not required to follow any part of the FA's advice. It is permissible for the trustee to specifically contract with others only those activities they deem as appropriate in their circumstances. The trustee can be more than one person, come from outside the company and the plan, a member of the sponsoring company's management, or a plan participant. In addition to the prudence imposed on the trustee, the good faith requirement mandates independence, and it is usually in the context of seeking independence that an FA is engaged. For purposes of this text, the trustee of the plan will engage the services of the FA specifically for sponsoring company share valuation(s).

QUALIFICATIONS AND RESPONSIBILITIES

There are specific qualifications and responsibilities that should be considered when hiring an FA. A trustee must take special care in choosing an FA because of the FA's important role in ensuring that fair market value of the company's shares is obtained, as seen from the perspective of the ESOP participants as beneficial shareholders. FAs also play a significant role in the resolve of the trustees' fiduciary duty. Their qualifications might include the following:

- Diverse background in financial analysis and modeling
- Training and experience in general business and the specific industry
- Communication skill set, both verbal and written
- Business valuation experience and credentials
- Accomplished in the type of contemplated plan transactions
- Reasonable knowledge of ERISA, DOL, IRS, USPAP, and other applicable rules specific to an ESOP
- Ability to identify, investigate, analyze, and fulfill the engagement requirements
- Ability to possess, exhibit, and maintain objectivity, integrity, and independence
- Ability to maintain an eminence as reasonable, neutral, and impartial

The essential role of an FA is to act as a financial advisor to the plan fiduciary (trustee). In most instances, the FA will report directly to the trustee, and it is the trustee's responsibility to ensure that the FA accomplishes certain tasks.

In most ESOP transactions, an FA, in some capacity, advises the trustee throughout the course of the transactions, often including the transactional negotiations for shares and share value with outside shareholders, debt structure and repayment, business succession issues, and so on. An FA is often engaged during and/or subsequent to ESOP transactions to evaluate the transactions from a financial perspective, approximating the overall reasonableness (adequacy) of the transaction as to terms, conditions, and pricing. An FA advises the trustee and, in many cases, explains valuation reasoning to the outside shareholders and management.

In the case of valuation of shares held or contemplated to be held by the plan, the FA is commonly engaged by the trustee to offer a conclusion regarding compliance with the Department of Labor pronouncements for *adequate consideration* often expressed as synonymous with fair market value. The FA's valuation letter and report provides a documented analysis of compliance of an offer made by outside shareholders or by the plan that the transaction is not outside the provisions of adequate consideration as promulgated by DOL.

The case of *Gary L. Eyler v. Commissioner,* 88 F.2d 445 (7th Cir. 1996), concerns ESOP valuation with an in-depth explanation from the court as to what is expected of an appraiser valuing shares for an ESOP transaction. In *Eyler,* the sponsoring company negotiated a loan from a bank to be secured by shares sold to an ESOP. The ESOP purchased approximately 13.7 percent of the common stock of the sponsoring company with the proceeds from the bank loan. The price paid for the shares by the ESOP was considered "fair," being based on the recent valuations prepared for the IPO. The court made very clear that this price did not constitute adequate consideration, and that the IPO valuations should not have been relied upon as a basis for the share value. A new valuation for the loan transaction should have been conducted by an appraiser, taking into account changes since the IPO valuation and stressing the importance of valuations being conducted at the time of the transaction. The appeals court stated the following:

> [We] find no merit to . . . [the] contention that the Board of Directors was well-informed and therefore, made a good faith determination of the fair market value of the stock. The record does not show that even one director, let alone a majority, sought independent information on the fair market value of the stock. . . . A prudent person would not have relied upon the dated Pru-Bache estimated price for the ESOP stock purchase in light of the failed IPO and changing financial conditions at the corporation. Moreover, there is no evidence that the board was knowledgeable about the effects of these changing conditions on the fair market value of CTS stock.

Although there is much language relevant to fiduciary duty, the court's language also clearly indicates the importance of an independent appraisal being conducted at the time of an ESOP transaction.

In order for an FA to provide a well-reasoned analysis of compliance, an FA must be informed on relevant regulations, court decisions, laws, practices, guidelines, and other controlling measures from agencies such as the IRS and DOL and must have access to the resources needed to support their conclusions. Initially, the valuation estimate may take the form of a compliance letter to the trustee, outlining the steps taken and documents reviewed by the advisor in determining whether the transaction is reasonably in compliance. An FA will generally be required to prepare a thorough valuation report that includes considerations found in IRS Revenue Ruling 59-60 and extended amendments in the *Federal Register*

(Department of Labor, Pension Welfare Benefits Administration's proposed regulations, 29 CFR Part 2510).

SUMMARY

The FA, whose principal responsibility is the valuation, is, debatably, the most important component to an ESOP. The valuation affects so many different transactions and decisions of the ESOP that the individual who will provide conference to the trustee should be chosen carefully. However, there is no requirement for a trustee, ESOP committee, or company to follow the recommendations or respond to the observations of the FA.

10

Financial Analysis of the Sponsoring Corporation: Framing the Appraisal Assignment

W here no active market exists for private equity securities, the Tax Reform Act of 1986 requires an annual valuation of the sponsoring company shares held by an ESOP. Additionally, a valuation is necessary when the ESOP makes its first acquisition of stock or liquidates its share position, and whenever there is a transaction with a controlling stockholder or member of a control group.

The essentials of analyzing the sponsoring company must be consistent with the scope and intent of a number of governmental compliance requirements. The overriding provisions dealing with adequate consideration are found in the Department of Labor's proposed regulation 29 C.F.R. 2510.3-18(b). See Appendix A for the full text of these provisions. The document contains general guidance of congressional intent, fiduciary good faith, and requirements to satisfy requisites for the statutory exemption for ESOP shares that allows the plan to transact with what would otherwise be a prohibited party by ERISA.

The DOL requirement, both express and implied, is that the share's fair market value be *incorporated* into the definition of adequate consideration; thus, fair market value is not necessarily synonymous with the adequate consideration. Additionally, the DOL acknowledges the imperfections of the valuation process and that valuation is a range concept rather than a specific amount.

Under the good-faith provisions of the DOL authority, the fiduciary must determine fair market value in good faith when establishing an objective (as opposed to a subjective) standard of conduct. As appraiser, the relevant facts and circumstances are to be identified, quantified, and analyzed. Since the primary engagement of the appraiser is centered on the valuation of ESOP plan shares, a prudent investigation of circumstances prevailing on or about the valuation date and application of sound business valuation principles, as well as a full description of the relevance and significance of each valuation methodology, should be taken into account.

In the analysis and framing of share valuation in the context of an ESOP engagement, the subtitles listed are only those that specifically identify matters that are unique to those that might be encountered in ESOP appraisals. Accordingly, the appraiser should exercise appropriate professional judgment of the contents of this chapter.

PURPOSE OF THE APPRAISAL

In an ERISA ESOP plan, the participants in the plan hold *beneficial interests* in plan assets through an investment pooling of those assets. At least annually, the participants are provided a statement of their accounts that indicate their proportionate share of sponsoring company stock, cash and other investments, and, of course, corresponding particulars of their vesting and other data at that plan's year-end. In essence, each participant is allocated a proportionate share of the plan assets on a line-item basis of the asset make-up at the end of the plan year resulting from this pooling.

> The ownership of the outstanding shares of sponsoring company stock is held by the plan and treated as one entity owner, not by the participants individually.

The plan is considered as one shareholder for all the shares of stock held by it. It is treated as assets held in trust, awaiting triggering events defined in the plan documents for the plan participants' exclusive and nondiscriminatory benefit.

The trustee of the plan generally retains an appraiser for transactional events other than participant distributions, and for annual updates for participant account statements, distributions, and governmental filing purposes. The decisions regarding appraisal dates and other pertinent details are governed by the plan trustee and the appraiser's engagement for services.

PREMISE OF ENGAGEMENT

Unless engaged to provide services for a plan termination, which, given certain circumstances, could alter the premise to liquidation, the primary appraisal engagement involves the going concern valuation of shares in the aggregate, illustrated by the proportionate number of shares outstanding to that held by the

ESOP. Often as a matter of assistance, a one-share value is calculated and illustrated. It is acceptable to round the per-share value because the degree of accuracy in a private company is not exacting, and the public trading marketplace counterparts acknowledge a range of transactional prices within any given day, week, month, quarter, or year.

Aggregating the equity shares' value for all shares—with or without the prerogatives of control—is an additional premise of the engagement. The motivation for providing appraisal services as a minority versus a controlling interest must be identified, applied, and supported.

It is necessary to provide detail as to whether the ESOP is with or without leverage, whether it is taxed for federal income tax purposes as a subchapter C or S corporation, and whether there is any status change made during the year. Sufficient details must be disclosed to afford an investor reasonable knowledge of relevant facts known on or about the valuation date.

Other sections of this book cover minority or control prerogatives, taxation of entities, and leverage available to the ESOP and the motivation for each; see Chapters 14 and 15.

STANDARD OF VALUE

The term *fair market value* is defined in proposed DOL Reg. 2510.3-18(b)(2)(i) as the price at which an asset would change hands between a willing buyer and a willing seller when the former is not under any compulsion to buy and the latter is not under any compulsion to sell, and both parties are able, as well as willing, to trade and are well-informed about the asset and the market for that asset.[1]

VALUATION ADJUSTMENTS

Contributions made to the ESOP in shares from the sponsoring company treasury or newly issued shares of the sponsoring company's stock can provide increased cash flow through their tax deductibility against current income as the shares require no cash outlay to achieve the deduction.

A corporation taxed as a subchapter C, through shares of sponsoring company stock contributions, creates cash flow to the extent of the applicable federal rate with the corresponding tax savings or shield. The same circumstances of deducting share value can be true in a subchapter S environment where shares held by the exempt ESOP will offset the tax savings to the extent of shareholders outside those of ESOP ownership of the shares. Whenever shares are contributed to an ESOP, it creates two happenings: (1) a dilutive impact on the percentage ownership of outstanding shares, and (2) a probable dilutive impact on per-share value that is netted against the probable cash-flow savings from the tax deduction.

Leverage in the ESOP Transaction

ESOPs are unique and complex qualified retirement plans for many reasons, but perhaps one of their most significant characteristics is their ability to borrow money as long as the proceeds are used for the primary benefit of its participants. See IRC § 54.4975-7(b)(3). It is the only retirement plan that, under certain criteria, can borrow money on a tax-advantaged basis to purchase shares of stock from and in the sponsoring company. With an ESOP debt obligation comes substantial commitments for the sponsoring company, the plan administrator, the lender, the plan trustee, and all shareholders, including those shares held beneficially through the plan by participants. See IRC § 54.4975-7(b).

In all cases, the sponsoring company has a commitment to meet the term payments of the ESOP for repayment of the loan principal as tax-deductible retirement plan contribution payments and associated interest (also tax deductible), assuming the contribution is within the annual compensation limits. The plan, in turn, pays down the note from the contributions, dividends and other plan cash and the lender releases shares held as collateral in suspense and now owned by the plan. These shares are now allocated to participant accounts as the principal of the note is reduced. Additionally, in an S corporation leveraged ESOP environment, any dividend distributions on shares that are unallocated, still pledged as collateral for the loan, in effect lose their dividend characteristics, are treated the same as allocated shares, and can be directed by the plan trustee to pay down the ESOP debt.

It is vital that a preliminary indication of fair market value provide the trustee (or contemplated trustee) with an estimated transaction range for compliance with the adequate consideration provisions of ERISA. The preliminary indication should be made prior to forming or initiating negotiations with an ESOP and outside shareholder or with the company when establishing a transaction with newly issued shares. In an ESOP share transaction with a shareholder or sponsoring company, the share valuation price ranges are made at pre-transaction and pre-debt, without consideration of the usage of sponsoring company cash or other assets to purchase the shares. Share valuation price ranges are also independent of considerations of debt impact if borrowing is made that obligates the sponsoring company for repayment from its future operations.

Transactions in which small shareholdings are sold to an ESOP generally do not require or incur leverage. These shares are released to the ESOP and allocated to the participants of the plan in the plan year of the acquisition and are made part of the participants' account balances. A leveraged transaction, in contrast, provides not only for larger shareholdings transfer but also for delayed allocations to plan participants able to meet the imposed compensation restraints of annual plan contributions. These changes permit spreading the release of shares and allowing new and existing employees to participate as the shares are allocated to participant accounts over the amortization of the loan.

Payments made as contributions to the plan by the sponsoring company in a leveraged ESOP can provide tax shielded cash flow through the ability of the sponsoring company to deduct both principal as a contribution to the plan and the interest of the loan repayments. (Not all appraisers agree on this point.) In both cases, the entity has a tax impact not seen in other entities with traditional non-ESOP financing with the net tax shield effect offset by the tax deduction of the loan principal payments.

As an example, suppose the same loan is made to the same company, but under two different scenarios. In scenario one, the proceeds of the loan are used to purchase outside shareholder shares, and the proceeds of the loan are paid out to the shareholder. In scenario two, the proceeds of the loan are used to purchase new issue shares, and the funds remain inside the company and are used for company operations, expansion, acquisitions or capital expenditures.

Perhaps stating the obvious, the investor risk associated with scenario one and that of scenario two can be very different, depending on the size and terms of debt and the utilization of funds. In a general observation, there will likely be a different (higher) return requirement from the equity holders in scenario one, when funds go for non-operations and to outside shareholders, than that of scenario two, when the funds are retained by the company for operations. Careful analysis is essential to quantify that measurement of equity risk; nevertheless, in general, the higher the debt, the higher the required rate of return to the equity owners.

As noted in *Insights Quarterly Journal,* the decrease in a company's post-transaction equity value is typically somewhat less than the amount of ESOP transaction indebtedness for two reasons: (1) debt financing usually has a lower cost of capital than equity financing and (2) ESOP transaction indebtedness can receive preferential income tax treatment because both its interest and its principal are tax deductible.[2] Additionally, compensation concessions and positive alterations in available cash flows may provide offsets for some of the additional cash requirements of a company. These issues should be considered in the evaluation of the posttransaction valuation.

Adjustments for Taxes

There is a correlation between the tax impact of subchapter C and S earnings, despite the fact that earnings are taxed as an entity, in the case of a C corporation, and as a flow through to the owners of the entity at their individual tax rates in the case of an S corporation. On one hand, federal tax rates generally favor a C corporation in amounts under the first $100,000, although receiving the net proceeds, if paid out as a dividend to the owners, incurs additional taxes. On the other hand, S corporations pass taxable income through to the owners where the graduated individual tax rate produces varying tax impacts, based on the individual shareholder's own tax situation.

> As an oversimplification, over time, S and C corporations annually pay income taxes in terms of cash flows in comparable manners and magnitudes.

A federal tax deposit is made directly by a C corporation to pay taxes, while an S corporation pays out "tax dividends" as a distribution to its owners, generally at the top individual rates, and those shareholders in turn pass on those deposits to the government via individual tax payments.

The economics of tax impact on cash flow produce similar, but not necessarily equal results. Additionally, in publicly traded corporations (there are no publicly traded S corporations) all financial detail and market data is considered to have the tax impact implicit with the rate of returns required by the equity investor. Thus, given the marketplace and the similarities between the tax impact on cash flow of an S corporation and a C corporation, earnings of an S corporation should be evaluated as if they were C corporations.

Additionally, the tax impact of S corporation shares held by the tax exempt ESOP is adjusted in a similar fashion. The reasoning behind this is twofold. First, the ESOP shares are not tax exempt; the holder of the ESOP shares, the ESOP trust, is. Upon plan-triggering events, the participant that receives termination benefits will no longer hold the shares that are tax exempt. Thus, to consider the share value as if the shares were exempt would make them prone to overstated value and would lead to a situation where the plan pays more than adequate consideration for the shares. Second, from the universe of hypothetical buyers that the appraiser considers in a market place (embedded in the definition of fair market value), any treatment other than tax effecting would be contrary to compliance with the dictates in the fair market value definition.

Effect of Stock Options and Warrants

Often the appraiser finds that anchoring key employees requires equity considerations outside those available in the ESOP. In many instances, nonqualified stock options are offered to essential management. In these instances, stock option plans create unique valuation and other challenges that must be addressed. Consideration of option price, option exercise, tax impact, cash flow requirements and dilutive impact of the additional shares (that are reasonably expected to become outstanding as the options mature and become exercisable) is required.

In order to better grapple with the optioned shares, a thorough understanding is needed of the option rights granted to these key personnel. From those option terms and conditions, the following process would provide a reasonable manner of consideration in the computation and impact to the existing shareholders, including the ESOP as an equity owner. To summarize the process:

1. Calculate value of the outstanding in-the-money options granted (number of option shares in-the-money multiplied by fair market value on the valuation date).

2. Tax effect the expensed portion of compensation amount of those options that are in-the-money on the valuation date regardless of exercise date or if they have been exercised (total market value price less option exercise price on all in-the-money options times the tax rate).

3. Add the cash flow generated from the transaction to the aggregate company value (option exercise price plus "2" above).

4. Calculate the aggregate total outstanding shares by adding the number of in-the-money option shares to the outstanding shares.

5. Divide "3" above, the aggregate company value plus option-related cash flow, by "4" above, the total fully diluted shares.

NONRECURRING EXPENSE ITEMS: ESOP PLAN EXPENSES

Normalization of a company's current and expected operating performance is an important function for an appraiser. In most cases, nonrecurring expenses may require consideration and adjustment. In addition to those nonrecurring expenses that may be more common are the initial ESOP plan expenses paid by the sponsoring company. These occur either in the form of contributions to the ESOP to pay the initial and nonrecurring plan expenses or, as is more frequently the case, in the form of direct payment for the initial expenses, which can be significant and material if absorbed by the sponsoring company.

A normalization adjustment for these plan expenses should be made whether a minority or controlling interest is being appraised, since the benefit comes to the shareholders through the ESOP, and all receive an economic benefit as a result of the nonrecurring expenditures. These adjustments to nonrecurring expenditures are not to be confused with those recurring ESOP plan expenses on a forward-looking basis.

COMPENSATION EXPENSE ISSUES

Unlike ESOPs with no debt, leveraged ESOPs may pose the need for economic and normalizing adjustments in the statements of income and balance sheet. The generally accepted accounting principles are founded in the accounting profession's Statement of Position (SOP 93-6). A reconciliation and adjustment of compensation expenses presented on the financial statements may be required for a clearer picture of operating performance, federal income taxation, and cash flows.

Compensation expense will fluctuate based on those shares' original cost basis when initially purchased using the debt and the value of those same shares as they are released and available for allocation when no longer held in suspense as *unallocated shares*. As the debt principal is paid down, a corresponding number of shares at original cost basis are released and the difference in the then-current market value is considered compensation expense.

Since in this instance there is no additional cash flow required for the difference in share basis, which is equivalent to the principal reduction and current value, there is an adjustment. Additionally, there is no federal income tax deduction available for these differences. Thus, adjusting for these three items, if material, would be appropriate and required.

OWNERS' COMPENSATION AND EMPLOYMENT AGREEMENTS

There is a tendency for outside shareholders of a sponsoring company that are accustomed to deriving the economic benefits of salary, bonus, and prerequisites to create golden parachutes prior to the sale of their shares to an ESOP. These details seldom show in the historic financial statements or data and have future benefits that may not follow those the plan trustee would consider customary.

Barring complications that run afoul of the anti-abuse rules explained in Chapter 15 of this text, there is nothing wrong with the selling shareholders doing this as long as the financial impact is included in the future earnings and benefit stream valuation for the remaining shareholders posttransaction, an impact which can (and often does) depress the value that the selling equity owners consider appropriate. In essence, the selling shareholder(s) will receive economic benefits (outside normal and customary) in the form of sponsoring company benefits going forward or incorporated in their share value, but not both.

Any pretransaction financial arrangements made that have a material impact on the future operations or performance of the company must be considered in the pretransaction valuation of the shares and will have a direct impact on the share value in its transaction with the ESOP or any other shareholder.

This is true of any other transaction outside the ESOP. The difficulty is obtaining that detail in advance of providing the initial valuation services. If, during any subsequent valuation, an appraiser discovers such activity, it would be necessary to obtain details of the change and discuss it candidly with the trustee before proceeding with the assignment.

CASH FLOWS AND FORECASTS: MINORITY AND CONTROL INTERESTS

Much debate has focused on the stream of benefits the equity owners or a company will enjoy in the future. As with any appraisal judgments, the handling of the net benefits to the equity owner is often measured in the form of the earnings and cash flows that are available to the equity owner. Making an analysis of those future earnings and cash flows available to the equity holders is largely determined by the ability of the equity owner to control future economic benefits.

In most appraisal circles, professional appraisers are in general agreement that the required rate of return to the investor or, put another way, cost of equity capital is the same, regardless of control or noncontrol. Deliberation among appraisers then shifts to a premium for control that assumes that there are prerogatives and differences to be derived from the diversion to the equity owners in excess of that benefit available to them as a minority investor.

In an ESOP, the trustee makes decisions concerning the valuation criteria in regard to the control or lack of control provided the ESOP shares and their treatment of participants upon distribution from the plan. The exception will be consideration of voting control in a multi-staged transaction where the plan achieves voting control, by agreement, in advance of the transfer of the shares. The transfer of technical voting shares could take several years to achieve.

> Don't assume that because the ESOP stock ownership interest is larger than that required to exercise control, it will be at control value or vice versa. Don't assume that a current minority holding will not be given control status by agreement. Circumstances are to be considered in every case. They are not absolute.

ENTITY STRUCTURE TAX STATUS

For years leading up to more recent tax law changes, ESOPs have been utilized by C corporations as an entity that pays federal income taxes on its own income directly to the federal government. Beginning in the late 1990s, however, tax law provided an exemption to the prohibited transaction rules for S corporation stock to be held by an ERISA plan. Shortly after this change, there was repeal of the UBIT (unrelated business income tax) for ESOPs that had subjected the plan to a special tax on income for S corporation earning held by an ERISA plan. By combining the new tax rules and repeals, ESOPs quickly expanded to include S corporations.

CONSIDERATIONS UNIQUE TO S SHARES

Given the exemption from federal taxation of S shares held by the tax exempt ESOP, there resulted a potential for accumulation of dividends by the sponsoring company that would have previously been paid out in federal income taxes. Depending on circumstances unique to the various percentage ownership interests held by the ESOP and other outside shareholders, this becomes what is commonly called a *tax distribution or dividend* from the sponsoring company to shareholders on flow-through income taxed to its shareholders.

As part of the IRS S corporation requirements, any distribution in the form of a dividend must be made proportionate to the ownership interest and paid accordingly. In this manner, the ESOP, due to its ownership of S corporation shares, receives a distribution for which no tax is due on the shares it holds because of its exempt status from federal income taxation. In turn, the ESOP allocates those paid dividends to employee participants under specific allocation rules.

The focus of the S corporation appraisal is the same as that of a C corporation in that a typical market condition, with a hypothetical and willing buyer and seller, mandates that transactions don't differentiate the feature for S or C corporations.

It is important to recognize that the S corporation shares themselves do not possess special rights or privileges and are not exempt from federal income tax on their allocation of taxable income. Rather, it is the ESOP entity that holds those shares which qualifies under ERISA as exempting those shares' earnings from federal income taxation.

Thus, in order to meet the adequate consideration provisions of ERISA, the valuation takes place in an environment void of consideration of its S corporation shares held by the ESOP and the plan's tax-exempt status. This being said, under circumstances where the ESOP holds all or substantially all the shares of S corporation stock of the sponsoring company, there is no requirement for a tax dividend and these funds can be reinvested by the company to pay off or down debt, accumulate in the accounts of the company, or to expand or cover other operational purposes. In these instances, the operations of the company are enhanced, creating a positive impact on the sponsoring company's share value. In the event that funds accumulate within the sponsoring company accounts that may be considered above those required for the customary operations of the company, these amounts, after adjusting their income or loss stream effect for expected future benefits, would be added to the share value like any other excesses or non-operation assets under generally accepted valuation theory and practice.

MANAGEMENT INTERVIEWS AND QUESTIONNAIRES

All valuation engagements require an understanding and assessment of the management and succession plan for management of the company. In an ESOP environment, an additional layer of understanding is necessary.

Working through an appraisal with a plan trustee—who very likely is a member of management—requires the appraiser to develop an interview technique consistent with the fiduciary responsibility imposed by ERISA. Like the qualification of an expert witness, an appraiser may rely on numerous representations, both columns and rows of financial detail and hearsay (interviews).

Assessing management's understanding of how an ESOP works, its benefits, and its requirements can have a binding and growing effect on an exiting shareholder, key management personnel, employment contracts, future expectations of repayment of debt or expansion of the business, change in business entity structure, and raising of capital.

The appraiser's questionnaire and interview must focus on events or developments that could affect the share value on a going-forward basis and analyze its impact given the company's history of operating performance and past economic conditions. The appraisal may include the possible dilutive impact on the shares value, employment practices, new employment agreements, options or bonus plans that could affect share value, and other related concerns.

VALUATION METHODS

Usage of Direct Equity or Total Invested Capital Method

Circumstances differ when appraising a nonleveraged versus a leveraged ESOP. Assessing the sponsoring company in a nonleveraged environment resembles valuations for purposes other than ESOP shares. In other words, it is an assessment of the unique attributes of the operations of the company and its capital structure. Assessing the company's specific features offers insight as to which invested capital method is best suited to provide an indication of value for the ESOP shares.

When valuing leveraged ESOP shares, utilization of an income and market data approach suggests that valuation methods include the total invested capital method, providing that the capital structure of the company can be reasonably quantified and considerations of minority or control value are measured. In this way, the differentiation of debt impact can be better assessed and can include consideration of utilization of the proceeds of the ESOP leverage being used for the operations of the company. This might be the case in the sale of new issue or treasury or for the purchase of shares from outside shareholders. Given company-specific capital and debt structure, the ESOP debt now borne by the sponsoring company reflects the probable impact on risk and the requirement for an amplified rate of return to equity owners.

End of Year and Midyear Conventions

For most closely held businesses, appraisers use discounted cash-flow models to provide indicated values. These cash-flow models are based on a present value computation estimating annual cash flows that are received throughout the forecasted period and are available to equity owners. Cash-flow estimates are always forward looking and generally span a number of years, with each year representing a forecasted period.

Using the end-of-year convention, computation of cash-flow present value presupposes that forecasted cash flows will be available to equity owners at the end of each forecasted period. Midyear convention presupposes that forecasted cash flows will be available to the equity owners at a midpoint, or half way into the forecasted period. By the design of these conventions, the midyear conventions will always produce a higher value indication than end-of-year conventions because cash flow is forecasted to equity holders more rapidly.

In most private companies, management adopts a "wait until we see how the year goes" style of making available cash returns to equity holders because business and economic conditions often tender an environment of intermittent and varying cash flows over the forecasted periods. It is important to differentiate these conventions because company-specific realities must be considered in adopting the appropriate convention model.

> In an ESOP environment, unless a compelling company-specific rationale supervenes, in order to stay within the guidelines of the plan not paying more than adequate consideration for ESOP shares, the default convention is end of year.

Considerations in the Calculation of the Terminal Value

Many fact-laden decisions are made in developing the final forecast period in discounted cash flow models. The estimate that produces the terminal value generated during this final period is often the chief component of the value indication using the discounted cash-flow method.

An ESOP is an ERISA-defined contribution plan with provisions allowing it to invest primarily in employer securities. By plan design, contributions are generally allowed to be made only by the sponsoring company. These retirement plan contributions are voluntary unless leverage is involved in ESOP share acquisitions or the plan is under a contractual multistage shareholder purchase agreement.

Voluntary retirement plan contributions are choices that typically reflect, among other things, the directives of management—operational results of the company, effort made by employees, compensation plans, and contemplated future expenditures. When plan contributions are required, the term and amounts of their requirements on future forecasted periods are identified. However, once the obligations are met, there may be no assurance that voluntary contributions will continue, or, if they do, will continue at the same level.

> In developing the terminal forecast cash-flow period, the appraiser must give careful consideration to the ongoing benefit of the voluntary/nonvoluntary nature of plan contributions and their impact on the benefit stream to equity shareholders, capitalized into perpetuity.

Adjustment for Lack of Liquidity

Discussions, theory, and practices abound on the topic of the need for an adjustment for lack of liquidity. For ongoing ESOP plans, this is generally expressed in terms of a discount for lack of marketability. Due to the put option requirement in an ESOP environment, an adjustment aligns better with liquidity of the sponsoring company or the ESOP itself. The put right and obligation causes a timely distribution of the share value in cash under ERISA-prescribed terms by the sponsoring company to participants.

> The put option obligation is termed a *repurchase obligation* or *liability of the sponsoring company* and is considered a contingent liability under current accounting practices, with no requirement to be reported in the financial statements or footnote disclosures.

Chapter 17 of this text covers the liquidity adjustment in more detail. However, it is important to identify differences in other valuations where there may not be a contractual obligation of the company, enforceable through a federal agency, in the area of discriminatory practices and obligation of the trustee to deal with all happenings of the plan for the exclusive benefit of the employee participants.

The comparison of availability of an active-trading public market for shares and that of the most efficient and well-financed private ESOP-sponsoring company demonstrates some differences. In the public sector, there is a three-day trade cycle, while in a private ESOP environment, the timing and ability to compensate qualifying distributions to plan participants would be delayed for months to years. Additionally, pubic market shares trade on an open and free exchange where investors buy and sell at will on a daily basis, which is not probable within a private company. Thus, although possible, there is a better likelihood that an adjustment is made for the lack of liquidity in ESOP shares with a range that will vary with the facts and circumstances unique to each company's and the plan's financial condition at the time of appraisal. The adjustment can vary from year to year and can trend up or down, as circumstances dictate.

> A liquidity adjustment is applicable to control and minority interest shares.

ESOP PLAN TERMINATIONS

Under varying circumstances, an ESOP can terminate, and the plan can transact its sponsoring company shares and other assets. In plan terminations, the plan trustee must grapple with a formal application to the Internal Revenue Service for a determination, as it provides an expedited review of the facts and circumstances and issues a favorable or unfavorable determination letter.

Generally, the sponsoring company of the ESOP is required to distribute assets from a terminated plan as soon as it is administratively possible. IRS Revenue Ruling 89-87 views the facts and circumstances normally to be concluded within one year of the plan's termination.

In any qualified (ERISA) plan, a termination or partial termination of the plan is a full vesting event, where account balances vest to the participants at 100 percent. Unlike formal plan terminations, partial termination is a fact and circumstances event that may create full vesting; however, the many variations of partial terminations are outside the scope of this text.

As a practical matter, solvent sponsoring companies that terminate ESOPs are motivated to have the ESOP shares put back to them, and participants are eager to exercise their put right, but the repurchase requirement for the sponsoring company can create significant financial requirements to the sponsoring company and the plan. If the company is sold and the plan is terminated, the proceeds from the acquiring company typically provide the monetary consideration to the fully vested participants as part of the transaction.

Under any of the termination scenarios, the focus of the transactions continues to be that distributions to participants meet the adequate consideration provisions and are provided on a nondiscriminatory basis. The trustee and named fiduciary must, in good faith, continue to act for the exclusive benefit of the participants in the plan.

SUMMARY

Revenue Ruling 59-60 provides the appraiser many logical details for preparing a value estimate for a private company. It concludes that certain factors, such as dynamics of the company, carry more weight than others. Listed in this chapter are several areas in which valuation of ESOP shares differs from more traditional appraisal assignments of non-ESOP companies and requires a second look by the appraiser. There are and will no doubt continue to be differences of opinion on a more precise way to analyze and develop each area of the sponsoring company.

As an observation regarding the appraisal of ESOP shares, there tends to be an inclination among some trustees of plans that consistency is to be maintained between the plan years, to the detriment of a more case-specific analysis of fair market value. For example:

- Adjustments for liquidity seldom vary with company and plan specifics changing.

- Risks in developing investors' cost of capital are seldom adjusted for anything more than the risk-free rate and general equity market risk premium.

- Cash flow assumptions drift or fall short in considering the reasonableness of management's forecasts.

- Growth in equity share value may remain constant in the face of positive or negative events that indicate otherwise.

A point to remember is the ESOP holds shares of the sponsoring company as an investment. As with any shareholdings, values change over time, whether up, stagnant or down. The job of the appraiser is to provide a value estimate consistent with the dictates of the adequate consideration provisions of ERISA should the share value change as a function of the market conditions on or about the valuation date.

11

Accounting Standards and Esops with Debt

The accounting profession continues to evolve in its development, interpretation, and promulgation of uniform accounting standards. These standards are commonly referred to as generally accepted accounting principles (GAAP). This cohesive self-governing effort is spearheaded by the accounting profession's national membership organization, The American Institute of Certified Public Accountants (AICPA). The AICPA, in conjunction with individual state Boards of Public Accountancy, acts as the accounting profession's uniform standards and compliance overseer. Its function is to maintain uniformity in understanding, reporting, and interpretations of the underlying basis for financial operations of entities and for fairness of financial presentations.

With regard to ESOPs, the AICPA has issued an accounting pronouncement titled Statement of Position (SOP) 93-6, *Employers' Accounting for Employee Stock Ownership Plans,* with an effective date for financial statement presentation of accounting years beginning after December 15, 1993. Existing ESOPs will apply this approach to all new ESOPs and all new acquisitions of shares, but not to refinancing of old acquisitions because prior ESOP transactions were allowed to retain their prior accounting treatment.

BALANCE SHEET ISSUES AND THE LEVERAGED ESOP

Under SOP 93-6, a company's direct and indirect loan arrangements for an ESOP loan should be shown as an obligation (liability) of the sponsoring company, with a contra account as a reduction in the equity section termed or similar to *unearned ESOP shares.* These unearned ESOP shares are often referred to as *suspense shares,* representing the collateral-pledged ESOP shares. As the ESOP debt is repaid, the suspense shares are released and allocated in a way that may not necessarily be proportionate to the debt reduction. Sponsoring company dividends on allocated shares and released but unallocated shares are charged to retained earnings. In cases where there has been an increase in the market value of the stock over that of suspense shares' initial acquisition price, that is added to the equity section to the paid-in capital account. No financial consideration is given to the future tax benefits that may be derived by the federal income tax deductibility associated with the repayment of the ESOP debt principal.

The plan can buy shares of the sponsoring company stock from its sponsoring company treasury stock account, from newly issued shares of the sponsoring company, from existing outside shareholders, or from any combination of the three. In this purchase transaction, a debt component can and may be incurred by the ESOP for the acquisition of the shares. Repayment of the debt by the ESOP generally occurs not less frequently than quarterly. The sponsoring company generally makes repayment of the loan to the ESOP through tax-deductible retirement plan contributions. In the case of a direct loan, the plan pays the lender directly from the funds contributed to it by the sponsoring company as loan repayment.

In the case of an indirect loan, the company pays the lender directly and generally accounts for the transaction as a plan contribution, thereby eliminating the step needed to contribute to the plan. In cases where the company pays in excess of the contribution limit imposed by compensation issues not known, the plan repays the sponsoring company.

SOP 93-6 requires the sponsoring company to record the transaction as a treasury stock acquisition for both direct and indirect loans used to purchase stocks held by shareholders in the open market. A subsequent issue of the shares to the ESOP is recorded by relieving the treasury stock account of the acquired shares and creating a contra equity account, "Unearned ESOP Shares." Should the ESOP acquire new issue (authorized but previously unissued) shares from the company, the company will increase the common stock and additional paid-in capital accounts at the current value of the shares with a corresponding entry to the "Unearned ESOP Shares" account.

EARNINGS PER SHARE ISSUES

Sponsoring company dividends on released common shares constitute an exchange of ESOP shares for compensated services (thus, they are now earned). As such, they are considered outstanding for earnings-per-share calculations. However, shares that are not yet released (suspense shares) are not considered "earned," thus "unearned" and are not considered outstanding in the earnings-per-share calculations.

Dividends on convertible preferred stock issued to an ESOP will affect earnings-per-share (EPS) calculations because they can be paid on allocated or unallocated shares and are recorded differently by the company on leveraged ESOP shares, depending on that allocation. In essence, the sponsoring company has control of dividends on the unallocated shares. Thus, when dividends paid on unallocated shares are used for debt service, the liability for the debt or accrued interest is charged, and if added to participant accounts, they are charged as compensation expense. In both instances, payment of dividends on unallocated shares requires no accounting adjustments to the net income in an earnings-per-share calculation.

Dividends paid on allocated shares added to participant accounts are handled no differently from any other dividend on convertible stock and are included in the earnings-per-share calculation using the if-converted method. If the dividends on the allocated shares are used for debt service, net income in the EPS calculation may need reduction.

STATEMENT OF INCOME ISSUES FOR
THE LEVERAGED ESOP

There are two primary issues relative to income statement presentation for ESOPs with debt (leveraged ESOPs):

1. The measurement of compensation expense associated with an ESOP plan

2. The period with which that expense is to be associated

Each accounting period has a different compensation expense that fluctuates with the market price of the shares to be released.

> The company measures compensation expense on the basis of the *fair value* (an accounting term considered synonymous with fair market value) of the shares to be released, which can cause some dramatic fluctuations in recorded compensation expense.

The average value of compensation expense for the year is generally used, as the stock is considered proratably earned throughout the year. This accounting treatment differs in nonleveraged plans where compensation expense is equal to the cash paid for the shares committed at the date of the commitment.

DIVIDENDS AND THE LEVERAGED ESOP

For financial statement purposes, dividends are chargeable to retained earnings and not compensation expense—with one exception. In the case where dividends are paid on unallocated shares arising from prepayment of debt, these dividends will be treated as compensation expense. If they can be used to satisfy an obligation of the plan, the payment no longer maintains the characteristics of a dividend. Additionally, the financial statement presentation affects the income statement presentation of the company as compensation expense, not as a charge against retained earnings on the balance sheet.

VALUATION IMPACT

Financial statement treatment and presentation for leveraged ESOPs under SOP 93-6 remains divisive. Although SOP 93-6 attempts to address financial reporting inconsistencies with leveraged and nonleveraged plans found in the superseded SOP 76-3, it does not create a clear picture for valuation purposes and presents several issues that must be reconciled.

When it comes to ESOPs that have no debt, there are no real GAAP differences between Statement of Position (SOP) 76-3 and the Statement of Position (SOP) 93-6 and, thus, no valuation adjustments warranted for the nonleveraged ESOP. However, for a leveraged ESOP, the difference between the two SOPs is significant.

Prior to the enactment of SOP 93-6, neither suspense shares nor fair value compensation expense required differentiation of the proper accounting period for share allocation. Treatment in SOP 93-6 results in fluctuations of compensation expense based entirely on estimates of a hypothetical market where hypothetical willing buyers and hypothetical sellers are used to match employee-earned services with an estimated value of shares. In addition, prior to SOP 93-6, the number of shares outstanding did not depend on whether shares had been released during debt repayment and had been classified as *allocated* shares. Instead, it followed an economic rationale of ownership with debt as collateral, rather than a debt controlling the ownership relationship.

Armed with a clear understanding of the financial presentation requirements of GAAP, the analyst may find it problematic to support certain provisions of SOP 93-6 in the valuation of leveraged ESOPs without economic and monetary adjustment. By not considering adjustments, the value indication could result in a material misstatement, an unsupportable valuation conclusion, and a possible breach of the *adequate consideration* rules promulgated by the DOL.

Often in a leveraged ESOP valuation, the loan is made with the company as guarantor or maker of the ESOP loan. The economic realities to the sponsoring company of the debt cannot be ignored. In most leveraged transactions involving ESOPs, the plan is a pledgor of the transacted shares that generally transfer from shareholders. It is generally necessary for proper liens to be perfected that lenders require the ESOP shares be placed as collateral. When the sponsoring company uses proceeds for nonoperating purposes, the share proceeds from the sale (perhaps in the form of qualified replacement property in the case of qualified tax-deferred gains under provisions of the IRS), sponsoring company business assets, and the sponsoring company (along with a personal guarantee of an officer of the sponsoring company or the selling shareholder or both) may be a condition of the loan.

If the ESOP loan were buying new issues of the sponsoring company, the company would be the recipient of the proceeds of the loan, thereby increasing company assets and cash flow for reinvestment in corporate growth.

In essence, these valuation adjustments may be considered:

- *Fluctuating compensation expenses*—accounting period expense charges, based on unallocated suspense shares using estimated fair values and adjusted to their original cost and allocated as an expense at that time and as the principal of the debt are reduced, are repaid.

- *Dilutive impact on share value*—all shares of stock owned by the ESOP, whether held as suspense unallocated shares, or allocated shares, may be considered outstanding to capture the fully dilutive effect.

FAS 150

The Financial Accounting Standards Board of the Financial Accounting Foundation has issued the promulgation Statement of Financial Accounting Standards No. 150, *Accounting for Certain Financial Instruments with Characteristics of both Liabilities and Equity,* with an effective date for first fiscal period beginning after December 15, 2003. However, FASB Staff Position (FSP–FAS150-3) defers this effective date, postponing indefinitely the implementation on these specific instruments for applying certain provisions in FAS 150 dealing with non–public companies' mandatory redeemable financial instruments. The Statement establishes standards for how an issuer of financial statements classifies and measures in its statement of financial position certain financial instruments with characteristics of both liabilities and equity. FAS 150 was and is intended to capture future obligations currently excluded from financial statement presentation and to require recording as a liability those now off the balance sheet and considered contingent obligations.

Under paragraph 17 of FAS 150, obligations under stock-based compensation arrangements are exempted from the FAS Statement if those obligations are accounted for under APB Opinion No. 25, FASB No. 123, and American Institute of Certified Public Accountants—Statement of Position (SOP) 93-6, or related guidance. There continues to be interpretation and deliberation with respect to this pronouncement and its impact on stock-based compensation arrangements. The provisions of FAS 150 require a company with an ESOP to book a liability for distributed shares if the shares are *mandatory redeemable*. There is no such obligation to record a liability while the shares are in the trust, or when shares are redeemed for cash prior to an employee leaving the plan. There is little doubt more discussion is forthcoming in this area of accounting for financial interests.

SUMMARY

Due to the unique method of illustrating the results of operations in both the statement of income and balance sheet when accounting for ESOPs that have used debt (leveraged), compensation expense may not necessarily represent usage of cash for cash-flow and earnings modeling. Additionally, since the repayment of ESOP debt principal is tax deductible, the federal income tax shield creates or can create a reduction in federal income tax not associated with repayment of conventional loans.

Thus, when analyzing financial statements that have leveraged ESOPs, the analyst should be keenly aware of the probable need to adjust both financial statements to reflect what a willing buyer armed with the relevant facts would consider as appropriate in assessing the operations of the company sponsor and its impact on share value.

12

Put Rights, Share Redemption Provisions, and Repurchase Obligations

What happens in an ESOP to the employer's securities held in a plan participant's account upon that participant's qualifying termination from the plan? Simply stated, an ESOP participant who is entitled to a plan distribution, and whose employer stock is not readily tradable on an established market, is provided the *right,* not the obligation, to require the sponsoring employer to redeem those plan securities. That right, when exercised, becomes the purchase obligation of the sponsoring company. Although the ESOP can have the right to assume the put obligation, it cannot be required to honor it.

The put right is commonly referred to as a *put option,* and is defined in IRC § 409(h) and Treasury Reg. § 54.4975-7(b)(10). The put is a distribution right that follows a participant termination and distribution from the plan that allows the distribution to a retiring participant or their beneficiary to require the employer to repurchase the distributed shares of a private stock. This right imposes on the sponsoring company of the ESOP the obligation of redemption of those shares held in the terminating participant's account, commonly referred to as the company's *repurchase liability or obligation.* However, there are alternative choices to this requirement, and the story is far from absolute concerning making good on those put rights. The put option provision gives the holder of the option the right, but not the obligation, to sell a stock or other instrument at a specific price within a specific time period.

REPURCHASE PREFERENCES

When a participant decides to put the stock, there may be a preference for the ESOP as an ERISA entity to make the acquisition directly if financially able and barring any existing debt covenants from lenders or plan document limitations. If this does not ensue, there is existing debt associated with leverage on unreleased shares.

> In reality, virtually all plan participants exercise their put rights, and in many plan documents, minimum account values provide for a cash out by the plan for accounts under a certain dollar amount.

If the ESOP does not transact the shares, then the sponsoring company will be required to do so. If the company buys back the shares, the sponsoring company must decide whether to redeem or recirculate the shares. In redemption, the company uses its assets to buy back the shares, and the financial impact is an offsetting reduction in the value of the sponsoring company by the amount of the purchase and a corresponding reduction in the number of shares outstanding. There is generally no resulting dilutive impact on the per-share value from the redemption to the remaining shareholders, as long as the transaction occurs at fair market value.

The other obligation selection available to the company is to repurchase the shares from the participant and then contribute, or *recirculate,* those shares to the ESOP for reallocation to remaining participants of the plan. Whether the shares are contributed or purchased by the ESOP, they are reallocated to the remaining participants. In this method, the remaining participants receive compensation. The end result is to make available to the company the opportunity to make tax-deductible contributions to a qualified plan and to maintain the relative size of the ESOP. Of course, this statement is subject to variation if the ESOP owns 100 percent of the shares and is taxed as an S corporation. Tax status is discussed in Chapter 15.

ROLLOVER PROVISIONS

In 2004, the IRS essentially consented to allow an ESOP to direct certain rollovers of distributions of subchapter S corporation stock to an individual retirement account (IRA) in accordance with a distributee's election, without terminating the corporation's S election.

> As a practical matter, any participant considering this rollover must make sure the custodian of the IRA will accept the S corporation shares in an IRA even though the shares will quickly be liquidated. Custodians are not required to take the shares, and if they do take them, the custodial fees for handling the transaction may pose considerations of working the transaction other than as a rollover.

Until this development, generally no S corporation shareholders were allowed to continue holding their shares posttermination distribution, as it would terminate the S election of the company for its taxation to the shareholders.[1] The significance of the S election is discussed in a later chapter; however, it is important to be aware that until 2004, this provision was not available to the departing participant.

FACTORS OF REPURCHASE LIABILITY

Several factors affect the dollar magnitude of the sponsoring company repurchase liability, pursuant to the put right of participants. Plan provisions are especially important, given the choices made at the time of the inception of the ESOP. They can affect the dollar magnitude to the sponsoring company for repurchase liability, pursuant to the put right of participants. The provisions have potential timing effects on when distributions may occur. Ultimately, the repurchase provisions merely act as a spreading of payments and deferral of the obligation. Several factors have a clear effect on the amount of the repurchase obligation:

- The size and age of the ESOP and its participants
- The rate of the turnover of plan-vested employee participants
- The underlying stock value change of the company

The size of the ESOP is measured as the percentage of ownership of the sponsoring company. Generally, the magnitude of the repurchase obligation would be smaller for a 20 percent ESOP-owned sponsoring company than that of a 100 percent ESOP-owned company. All other things being similar, participants would hold a greater number of shares as the ESOP ages and participant ownership percentage increases.

Generally, the greater the employee turnover, assuming a plan vesting schedule that produces distributable plan assets to those terminating participants, the higher the anticipated level of repurchase obligation. The higher the growth level of value of the sponsoring company, the higher the per-share price of the ESOP shares distributed to participants. In some instances, the dollar impact of the redemption obligation can be significant. If the growth rate in the company value is minimal, there may be little anticipated adjustment in the underlying repurchase requirements.

The timing of the put share payment, if made from the sponsoring company to the terminated ESOP participant, is a vital consideration when the plan documents are drafted.

Plan design can eliminate this timing provision and/or make modifications in account minimums of cash in or out participants.

Most plan distributions cannot occur until the employee has officially separated from the employer by a qualifying event. IRC §§ 401(a)(9) and (14) require the following:

> [The] distribution must generally occur or begin no later than the "required beginning date" or, if earlier, last day of the plan year in which: the participant attains the earlier of age 65 or the normal or early retirement dates specified in the plan; the 10th anniversary of plan participation occurs; and the participant separates from service.[2]

Distribution requirements in part depend on whether the stock was acquired before or after December 1987.[3]

The form of distribution can be cash or stocks.[4] However, particular care must be taken in the attempt to convert the form of the distribution. The Tax Court in *Lemishow v. Commissioner*[5] held that an eligible rollover distribution received in cash may only be rolled over in cash. In this case, the taxpayer had received an eligible rollover in cash and used a portion of the cash proceeds to purchase stock, which was then deposited into an IRA account within 60 days of the distribution. The Tax Court focused on the legislative history of the Code's rollover provisions, which require a permissible rollover in terms of the "same amount of money, or the same property." Therefore, the court held that the taxpayer had not validly rolled over the cash distribution because he had deposited the property from the cash proceeds, instead of the cash distribution itself.

It is possible and important to reflect on the fact that an amortized payout can be made by ESOP-owned companies for the redemption of company stock from departing participants by issuing promissory notes for the value of the shares of the employer securities.

USE OF PROMISSORY NOTES

When promissory notes are made to terminated participants, they require collateral, and the sponsoring company must determine what type of collateral is available and what will be used. In 2002, a principal issuer of surety bonds, which were often used as collateral for the notes, indicated that it would no longer issue the surety bonds, closing an avenue to many companies and forcing consideration of alternative collateral.

IRC § 409(h)(5) indicates that the amount to be paid to the departing participant for the stock may be satisfied with a promissory note if the following conditions apply:

- The note provides for substantially equal periodic payments that begin within 30 days and end no longer than five years from the exercise of the put option.
- There is "adequate security" for the note.
- The note bears a reasonable interest rate.

See also Department of Labor regulation § 2550.408b-3(l). It is evident that importance lies in ensuring that the notes are secured by collateral, so that the participant is not harmed by the company's defaulted note.

In considering adequate security, the position of the IRS is a narrow one. Technical Advice Memorandum 9438002 (1994) ("TAM") defines adequate security as: ". . . a pledge of security that may be sold, foreclosed upon, or otherwise disposed of upon default." Further, the IRS takes the position that the security must be "tangible," such that it may be reasonably anticipated that loss of principal or interest will not result from the loan The Internal Revenue Manual (IRM), § 4.72.4.2.8.1 (8/13/2001), goes to further lengths to detail the intentions of the IRS. It is a training manual for IRS auditors of ESOP companies. The IRM states the following:

> If the employee puts shares to the employer received in total distribution, make sure the employer provides adequate security and pays reasonable interest on the unpaid portion. A put option is not adequately secured if it is not secured by any tangible assets. For example, adequate security may be an irrevocable line of credit, a surety bond issued by a third party insurance company rated "A" or better by a recognized insurance rating agency, or by a first priority perfected security interest against company assets capable of being sold, foreclosed upon or otherwise disposed of in case of default. Promissory notes secured by a company's full faith and credit are not adequate security, nor are employer securities adequate security.

It is apparent that the position of the IRS is that necessary precautions must be taken to avoid the plan and sponsoring company from defaulting under a loan, thus protecting the participants' retirement benefits.

For some sponsoring companies, the restrictions on collateral just described, coupled with the loss of surety bonds previously available to ESOPs, can result in the ESOP having to consider using the sponsoring company's assets or other collateral sources to secure the notes. These repurchase liability alternative solutions can create financial adversity because the debt incurred does not provide the company with any economic benefit.

Noteworthy: There is no financial reporting requirement for this estimated repurchase obligation under GAAP.

Trustees of the plan and management of the sponsoring companies should consider the put provision long before it arises and provide a plan for funding the ESOP or set aside reserves for departing participants of the plan. This may be difficult during periods of ESOP debt repayment; thus, acceptable deferrals are often included in the plan documents and within the bank covenants until an event or reduction in the debt is made. The financial realities of the required ERISA put provisions may force companies to reconsider how plan distributions are made in the normal course of business and how to continue to survive financially in times of economic downturns.

The Department of Labor's Proposed Regulation 2510.3-18(b) provides that the financial viability of the put must be evaluated. See Chapter 17 for more discussion on this important subject.

DISTRIBUTION OPTIONS

Companies have flexibility in choosing the desired manner of plan participant distributions. The plan documents should define whether the distribution has to be paid in a lump sum or can be paid out in installments. The period of years allowed for installments is often limited by the amount of the total distribution. If the participant is receiving the distribution in the manner of shares, then they have the right to exercise the put option at two distinct 60-day periods, the first beginning on the date securities are issued to the participant, and the second, after the valuation determination in the immediately ensuing year.

DIVERSIFICATION

For employer securities acquired after December 31, 1986, IRC § 401(a)(28)(B) provides the following:

> Each "qualified participant" in a plan may elect, within 90 days after the close of each plan year in the qualified election period, to direct the plan with regard to the investment of at least 25% of the participant's plan account. The account balance subject to the diversification election increases to 50% in the final year of the election. A "qualified participant" is any employee who has completed 10 years of participation in the plan and has attained the age of 55. The "qualified election period" is the 6-plan-year period beginning with the later of the first plan year (1) in which the individual first becomes a qualified participant, or (2) beginning after 1986.

The plan can meet the diversification requirements in one of three ways. It must either (1) distribute amounts covered by the election to the participant within 90 days of the end of the election period, or (2) offer three investment options to each qualified participant within the plan, or (3) allow for the transfer of assets to another plan that has three investments options.

The repurchase obligation of an ESOP company is a compensation decision and should be viewed in relation to the compensation levels that are prevalent in the company's industry. It is crucial to understand the differences in the methods of redeeming ESOP shares and recognition of the impact of the repurchase obligation on the value of the company. Quantifying the repurchase obligation is possible and requires projections of the number of shares expected to be eligible to be put to the company in the future.

> As a practical matter, the quantification of repurchase liability is laden with suppositions that are, at best, good-faith estimates. In general, the appraiser is concerned with repurchase that is imminent and identifiable. As with public accounting promulgations and accounting literature, a significant characteristic is the assessment of *going concern* issues for the current and immediately following operational year.

The effort to understand and plan strategies for dealing with repurchase obligation is needed early in the life of an ESOP company. Companies must use available resources to estimate the share value and shares that will be eligible for the put right over the ensuing periods.

SUBCHAPTER S CORPORATIONS AND REPURCHASE OBLIGATIONS

With the emergence in the year 2000 of permitted ESOPs' viable ownership of S corporation stock, their repurchase obligation has been made less intrusive to manage. However, with this allowance arises a new key issue: Who will buy the shares—the company or the ESOP?[6] Before the emergence of the S corporation rules, National Center for Employee Ownership (NCEO) survey data revealed that about half of all ESOP companies bought back shares, while the other half had the company buy them back.[7] The survey also showed that almost all ESOP companies planned to maintain or expand current levels of ownership. The main issue of C corporation companies then was more a matter of managing the timing of the plan's reacquisition of the shares rather than of deciding to retire them or sell them to someone else.[8] The difference in S corporations may depend somewhat on whether it is a 100 percent ESOP-owned S corporation.

For 100-percent owned S corporations, there is no tax advantage to the ESOP buying the shares, unlike the same situation in a C corporation. Therefore, it may prove more advantageous for the sponsoring company to buy back the shares unless the ESOP has cash available that the company wants to use to buy shares for investment in company stock. In an S corporation with less than 100 percent ESOP ownership, the decision is often driven by the S corporation rules on percentage of stock held by the plan. The decision is more of a balancing act dependent on the plan demographics and the company profitability.[9] Companies in this circumstance will want to cautiously plan their future share redemptions.

NONTERMINABLE ESOP PUT RIGHT PROVISIONS

Treasury Regulation § 54.4975-11(a)(3)(ii) describes the put rights for a privately held employer security included as sponsoring company shares held in an ESOP as a nonterminable right. Thus, these put provisions available to a qualifying participant of an ESOP cause the plan to cease being an ESOP. Where the plan is amended and converted to a non-ESOP, the plan continues.

Additionally, IRC § 411 (d)(6) provides that a plan will not satisfy the requirements of this section if the accrued benefit, early retirement benefit, retirement-type subsidy, or optional form of benefits of participants is eliminated or reduced by an amendment to the plan. IRC § 411(d)(6)(C) provides that an ESOP may modify its plan's distribution options provided it is done in a nondiscriminatory manner. This is an exception to the IRC § 411(d)(6) prohibitions.

SUMMARY

The put right provision is designed to create liquidity for the terminating employee participant. Without it, retirement would be constricted, and Congress could deem ESOPs' ability to achieve equity ownership spread among participants a failure. In most cases, the requirement to repurchase is not insurmountable, and with proper planning and good counsel, the apparent objections can be overcome.

In reality, the sponsoring company generally has the available resources and/or borrowing capacity to redeem the shares with internal cash or borrowed funds or the ESOP itself may have sufficient funds to meet the obligation. In this manner the participant is made whole and the many attributes of the ESOP remain unfettered.

13

Adequate Consideration

Can "adequate consideration" be inadequate? Much discussion and, regrettably, much misunderstanding stems from the inadequacy of the definition of *adequate consideration* in ERISA § 3(18)(B) and § 8477(a)(2)(B) of the Federal Employees' Retirement System Act of 1986 (FERSA). Considering the nuances of the expression "adequate consideration" reveals a wealth of understanding as to the uniqueness of an ESOP and the requisite impartial services of the financial advisor-appraiser. Adequate consideration is directly associated with the benchmark standard, fair market value, essentially reflecting the generally accepted meaning of the term, but with multifaceted ERISA plan significance.

What exempts the sale of sponsoring company stock to an ERISA ESOP-prohibited transaction requirements is an exclusion that is offered as long as the sale of shares meets, among other requirements, the definition of adequate consideration, as determined in good faith by the trustee or named fiduciary.

ADEQUATE CONSIDERATION
AND THE DEPARTMENT OF LABOR

The DOL promulgated a proposed regulation[1] in 1988 relating to adequate consideration. This is still arguably the most relevant piece of literature published by the DOL to date, although by the mid-1990s, the DOL no longer considered it authoritative and purged it as guidance.

Department of Labor Initial Explanation

The 1988 proposed regulation, in part, dealt with the concept of fair market value, how fair market value relates to a determination of adequate consideration, and how these requirements must be satisfied to meet the criteria of the proposed regulations. The value assigned to an asset must reflect its fair market value, and the value assigned to an asset must be the product of a determination made in good faith. This underscores the point that Congress did not intend to allow arbitrary values to be assigned to, or for, plan assets when transactions occur inside or outside the plan.

ERISA § 3(18)(B) provide "for assets other than securities for which there is a generally recognized market . . . the term 'adequate consideration' for such assets means the fair market value of the asset, as determined in good faith by the Trustee or named fiduciary pursuant to the terms of the plan and in accordance with regulations promulgated by the Secretary of Labor." The proposed regulations are clear that good faith alone may not provide a safe harbor in instances that fail to ensure equitable results and produce valuation amounts outside acceptable generally recognized valuation methods.

The first part of the DOL's proposed regulation 2510.3-18(b), proposed 29 C.F.R. 2510.3-18, two-part test under § 3(18)(B) and § 8477(a)(2)(B) requires that a determination of adequate consideration reflect the asset's fair market value.

The term *fair market value* is defined in proposed § 2510.3-18(b)(2)(i) as the price at which an asset would change hands between a willing buyer and a willing seller when the former is not under any compulsion to buy and the latter is not under any compulsion to sell, and both parties are able, as well as willing, to trade and are well informed about the asset and the market for the asset.

The importance of this usage of fair market value is the same concept of a universe of hypothetical buyers and sellers and the business on a stand alone basis, without the influences of intrinsic or investment value. In keeping with the realities of business equity transactions that are subject to arm's length negotiations, the proposed regulation did not stop at just the definition of *willing, well informed,* and *under no compulsion.*

The DOL proposed regulation went on to say:

The Department is aware that the fair market value of an asset will ordinarily be identified by a range of valuations rather than a specific, set figure. It is not the department's intention that only one valuation figure will be acceptable as the fair market value of a specified asset. Rather, this proposal would require that the valuation assigned to an asset must reflect a figure within an acceptable range of valuations for the asset.

In what appears to be an effort to bring realism into the proposal and transactions of ESOPs and shareholders, the DOL further communicates that reasonableness must enter into the course, as if to say that the DOL has an understanding that transactions structured on a practical basis with realistic expectations, conceivable processes, and credible considerations would be appropriate in the circumstances and satisfactory to DOL, all other things being in order.

The second part of the DOL's proposed two-part test under § 3(18)(B) and § 8477(a)(2)(B) requires that an assessment of adequate consideration be the product of a determination made in good faith by the plan trustee or named fiduciary. The good faith requirement proposed by DOL wraps the general overview of adequate consideration in a bow as it completes the relationship cycle of the ESOP and the sponsoring company. The fiduciaries must play an active and engaging role with adequate toil to make good-faith estimates of well-reasoned transactions at an exchange amount that would not be out of line with other similar deals given the same circumstances.

DOL Rulings and ESOP Valuation

Adequate consideration, as defined by the DOL, has specific meaning in the valuation of ESOP securities. The definition of the term in the proposed regulation was designed to assist the trustee in fulfilling their statutory duty to plan participants by ensuring that the participant are not disadvantaged by what the plan pays for sponsoring company assets (i.e., shares of employer securities), nor by what they receive upon plan termination.

> Put another way, the trustee of the ESOP must not pay more than fair market value in a purchase of sponsoring company shares and must not pay less than fair market value in the case of participant termination receipt of benefits from distribution of the plan assets.

As an example, say the plan trustee accepts the appraiser's valuation of the common stock of the sponsoring company (employer securities) as reasonable at $50 per share for purposes of adequate consideration. An outside (non-ESOP) shareholder is selling shares, and the plan has an interest and purchases them for $45 per share. In this instance, the ESOP has not paid more than adequate consideration and is compliant within the prudent, good faith rules and intent of the DOL. In contrast, an ESOP participant terminates the plan and tenders plan-held sponsoring company shares, and, for the sake of this illustration, the ESOP purchases the shares. In this instance, the trustee will pay $50, the fair market value for the ESOP shares as is required, and does not disadvantage the ESOP participant. Paying more than fair market value would be greater than adequate consideration and would not be in compliance with the adequate consideration provisions.

DOL Additional Explanation

Further explanation and direction by the DOL in determining what exactly constitutes adequate consideration is difficult to obtain. As already stated, in 1988 the DOL drafted a proposed regulation defining adequate consideration as the fair market value of the assets, as determined in good faith by the trustee or named fiduciary pursuant to the terms of the plan and in accordance with regulations promulgated by the Secretary of Labor. See ERISA § 3(18)(B) and 29 U.S.C. 1002(18)(B). However, in 1990 at a hearing before the Subcommittee on Labor-Management Relations of the House Committee on Education and Labor, the DOL determined that ESOP participants should receive "dollar-for-dollar" equity in multi-investor ESOP transactions. The "dollar-for-dollar" concept is that employees should receive a benefit from shares equal to that of the amount paid for them. This position was later addressed in a complaint filed by the DOL against Wardwell Brading Machine Company (*Dole v. Farnum,* 17 BNA Pension Reporter 1494 (D.R.I. 1990)) alleging that plan fiduciaries breached their fiduciary duty by agreeing to pay more than adequate consideration for shares by not taking into account the cash drain to the sponsoring company as a result of expected ESOP contributions. Although it is essential to realize that the complaint was later withdrawn, it did result in confusion on the position of the DOL in defining adequate consideration, pre- and posttransactions.

Then, in 1995, the DOL withdrew its 1988 proposed regulation without an accompanying explanation. In the absence of a final version or any new regulations promulgated by the DOL, the 1988 regulation is still considered the most relevant available and is utilized by many that value ESOP shares, although an Internet search and phone call to the DOL do not reference it.

The adequate consideration provisions of DOL merit further, but brief, explanation and comment. The DOL makes specific mention of securities other than those with recognized and established markets. In cases of private company shares, comparable similar securities of corporations engaged in the same or similar lines of business whose securities are actively traded in a free and open market must be assessed. Additionally, there are requirements for assessment of the effect of the securities' lack of marketability, as well as awareness of the put right provisions available to individual participants of the plan and control/noncontrol issues, both in substance and in form, with an eye for significant adverse affects. These issues are covered in depth in Chapters 12 and 17.

Employer Securities: Exclusive Benefit Rule

An exclusive benefit violation may occur if an ESOP acquires stock for more than its fair market value. Revenue Ruling 69-494, while not in all requirements applicable to ESOPs, provides guidelines for determining whether a plan investment is consistent with the exclusive benefit rule. As applied to ESOPs, these guidelines require a determination of whether the amount paid for the stock exceeds the shares' fair market value at the time of the acquisition.

The purpose of Revenue Ruling 69-494 was to update and restate a position relating to the requirements an exempt employees' trust must comply with in order to invest funds in the stock or securities of an employer corporation. Under § 1.6033-1(a)(3) of the Treasury regulation:

> The primary purpose of benefiting employees or their beneficiaries must be maintained with respect to investments of the trust funds as well as with respect to other activities of the trust. This requirement, however, does not prevent others from also deriving some benefit from a transaction with the trust. For example, a sale of securities at a profit benefits the seller, but if the purchase price is not in excess of the fair market value of the securities at the time of sale and the applicable investment requisites have been met, the investment is consistent with the exclusive-benefit-of-employees requirement. These requisites are:
>
> - the cost must not exceed fair market value at time of purchase;
>
> - a fair return commensurate with the prevailing rate must be provided;
>
> - sufficient liquidity must be maintained to permit distributions in accordance with the terms of the plan, and
>
> - the safeguards and diversity that a prudent investor would adhere to must be present . . .

ADEQUATE CONSIDERATION VERSUS FAIRNESS OPINION

"Fairness Opinion—an opinion as to whether or not the consideration in a transaction is fair from a financial point of view," is the memorialized definition from a glossary of terms in the International Appraisal Standards accepted by all valuation societies and associations.

Defining the word *opinion* is relatively straightforward. However, defining the word *fair* is case-specific and distinct in the setting of its use.

Although fairness opinions are often used in an ESOP setting, the proposed criteria of transaction reasonableness may differ. Fairness opinions stem primarily from an investment-banking environment. Their usage has been an important part of specific transactions to offer reasonable assurance that a transaction is fair between the parties. Adequate consideration does differ from the definition of a fairness opinion as its concept is unique to ESOPs.

Transactions with ESOPs stipulate that the plan cannot be disadvantaged by paying in excess of adequate consideration, or, to put it in more street terms, the ESOP cannot pay more than fair market value. *Fairness,* a testy, squeamish term, implies that all parties to the transaction are at ideal conditions, while *adequate consideration* implies fair market value to the ESOP and its participants in a broader range allowing a compliance concept. Put another way, the ESOP can deal in its best interest and can purchase shares at less than fair market value. However, upon qualifying distributions to terminating participants, the ESOP requirement is to distribute to these individuals or their beneficiaries, at fair market value.

The key is the concept of compliance with the adequate consideration provisions found in ERISA and enforced by DOL. Without meeting the criteria of adequate consideration, the ESOP transaction can fall outside the ERISA-prohibited transaction exemption that allows a qualified retirement plan to transact in share of a typically disqualified entity the sponsoring company, and therefore imposes penalties for noncompliance.

CASE LAW

The courts have further added to the search for a clear definition by requiring an objective test of good faith consistent with ERISA's "prudent investor" standard. In *Donovan v. Cunningham,* 716 F.2d 1455, 1467 (5th Cir. 1983), the court ruled that ERISA's adequate consideration requirement:

> Must be interpreted so as to give effect to the Section 404 duties to which those persons remain subject. In this regard, it is especially significant that the adequate consideration test, like the prudent man rule, is expressly focused upon the conduct of the fiduciaries. A court reviewing the adequacy of consideration under Section 3(18) is to ask if the price paid is "the fair market value of the asset as determined in good faith by the fiduciary;" it is not to redetermine the appropriate amount for itself *de novo.* Contrary to the appellees' contentions, this is not a search for subjective good faith "a pure heart and an empty head are not enough." The statutory reference to good faith in Section 3(18) must be read in light of the overriding duties of Section 404.

ADEQUATE CONSIDERATION AND VALUATION REPORTS

Is the DOL valuation expression of adequate consideration date and written report-sensitive? Yes. The burden of proof is on the person, typically the plan trustee, who uses the adequate consideration provisions to meet specific ERISA exemptions. As an example, the DOL requirements place adequate consideration in a number of very important compliance roles, including using it as an exemption from some of the prohibited transaction provisions found in all ERISA plans.

In this regard, the view of the DOL is that a written valuation document that provides the foundation to a valuation is prudent and necessary for a determination of how, and on what basis, an asset was valued, and whether the valuation reflects an asset's fair market value. The DOL goes on to establish valuation report content, modeled around IRS Revenue Ruling 59-60 and relevant in each engagement, which is the subject of Chapter 18.

SUMMARY

Adequate consideration is a crucial concept in understanding its applicability and definition in the valuation of sponsoring-company ESOP securities. The appraiser's requisite knowledge and understanding of the definition and role that adequate consideration plays in ESOP valuation, is paramount to successfully operating within the regulatory environment of ERISA and IRS regulations so that severe repercussions do not occur.

14

Control versus
Minority Positions

W hen determining the value of shares of a privately held company, the degree of technical and substance control purchased by the ESOP is another critical aspect of this unique plan. As one would expect, buying or selling a controlling interest is generally regarded as paying or receiving a control premium above the same class of stock in a company when compared to that of a noncontrolling, minority interest. A controlling interest's premium is primarily driven by the privileges that are inherent in implementing change or directing the benefit stream that is derived from the interest's power to direct and implement those changes. These privileges include the ability to elect most, if not all, of the board of directors, direct the discretionary capital and operating expenditures, adjust salaries, hire and fire personnel, change marketing direction, negotiate or renegotiate debt, change vendor, supplier, customer, or professional relations, control perquisites, and set dividend policies.

What is often termed a *super majority* or *super control* occurs when a shareholder/the plan owns sufficient shares to control liquidation, merger, or sale. Generally, when the shareholding interests exceed 66.67 percent of the voting shares of stock, a blocking of a super majority is available. The percentage ownership that makes up a super majority is promulgated by (1) the state incorporation acts, (2) jurisdiction of the incorporation, or (3) given changes in the bylaws of the corporation in cases of a "close" corporation, those corporations that by state statute and bylaws provide voting control on a basis other than size of shareholder.

Control premium is "the additional value inherent in the control interest, as contrasted to a minority interest that reflects its power of control."[1] The trustee must in good faith and to the exclusive benefit of the employee participants in the plan, consider the impact of control versus noncontrol in determining what and whether an ESOP should pay a premium for control or for controlling shares. The substance and form of the contemplated transaction should be discussed and fully understood. It is the trustee's decision to make, and it is the trustee who directs the valuation for a specific transactional purpose.

Typically, consideration for acquiring the shares as a controlling interest will not arise until the ESOP could or would possess greater than 50 percent of the voting shares of the sponsoring company common stock. There is no aggregation of block-voting consideration of shares held inside the ESOP with plan participant member's stock ownership shares held outside the ESOP. Considerations include any impact of dilution that could occur from stock options, warrants, and other fading or synthetic stock rights covered in Chapter 16. However, this is only where the consideration and control analysis begins. The trustee, with the appraiser acting in his or her capacity as financial advisor, must assess the posttransaction actuality that the price paid correctly reflects the ESOP ability to initiate and exercise control prerogatives. If the ESOP will not enjoy the ability to make changes as described, then the premium paid for control must either be reduced or eliminated, as the circumstances of the case may dictate.

THE DOL POSITION

The DOL proposed regulation on adequate consideration states that an ESOP may pay a control premium only if the plan obtains control "both in form and in substance," and that the premium must be consistent with what a third party would pay.[2] There is a certain amount of controversy as to whether an ESOP can have control "in substance," although it may have it "in form" by a percentage of votes. Each appraiser must approach this subject with added precaution. The amount of control premium, if any, should include all the circumstances unique to that case when developing valuation assumptions. Many appraisers take the cautionary measure of providing in the appraisal report an explanation as to the analysis of and likely implementation of obtaining control.

THE IRS POSITION

The IRS, motivated by the generation of revenue, holds a different position from that of the DOL, whose pledge is the protection of the employee participant to the plan. The IRS draws no distinction between numerical and actual control.[3] Simply stated, if the ownership of the ESOP is more than 50 percent, then the IRS considers the ESOP as owning control. Since the IRS and the DOL are motivated by differing purposes in their directive in this sensitive area, it is critical that an appraiser understand and take special care to provide a thorough analysis of and substantiation to the appraisal and should ensure that the valuation report includes mention and support for the control ownership position.

EMPLOYMENT AGREEMENT

Anytime a sale from an employee owner is being contemplated and control is at issue, it often proves revealing when the financial advisor/appraiser recommends or requires an employment agreement that includes a noncompetition clause. If the owner is skeptical about putting the parameters of their role, salary, bonuses, and benefits in writing, then it could be an indication that they are not as willing to give up control. Employment contracts with key management executives are powerful arrangements that offer clarity to their roles post-transaction with the company. They provide a road map that allows a good look into the expense arrangements posttransaction and lessens the risk to all the parties to the transaction.

LEVELS OF NONCONTROLLING MINORITY INTERESTS

Often, minority interests are ranked by their strengths and weaknesses based on the comparison of the size of the block of shares transacted and those held by other shareholders. The operative word is *transacted*. Although there is latitude as to what the ESOP plan may hold after acquiring plan shares, the corresponding voting rights issues, or lack of voting rights (see Chapter 5), may preclude considerations that are commonly found in the marketplace, such as *swing votes,* voting for management or the board of directors.

However, should the ESOP acquire enough shares to vote as a single supermajority in both substance and form and thus on key and permitted votes begin to collectively affect merger, acquisition, restructuring, and liquidation decisions, the appraiser might include a premium above that of an interest that cannot impose those features. The key point remains that the decision of the purpose of the valuation engagement resides with the trustee.

MULTISTAGE TRANSACTIONS

A properly structured and implemented multistage sale of employer securities to an ESOP that would achieve voting control in both substance and form would be acceptable to both the DOL and IRS. The valuation reasoning for multistage transaction is the buyer (an ESOP) and seller(s) could transact at a control rather than a minority value.

The Department of Labor's proposed Regulation 2510.3-18(b)(4)(i)(I) addresses the role of control premiums in valuing securities other than those for which there is a generally recognized market. The DOL proposes that a plan purchasing control may pay a control premium, and a plan selling control should receive a control premium. Specifically, the DOL proposes that a plan may pay such a premium only to the extent that a third party would pay a control premium.

Similarly, if the plan purchases employer securities in small increments pursuant to an understanding that the employer will eventually sell a controlling portion of shares to the plan, a control premium would be warranted only to the extent that the understanding with the employer was actually a binding agreement obligating the employer to pass control within a reasonable time.[4]

There has been no direct quantification of the length or reasonability of time that control needs to be transferred to meet the multistage contract obligations. However, in several DOL cases, there is a trend that would at least imply that *within two years* would be acceptable, and that *five years* would also be acceptable, given compelling circumstances. There does, however, appear to have emerged loose consensus on what might qualify allowing the ESOP trustee to consider in negotiating and meeting the adequate consideration provisions of DOL:

- Upon initial transaction, the plan trustee must be provided immediate voting control rights

- The ESOP must buy sufficient shares in the initial transaction to reasonably have the ability to obtain control within a short time frame.

- Future transactions do not have fading ownership through the inclusion of anti-dilution provisions.

- The trustee must provide control valuations for annual participant accounts post initial multistage transaction, including put rights at control.

VOTING AND OTHER RIGHTS OF THE ESOP SHAREHOLDERS

An employee stock ownership plan must provide that each participant or beneficiary in the plan is entitled to direct the plan trustee as to the manner in which securities allocated to his or her account are to be voted if the employer has a registration class of security (generally, a class of securities required to be registered under the Securities Exchange Act). If the employer does not have a registration class of security, each participant or beneficiary in the plan must be entitled to direct the plan as to the manner in which voting rights under the securities allocated (only allocated shares can vote) to his account are to be exercised. This is true with respect to any corporate matter that involves the voting of such shares in the approval or disapproval of any corporate merger or consolidation, recapitalization, reclassification, liquidation, dissolution, sale of substantially all assets of a trade or business, or similar transactions.[5]

For private companies, voting rights are required to be passed through to the ESOP participants as beneficial owners with allocated shares, only on issues that require consideration of corporate mergers, consolidations, recapitalization, reclassification, liquidation, dissolution, or sale of substantially all assets of the business. In cases where a vote pass-through is required, appropriate information on the issues must be provided, just as it would be provided to other shareholders. In this event, the trustee generally votes the shares for the plan. The plan design can provide voting rights be passed through on all voting matters although this is not a requirement by ERISA. In public companies, voting rights are passed through to plan participants no differently than any other shareholder.

The ESOP trustee is permitted to vote the shares held by the ESOP on a one-man, one-vote basis. To use this rule, each participant of the ESOP must be allowed one vote with respect to each issue on which the shares held by the ESOP are entitled to vote, and the trustee must vote the shares in the proportion determined by the participant's votes. These voting rights do not extend to beneficiaries or employers with registration type securities. It is important to note that the one-man, one-vote rule is located in the IRS Code only, and not found in ERISA.

What if the trustee receives no direction from the participants regarding their allocated shares? The DOL has determined that if the participants have the opportunity to vote their allocated shares and do not, the trustee is not obligated to vote their shares.[6] Likewise, the IRS has held that a trustee can vote the shares for which no directions were received.[7]

OTHER RIGHTS

Another ESOP participant right is the right to receive securities and put options. An ESOP must give employees who are entitled to distributions the right to receive the distributions in the form of employer securities if maintained by the employer as restricted stock. If the employer securities are not readily tradable on an established market, employees may exercise a put option, which is the right to have the employer repurchase the securities under a fair valuation formula. See IRC § 409 (h). The put options, or put rights are discussed in depth in Chapter 12 of this book.

There are also basic information requirements, such as summary plan descriptions, the summary annual report, and individual benefit statements that all ERISA plans are required to provide to ESOP participants.

Summary plan descriptions provide such information as the rules of the ESOP, how and when employees become participants, how and when distributions are made, the procedures for questioning or complaining about management of the ESOP, and names and addresses of the sponsor and fiduciaries. All ESOP participants must receive the summary plan description within 90 days of becoming a participant, changes must be updated, and if no changes, then participants must be provided a copy every five years.[8]

Within seven months after the close of each fiscal year of the plan, the sponsor must provide ESOP participants a summary annual report on a DOL form. Also, each year, upon termination, request, or a one-year break in service, ESOP participants must receive their individual benefit statements, which include the fair market value of their shares and vesting information. Although these are the basic information documents that ESOP participants must be provided, there is a list of information below that is not required by ERISA.

FINANCIAL INFORMATION

Contrary to popular belief, participants in an ESOP do not have rights to the sponsoring company's financial statements, stock record books or information on salaries. Disclosures of these items are at the discretion of the sponsoring company. However, as a practical matter, summary financial information is often made available to the plan trustee. The issue of whether to share financial information with ESOP plan participants has been a topic of much debate as it relates to employee ownership culture and the psychology of ownership. The *Employee Ownership Report,* published by the NCEO, in a November/December 2003 issue, published an article titled "Critical Numbers," which addresses this issue. The article correlates providing financial information with improved employee owner performance: "Curiously, despite their importance and simplicity, few companies share these critical numbers with employees. They are somehow regarded as secret or even sacred. That's too bad, especially in employee ownership companies. These easy-to-develop and communicate numbers may be the most powerful way to engage employees in finding ways to improve business."[9]

Companies should consider carefully whether they will practice sharing critical numbers with ESOP participants, especially in light of the current trend of increased suspicion among participants that has arisen as a result of Enron and other large ESOP fallouts. Not only can sharing financials increase understanding, trust, communication, and collaboration between management and participants, it may actually increase productivity and a sense of personal pride through involvement among participants.

EFFECTS OF STATUS OF SHAREHOLDINGS FOR PLAN PARTICIPANT'S DISTRIBUTIONS AT QUALIFIED TERMINATION FROM THE PLAN

The obligation of the plan trustee is to provide services to the exclusive benefit of the plan participants under the DOL provisions specific to adequate consideration and equitable treatment of employee participants of the plan. In the absence of compelling reason otherwise, the participants of the plan transact on their plan termination at a control or elevated premium. Assessment of whether the fiduciary acted in good faith will be made in light of all relevant facts and circumstances. Exceptions to that statement are applicable in plans where the ESOP is leveraged and shares are not released for allocation, and thus control may not have been effectuated.

~ SUMMARY

ESOP participants, either through the plan trustee, individually, or collectively, have important rights. The DOL promulgates and administers compliance and enforcement actions, when necessary, to ensure participant rights are not violated. Within the ESOP culture generally comes the sharing by the sponsoring company and its management a broader understanding and summary details on the progress of the company and its operational impacts on the share value and how the employees can provide the input and impact of enhanced financial performance and share value that translates directly to their own participant account.

Determination of all relevant facts and circumstances surrounding the control issue is essential. All transactions can be viewed as under no compulsion for the plan to transact in making an acquisition of shares from outside shareholders. Likewise, the seller is under no compulsion to transact his or her shares. Provided there is arm's-length negotiation, the share value should provide an incentive for completing a transaction. Participants that qualify for distributions from the plan must be treated in a manner that does not financially disadvantage them. The application of sound, prudent business practices and acting in good faith is the optimal means of handling this complex valuation issue.

15

Esops and Taxes*

In order to encourage the use of Esops, the federal government has instituted tax benefits for the sponsoring company and their owners who participate in ESOP transactions.

ESOP TAX INCENTIVES: AN OVERVIEW

The purpose of this chapter is to explore these benefits, which include:

- Entity tax structure of S corporations versus C corporations
- Deductible contributions to the plan
- Tax benefits available for C corporations
- IRC § 1042 provision of selling shareholder incentives that allow deferral of income if qualifying replacement property is purchased, available to C corporations only
- Earnings (flow through) attributable to S corporation shares held by ESOP exemption from tax
- Conversion of C corporations to S corporations and visa versa

ENTITY TAX STRUCTURE OF S CORPORATIONS VERSUS C CORPORATIONS

A company must have stock in order to have an employee stock ownership plan. There is some indication through private letter rulings that an LLC that elects to be taxed as a corporation may include employees in an ESOP, provided there is a parent company that has stock that the ESOP can own (see PLR 200111053 and 199949046). A stand-alone LLC cannot sponsor an ESOP because an ESOP must own stock of the employer, and the LLC has member interests. ESOPs can own

---

*This chapter was contributed by Judy Lee.

stock in subchapter S or C corporations. Although S corporation ESOPs operate under most of the same rules that C corporations do, there are important differences. Interest payments on ESOP loans count toward the annual plan contribution limits in S corporations, but not in C corporations. Certain flow-through distributions to participants (i.e., dividends on ESOP shares that are deductible to a C corporation) are not deductible to an S corporation. Sellers to an ESOP in an S corporation do not qualify for the tax deferred rollover treatment under IRC § 1042 discussed later in this chapter.

An ESOP is a unique S corporation owner, as neither it nor the sponsoring company pays federal income tax and, in some states, does not pay state income or franchise tax on any profits attributable to its allocation of income. As an S corporation shareholder, dividends paid on unallocated shares in the plan can be used to repay ESOP debt to the lender. These differences can make converting to an S corporation very enticing when a C corporation ESOP owns a significant portion of the sponsoring company's stock. The entity tax structure may also affect the annual accounting period of the company. Traditionally, a C corporation will follow the year-end that reflects the accounting cycle of the business, and an S corporation follows the calendar year-end promoted by the Internal Revenue Service. However, Revenue Procedure 2002-38 § 5.06 allows a 100 percent ESOP-owned company to retain their fiscal year-end upon conversion to an S corporation.

DEDUCTIBILITY OF CONTRIBUTIONS TO THE PLAN

One of the many benefits to the company in considering an ESOP is the tax deduction for employee retirement contributions made to the plan. Under IRC § 404(a)(3), contributions to the plan are deductible in calculating taxable income. This deductibility follows the same limits as any defined contribution stock bonus or profit-sharing qualified plan. Thus, contribution deductions are limited to 25 percent of the eligible compensation otherwise paid or accrued during the plan year. In the case where the company also has a 401(k) plan, the employee deferrals to the 401(k) do not count against what the company can deduct or contribute. They only count against IRC § 415 limit, the amount individuals can have added to their account. These contributions to the plan can be made in the form of employer stock, cash, or a combination of the two. IRC § 404(a) permits a corporation to deduct contributions of its stock to an ESOP.

DEDUCTIBILITY OF DIVIDENDS PAID ON EMPLOYER SECURITIES

A C corporation can deduct dividends paid on shares held by the ESOP. IRC § 404(k) permits the deduction of the amount of *applicable dividends* paid in cash with respect to *applicable employer securities*. An *applicable dividend* is one that is paid within the scope of plan provisions and meets one or more of these provisions:

- Is paid to the participants in the plan or their beneficiaries
- Is paid to the plan and then distributed by the plan within 90 days of the close of the plan year
- Is at the election of the plan participant or their beneficiaries payable as above or paid to the plan and reinvested in qualifying employer securities
- Is used to make payments on an ESOP acquisition loan; a loan in which the proceeds were used to acquire employer securities

Applicable employer securities are employer securities held by an ESOP that is maintained by the corporation paying the dividend or any other corporation that is a member of a controlled group of corporations, which includes that corporation. Such deductions are in addition to the deductions allowed under IRC § 404(a), thus not subject to the 25 percent of compensation cap.

USE OF DIVIDENDS TO MAKE LOAN PAYMENTS FROM A C CORPORATION

C corporations may use dividends paid on shares held by the ESOP under IRC § 404(k) to make payments on ESOP acquisition loans. These payments of cash dividends on both allocated and unallocated ESOP shares may be used to make loan payments. IRC § 404(k) does not apply to S corporations.

Dividends paid on shares in the ESOP loan suspense account (unallocated shares that have not been released because the lender holds them as surety until a principal payment is made to release them) at the time the dividend was declared (record date) may be used to make the loan payments. The IRS has ruled the use of dividends paid on allocated shares would be a prohibited transaction. However, on October 22, 2004, President Bush signed into law H.R.4520, the American Jobs Creation Act of 2004 (Jobs Act) that changed this ruling. A provision of this bill permits S corporation distributions on allocated and unallocated ESOP stock to be used to pay ESOP debt. Section 654 of Jobs Act allows distributions from an ESOP held by an S corporation for the purposes of repaying a loan used to purchase employer securities without losing ESOP qualification or violating rules against prohibited transactions. The ESOP must allocate shares with a value equal to the distribution to the participant's account. Note this provision applies retroactively to distributions made after December 31, 1997.

The payment or reinvestment of dividends is not considered to be an employer contribution to the plan, employee contribution or forfeiture under IRC § 415 (c) (2). Thus, dividends do not affect the amount of contributions an employer can make under the 25 percent of compensation limits.

PASS-THROUGH OF DIVIDENDS AS A C CORPORATION

What is the effect of dividend payouts? Dividends paid through the plan on shares allocated to ESOP participants or their beneficiaries under IRC § 404(k)are taxable to the required participant in full as ordinary income in the year they are received and are not available to be rolled over to an IRA or another benefit plan. They are not subject to the mandatory 20 percent federal income tax withholding provision of IRC § 3405(e)(1)(A) or the disclosure provisions of IRC § 402(f) nor subject to IRC § 72(t) provisions, which require a 10 percent additional tax on distributions made to participants prior to attaining age $59^{1}/_{2}$, nor the consent provisions of IRC § 411(a)(11).

ADDITIONAL PROVISIONS REGARDING C CORPORATION DIVIDENDS

> Participants must be fully vested with regard to dividends in order for the corporation to claim a deduction under IRC § 404(k).

An ESOP can comply with this rule in two ways, either by providing that participants are fully vested in dividends with respect to which an election under IRC § 404(k) is offered (i.e., making a specific plan provision that allows full vesting in dividends without regard to vesting in the stock with respect to which the dividend is paid) or, alternately, by offering an election under IRC § 404(k)(2)(A) (iii) only to vested participants.

The IRS may disallow a deduction for any dividend if it is determined that such dividend constitutes an avoidance or evasion of taxation. IRC Notice 2002-2 Question 11 addresses the issue of what constitutes *avoidance*. The service position is that IRC § 404(k) gives authority to disallow a deduction for unreasonable dividends:

> a determination regarding whether the dividend is reasonable is made by comparing the dividend rate on the stock held by the ESOP with the dividend rate for common stock of comparable corporations whose stock is primarily and regularly traded on an established securities market. Whether a closely held corporation is comparable to a corporation whose stock is primarily and regularly traded on an established securities market is determined by comparing relevant corporate characteristics such as industry, size of the corporation, earnings, debt-equity structure, and dividend history.[1]

An observation would be that many small businesses either do not have a history of paying dividends or are not comparable with the publicly traded market in the area of dividend payouts. This may lead to concerns if the IRS chooses to make an issue of C corporation dividend deductions in small corporations.

Payments in redemption of stock held by an ESOP that are used to make distributions to terminating ESOP participants constitute an evasion of taxation under IRC § 404(k)(5)(A) and are not applicable dividends under IRC § 404(k)(1). Any deduction for such payments in redemption of stock is barred under IRC § 162(k).[2]

IRS Notice 2004-38 attempts to clarify these issues related to payments in redemption of stock held by an ESOP.[3] The service position uses the arguments from *United States v. Davis,* 397 U.S. 301, 313 (1970), which "provides that a redemption is not essentially equivalent to a dividend if it result(s) in a meaningful reduction of the shareholder's proportionate interest in the corporation." Therefore, in order for the dividend paid to the ESOP to be deductible to the corporation it must not reduce a shareholder's proportional interest.

IRC § 1042 DEFERRED GAINS
AVAILABLE TO C CORPORATIONS

Small business owners often spend a lifetime building a business, putting all their energies into making it work. When the business is built, a corporate environment is developed and the owners are ready to retire, they think about selling and realize that there is a silent partner waiting for their share of the sale proceeds—the federal transfer taxes, which may take a large portion of their hard-earned company.

This is when an ESOP may provide an answer. IRC § 1042 allows a taxpayer to elect not to recognize gain on the sale to an ESOP if certain requirements are met and qualified replacement property is purchased within the replacement period.

The selling shareholder (taxpayer) and the sponsoring company must make an election with timely filed returns, including the following statements for the year of sale:

- A statement of election
- A statement attesting to the purchase of the qualified replacement securities
- A statement of consent to the application of IRC §§ 4978 and 4979A excise tax provisions

The election required under this section is made as a *Statement of Election* attached to the taxpayer's income tax return filed (with extensions) in a timely manner for the taxable year of the sale. *The election may not be made on an amended return.* Once made, the election is irrevocable. However, sale of replacement property will trigger gain if applicable at the time of the sale.

If replacement property has not been purchased by the date of filing the required return, it may be filed with the tax return for the following year. However, if the return is filed in a different IRS regional office, a notarized *Statement of Purchase* must be filed with the regional director where the election was originally filed.

The taxpayer making the election must also file a written *Statement of Consent* to the application of the excise taxes that apply under IRC §§ 4979A and 4978, taxes paid by the employer whose employees are benefited under the ESOP. There are two excise tax provisions that apply when a business owner chooses to utilize IRC § 142 income deferral provisions.

The first excise tax provision under IRC § 4979A states that the ESOP cannot allocate the securities purchased in a nonrecognition transaction to the account of the taxpayer who sold the securities to the plan or a person related, or any other person who owns 25 percent of any class of stock of the corporation during the 10-year period after the date of the sale or the date the acquisition indebtedness is paid in full. The penalty for the employer is an excise tax of 50 percent of the amount allocated to such ineligible person.

The second excise tax provision is under IRC § 4978. An employer is subject to an excise tax if the ESOP disposes of the securities during the three-year period after it acquired them under a nonrecognition transaction, if, immediately after the disposition, the ESOP holds a smaller number of shares than it did immediately after the nonrecognition transaction or it holds less than 30 percent of the total value of all securities of the employer. The amount of the excise tax is 10 percent of the amount realized in the disposition from the nonrecognition transaction. This provision excludes distributions to employees made by reason of death, disability, retirement after age $59\frac{1}{2}$ or separation from service, dispositions in corporate reorganizations, or as requisite under diversification requirements.

Requirements to qualify for a nonrecognition sale must include five components:

1. Qualified securities (defined later)
2. An employee organization, either an ESOP as defined in IRC § 4975(e)(7) or an eligible worker-owned cooperative
3. A plan holding a minimum of 30 percent of the stock immediately after the sale
4. A written statement from the employer filed with the secretary
5. Stock held for at least three years prior to the sale

What securities represent *qualified securities* for 1042 treatment? The term *qualified securities* means employer securities issued by a domestic C corporation that has no stock readily tradable on an established securities market. (Note this provision is not available to S corporations.) Additionally, the stock cannot have been received by the taxpayer as a distribution from a plan described in IRC § 401(a) or acquired through an employee stock purchase plan or incentive stock option plan or for the performance of services.

The basis of replacement property is reduced by the amount of gain not recognized by the taxpayer during the replacement period. If more than one qualified replacement property is purchased, the basis of each property shall be determined on a pro rata basis.

The term *replacement period* means the period beginning three months before the date of the sale of qualified securities occurs and which ends 12 months after the date of the sale.

To summarize, IRC § 1042 allows the taxpayer who wishes to sell an opportunity to preserve his or her equity investment in the form of a replacement property as a new investment without the current tax impact.

OTHER NONRECOGNITION RULES

A seller of stock to an ESOP could use the installment sale rules. Under installment sale, gain on the sale of corporate stock is normally required to be recognized when cash is received. If the stock is sold for an installment note, the gain is recognized as payments on the note are received. Installment transactions may be subject to interest on deferred tax liability under IRC § 453A.

TAX ISSUES—ESOP SHARES HELD IN AN S CORPORATION

An ESOP that holds stock in an S corporation does not pay tax on the earnings from the pass-through on the proportionate share equivalent to stock held by the plan. This allows the plan an added benefit of income accruing tax-deferred. In lieu of taxes paid by the corporation, the corporation has an opportunity to utilize the cash flow that would have been sent to the government to facilitate operations and potentially add growth and stability to the business or to pass through to the ESOP and other outside shareholders.

Shareholders receive pro-rata distributions when, and if, dividends are paid and the ESOP proportionately participates in the dividend with other stockholders. The ESOP can apply dividend distributions to purchase additional outstanding or new issue shares, pay down ESOP debt to create a fund for future repurchases requirements, or invest as additions to individual participant accounts. Although the S corporation rules make an ESOP very attractive, legislation passed in 2001 is clear that these rules are not to be abused by companies creating the ESOPs to benefit only a few people.

Congress has allowed S corporations to be owned by an ESOP, but only if the ESOP gives rank-and-file employees a meaningful stake in the S corporation. In an attempt to ensure the benefits to current employees, the ruling prohibits using stock options on a subsidiary to drain value out of the ESOP for the benefit of the S corporation's former owners, key employees, or other disqualified persons.

Temporary regulations have been issued to provide guidance on identifying disqualified person and determining whether a plan year is a nonallocation year under IRC § 409(p), as well as guidance on the definition of synthetic equity under IRC § 409(p)(5). The stocks on which a synthetic equity interest is based are treated as outstanding stocks of the S corporation and as such, owned by the person holding the synthetic equity interest, if this treatment results in the treatment of any person as a disqualified person or the treatment of any year as a year in which allocations are prohibited excise taxes may result.

Synthetic equity is any stock option, warrant, restricted stock, deferred insurance stock right, or similar interest that gives the holder the right to acquire or receive stock of the S corporation in the future. Synthetic equity may include deferred compensation. (See Chapter 16 on synthetic equity.)

Where cash dividend payments are made by an S corporation, the distributions are generally made to meet the personal tax obligations of the non–ESOP shareholders and flow, or in the case of the non–ESOP stockholders, directly to the shareholder, and, in the case of the ESOP, to the ESOP trust. In both scenarios, the cash is no longer available to the company for investment in the operations of the enterprise. The ESOP, with some restrictions, can use these dividend distributions to lower company contributions to the plan, to pay down existing debt, to purchase or repurchase shares, or to pay plan benefits.

In the case of an S corporation that is owned 100 percent by an ESOP, the cash retention to the company can be significant, as no payments are required for federal income taxes. Therefore, the company realizes on an annual basis a cash savings equal to the dollar amount of the taxes the company would have paid if it were a C corporation. The *tax shield* is available only to an S corporation's ESOP and provides a significant benefit that may make S corporations the entity structure of choice.

RETIREMENT DISTRIBUTIONS ROLLOVER TO AN IRA

Distributions by an ESOP to an Individual Retirement Account (IRA) do not terminate an S election if certain conditions are met. In Revenue Procedure 2003-23, the IRS outlines the requirements that the participant must meet in order to have the S corporation stock distributed to an IRA in a direct rollover and not affect the S corporation's election to be taxed as an S corporation. In order to retain S corporation status when the participant directs that the stock be distributed to an IRA in a direct rollover, the following three provisions must be met:

1. The terms of the ESOP require that the S corporation repurchase its stock immediately upon the ESOP's distribution of the stock to an IRA.

2. The S corporation actually repurchases the stock contemporaneously with and effective on the same day as the distribution.

3. No income or loss (including tax-exempt income), deduction, or credit attributable to the distributed S corporation stock under IRC § 1366 is allocated to the participant's IRA. Although the ESOP can assume the repurchase obligation, the company must retain the responsibility for making sure shares are bought back.

CONVERSION OF C TO S CORPORATIONS

The seller of stock benefits most from a C corporation structure under IRC § 1042, and the most significant benefits to the companies on a long-term basis accrue to an S corporation. Therefore, it would seem that a strategy to maximize benefit would be to a C corporation when the ESOP is formed and then convert to an S corporation at an advantageous moment. This election must consider IRS rules in place to prevent usurping the double taxation of C corporations through electing S status. IRC § 1374 imposes a special corporate-level tax on gains that were built into the corporation's assets at the time of conversion if the corporation disposes of the assets within a 10-year recognition period following the S election. Attention must be paid to LIFO rules and valuation of assets at the date of conversion.

If a corporation has made an election to be taxed as an S corporation, then converts to a C corporation to take advantage of IRC § 1042 income deferral for the shareholder, it is not permitted to regain S status for five years.

SUMMARY

ESOPs provide benefits in the form of tax savings through a variety of avenues. The savvy business owner can create a culture of employee ownership and benefit that allows the company to outlast the owner's involvement. Careful attention must be paid to the specifics of the company and the tax implications of each transaction to utilize the benefits available and to avoid difficulties with the IRS.

16

Shareholder Employment and Other Agreements: Phantom and Synthetic Equity

Agreements are an important tool and a way of life for the family and management of closely held businesses. These agreements are implemented for many purposes, including assuring continuity of management, providing estate liquidity, procuring special financing, offering key employee incentives and succession planning, providing a road map in the event of unexpected or unpredictable happenings, and creating a market for company stock. However, shareholder or buy-sell agreements and other price fixing or formula-driven methods—as well as employment and other deferred compensation benefits—can have impact on and be unrepresentative of fair market value and should be viewed with prudence when considering them as a basis for the valuation of shares.

Suppose a minority shareholder has an agreement with another minority shareholder that fixes their share price at a certain amount; the concurrence should not be taken, at face, as an indication of fair market value of the shares. There are outside influences and circumstances that motivate the share price or amount set in the agreement that may well provide a strategic plan of succession and whose binding effect may have little to do with market conditions or constitute those considerations requisite of willing buyers and sellers.

The concern over using buy-sell agreements in determining value is addressed by the IRC § 2703. This section requires business appraisers to disregard certain rights and restrictions in valuing such interests, including buy-sell and shareholder agreements among related parties drafted or substantially modified on or after October 8, 1990. The agreements can only be considered if they meet the following three-pronged test:

1. They are a bona fide business arrangement.

2. They are not used as a device to transfer property to family members for less than full and adequate consideration.

3. They are comparable to similar arrangements entered into by persons in arm's-length transactions.

The IRS and the tax court are obviously more suspicious of agreements relating to family members that appear self-serving. However, even when shareholder agreements do not involve family members, they must pass four tests before being considered determinative in value for estate tax purposes. See *Estate of Lauder* (TC Memo. 1992-736.).

1. The price must be fixed or determinable.

2. The agreement must be binding on the parties during life and death.

3. The agreement must have been entered into for a bona fide business reason.

4. The buy-sell agreement must not be a substitute for a testamentary disposition.

The *Estate of Blount*, a 2004 tax court case, is instructive in this matter.[1] The central issue in the case was whether a buy-sell agreement fixed the estate tax value of the corporation's shares, or whether the agreement should be disregarded. The court held that because Blount, the controlling shareholder, had a controlling interest and the unilateral ability to modify the agreement, the agreement did not fix the estate tax value of the shares. In the *Blount* opinion, the tax court discussed at length the interplay between agreements and fair market value, the standard for valuing shares.

From a valuation perspective, synthetic equity has become the catch-all phrase for virtually every benefit, contract, agreement, right, incentive, stock appreciation rights, and so on that is directly or indirectly associated with the shares of the company and that could affect share value. At issue is the potential impact of arrangements on share value from dilution, obligations, compensation, or enhanced rights. IRC § 1.409 (p)-1T, often referred to as Anti-Abuse Rules, states:

> Synthetic equity—(i) Rights to Acquire Stock of the S Corporation. Synthetic equity includes any stock option, warrant, restricted stock, deferred insurance stock right, stock appreciation right payable in stock, or similar interests or right that gives the holder the right to acquire or receive stock of the S corporation in the future. Rights to acquire stock in an S corporation with respect to stock that is, at all times during the period when such rights are effective, both issued and outstanding and held by persons other than the ESOP, the S corporation, or a related entity, are not synthetic equity. . . .

In essence 1.409(p)-1T treats a person that is entitled to synthetic equity in shares of an S corporation as deemed owning those shares. This section also imposes an excise tax on the total amount involved in a prohibited allocation to a disqualified person under certain circumstances. In general, this anti-abuse rule is directed to highly compensated and larger shareholders. It provides the basis for an annual test to ensure that synthetic equity in an S corporation environment must meet specific criteria by not disproportionately benefiting "highly compensated" individuals or their family members. The risk of triggering substantial penalty should outweigh any attempts to maneuver around the code parameters.

Revenue ruling 2003-6 provides guidance to S corporation ESOP companies in the area of allocations to disqualified persons. IRC § 409(p) requires that an ESOP that holds stock in an S corporation may not allocate assets of the plan for the benefit of disqualified persons. The Internal Revenue Service issued this revenue ruling to prevent abuses caused by companies circumventing IRC § 409(p) by not immediately using the provisions of the Economic Growth and Tax Relief Reconciliation Act (EGTRRA), even though they were not required to be effective until December 31, 2004.

Additional guidance is provided in the area of synthetic equity by Revenue Ruling 2004-4, specifically related to S corporation ESOPs. The ruling addresses prohibited allocation of securities to an S corporation ESOP; defining individuals that are disqualified persons, nonallocation year of the ESOP, and the effect of qualified subchapter S subsidiaries (Q-Subs) and, the effect of synthetic equity. The IRS aims to ensure that rank and file employees receive benefits proportionate with their earnings. Additionally, the IRS has promised additional regulations are forthcoming in this area.

Although these revenue rulings deal with S corporation ESOP plans, there are no such provisions dealing with C corporations with ESOP plans, presumably because S corporation income allocated to shares held by the plan are not currently taxes.

STOCK OPTIONS IN THE C CORPORATION

Attracting key personnel in the current employment environment has and will continue to change as the marketplace of competition for talented personnel expands. The traditional salary, work hours, vacation, holidays, and base retirement have evolved to include cafeteria plans, health insurance, life insurance, flex-hours, virtual offices, office sharing, expense account, and equity stakes in the company. In a corporate environment, providing nonqualified stock options to anchor and incentive key members of a company though the usage of equity options continues as a very viable employment benefit.

These equity benefits options extend to many private and nonmarketable shares of stock in much the same way as their publicly traded counterparts provide these benefits, which can include different stock features, with restrictions, voting rights, and so on. In most cases, private company stock option plans provide for an ongoing plan that is available to a specific class or group of employees. These option plans generally set aside 10 percent or less of the company shares for a period of not longer than 10 years and set vesting, grant dates, exercise dates, and terms.

In keeping with the dictates of IRC § 83, the options do not create a taxable event at their issuance. However, upon exercise the difference in the exercise price and the market value on the date of exercise becomes a compensation event and the difference in exercise price and fair market value is added to the exercising employees salary, thus grossing up for the difference. This taxable event is a deduction to the corporation providing a tax shield against income because the company requires no cash flow. These events should be anticipated in the valuation of the ESOP shares as if all shares that are in the money are exercised on the valuation date.

It is important to note that the dilutive impact of all the shares that are in the money should be included in the computations, net of their tax shield. Additionally, the value of the option shares does not necessarily follow that of the ESOP shares as the ESOP shares' adequate consideration provisions provide the "put" right, which does not and cannot obligate the plan to buy shares under the nonqualified stock option plan of the company. The nonqualified stock option plan is a stand-alone plan with its own set of restrictions and shareholder buy/sell terms.

Option shares that are in the money represent those shares where the transaction price of the shares exceeds the exercise price. The reverse is that the share options are under water or out of the money. Since elections to exercise are optional, the economics of the option arrangement would make the feasibility less attractive to the optionee to purchase share by exercising the option at an exercise price greater than the share value at the time of exercise.

Quantifying the impact of share dilution and the potential exercising of in-the-money options is to be balanced with the cash flow benefits of compensation expense and income tax shield. In this regard, fair market value will need to be estimated on a stand-alone basis and outside considerations of the ESOP provisions. In these instances, there will likely be a greater adjustment in the lack of liquidity for the nonqualified shares than those shares in an ESOP, which will generally produce a minority interest value indication.

One method of quantifying the dilutive impact of outstanding options and providing a reasoned basis for eliminating the fading of ownership interest in the ESOP and with other outside shareholders is a multistep process:

1. Sum the unexercised options outstanding on the valuation date.
2. Calculate the impact of these shares by multiplying them by the estimated market price of the options shares on a stand alone basis.
3. Deduct from the same options shares at their option exercise price—with one exception, where the option exercise price is greater than the market value
4. Calculate using the market price.

The resulting sum represents the compensatable excess, an amount that requires no cash flow of the company. Once the amount of compensation is determined, the amount of compensation difference represents an available tax deduction and is tax affected. By adding the tax effect, creating cash flow with the compensation expense amount, cash flow is created as the residual and is added to the aggregate company value for ESOP purposes. The resulting share value aggregate total is divided by the aggregate shares outstanding plus those shares of the outstanding options. The result provides a fully diluted value. (Not all appraisers agree with this approach).

To summarize the process:

1. Calculate value of the outstanding "in the money" options.

2. Tax effect the expensed portion of compensation.

3. Add the cash flow to the aggregate company value.

4. Calculate the aggregate total outstanding shares by adding the number of option shares to the outstanding shares.

5. Divide the aggregate company value, the aggregate company value plus option related cash flow, by the total fully diluted shares illustrated in the aggregate total outstanding shares.

In the DOL and IRS environment with fading or synthetic equity arrangements, consideration must be given to options. It would appear appropriate that option arrangements be entered into prior to the initial share transactions with the ESOP, as the impact of these option shares would be considered from the onset and incorporated in the adequate consideration estimate.

SUMMARY

Given the IRS activity in this area and the comments of more to come, tremendous effort is exerted to slow or stop plans of nonqualified benefits to employees, especially in the area of S corporations with ESOPs. As noted, maintaining key personnel is an important aspect to any long-range business plan, regardless of the company's size. Although ESOP benefits are spread among all employees under the ERISA provisions of nondiscrimination, there may still remain the necessity of anchoring key management and officers that, alternatively, may be able to find a more favorable tax atmosphere with a larger, perhaps public company that offers nonqualified equity or bonus arrangements based on quantifiable performance and production.

S and C corporation options and other arrangements are not treated the same under the anti-abuse rules. The IRS appears to consider that since C corporations pay taxes at their entity level, they are tax revenue neutral. It is best advised to seek competent help in assessing the impact on the share values and to stay clear of the anti-abuse rules.

17

Adjustments for
Lack of Marketability

Addressed in this chapter are considerations for the assessment of an adjustment for marketability of sponsoring-company ESOP shares and applicability to an ongoing ESOP. Not addressed are special considerations such as liquidations, sale of substantially all the assets of the company, or common shares. Volumes of information have targeted the size and applicability, if any, of an adjustment for a lack of marketability (liquidity) to a valuation assignment. These adjustments for lack of marketability commonly are pursued as, and are concluded in, the form of a discount when applied to a private company equity interest, such as the common stock of a closely held or thinly traded public corporation.

There are two broad camps of thought on generic marketability adjustment discussions. One camp follows a hierarchical approach of theoretical, multiplicative, and scholarly dissertation on qualifying the adjustments, while camp two emerges more focused on a systematically judgmental, common sense, and intuitive feel for the company in relation to its readily tradable peers.

Whatever the evaluator chooses as the methodology or blended system of quantifying and estimating an adjustment for a lack of marketability,there are unique aspects of liquidity and marketability to an ESOP framed primarily by governmental design, restrictions, prerogatives, incentives, statutory exemptions and intervention in qualifying an investment under the umbrella of a qualified retirement plan. These unique ESOP attributes are both similar to and in addition to those characteristics found in publicly traded securities. The details specific to an ESOP are placed in this text as ingredients for the appraiser's consideration in the assessment of, the need for, and the development of a marketability adjustment.

DEPARTMENT OF LABOR PROPOSED
REGULATION 2510.3-18(b)

Subparagraph (H) of this proposed regulation states that in the valuation of ESOP shares where there is no public market, DOL "requires an assessment of the effect of the securities' marketability or lack thereof."

The subparagraph continues:

> [T]he Department believes that the marketability of these types of securities will directly affect their price. In this regard, the Department is aware that, especially in situations involving employee stock ownership plans, the employer securities held by the ESOP will provide a "put" option whereby individual participants may upon retirement sell their shares back to the employer. It has been argued that some kinds of "put" options may diminish the need to discount the value of the securities due to lack of marketability. The Department believes that the existence of the "put" option should be considered for valuation purposes only to the extent it is enforceable and the employer has and may reasonably be expected to continue to have, adequate resources to meet its obligations. Thus, the Department proposes to require that the plan fiduciary assess whether these "put" rights are actually enforceable and whether the employer will be able to pay for the securities when and if the "put" is exercised.

ASSESSMENT OF ESOP SHARES MARKETABILITY

The courts' position in assessing marketability of securities whose shares have no access to an active market is what is important to the appraiser of ESOP shares. Listed is only one of a number of court acknowledgments and summaries in assessing marketability issues. All are important to every valuation assignment, although this chapter specifically addresses areas that are more specific to ESOPs.

> When valuing unlisted stock, it is sometimes appropriate to apply a lack of marketability discount to the price in order to reflect the absence of a recognized market for closely held stock and to account for the fact that closely held stock is generally not readily transferable. See *Mandelbaum v. Commissioner,* T.C. Memo. 1995-255, affd. 91 F.3d 124 (3d Cir. 1996); *Estate of Trenchard v. Commissioner,* T.C. Memo. 1995-121; Rev. Rul. 77-287, 1977-2 C.B. 319, 320-321.

The courts have indicated that several factors should be considered when attempting to decide how much of a marketability discount to apply in a particular case:

- The cost of a similar corporation's public and private stock

- An analysis of the subject corporation's financial statements

- The corporation's dividend-paying capacity, its history of paying dividends, and the amount of its prior dividends

- The nature of the corporation, its history, its position in the industry, and its economic outlook
- The corporation's management
- The degree of control transferred with the block of stock to be valued
- Any restriction on the transferability of the corporation's stock
- The period of time for which an investor must hold the subject stock to realize a sufficient profit
- The corporation's redemption policy
- The cost of effectuating a public offering of the stock to be valued

See *Estate of Gilford v. Commissioner,* 88 T.C. 38, 60 (1987); *Mandelbaum v. Commissioner, supra;* Rev. Rul. 77-287, *supra.*

Assessing and quantifying discounts have developed along several paths over time and assess active-market trading delayed for specific periods in time. From the perspective of ESOP shares, the approaches may track by following inherent similarities, thus comparability with securities that are restricted.

RESTRICTED STOCK ANALYSIS

This restricted stock analysis points out that there are differences in transaction prices between common stock and restricted stock in the same company that is exposed to a ready trading market. The basis for restricted stock is grounded in the fact that restricted investments are barred, by written restriction or agreement, from access and sale of the interest for a specified period of time.

The correlation surmises that the principal difference in the same company between freely traded common shares and those that are restricted from transacting at the current market prices is the commonly discounted price paid for the restricted stock. This resulting restriction-driven discounted price is thus the result of a lack of liquidity imposed by the length of time the shares are restricted from a freely traded market. The difference in prices paid for restricted shares and those that have a ready market is therefore considered as the market-driven adjustment for a lack of marketability. This analogy can produce and is often reasoned to be a neutral indicator of a discount for the restrictions placed against the shares.

RESTRICTIONS AND ESOP SHARES

Various requirements and unique characteristics of ESOP shareholdings correspond to the participants of beneficial interests, cover restrictions in voting rights, restrictions on diversification of the participant's portfolio of sponsoring company securities, vesting in participant accounts, special allocations of shares to the participant accounts, triggering events that will commence the subsequent distribution of benefits from the ESOP, put rights on transacting shares and the sponsoring company's options on payment of the participant account share value over time. These unique characteristics of ESOP shares liken themselves as comparable to letter or restricted stocks with delayed access to tender in a market place.

Various inputs influence the assessment of a lack of marketability, most based on the assumed holding period of an investment. However, there are other influences that additionally differentiate the ESOP shares from those unrestricted shares in a freely traded marketplace such as the interim available cash flows and paid-out distributions to shareholders, and the potential for growth or decline in the underlying securities marketable.[1] The following bullet list is provided as a means of paralleling the points previously stated as characteristics of retirement plans and those found in a private equity security.

Comparison Bullet Points of Differences:

- Beneficial interests versus direct title and ownership
- Voting rights—Limited versus full ownership characteristics
- Diversification—Limited versus ability to trade in best interest
- Vesting versus no partial interests
- Special allocations versus no allocations at all
- Triggering events versus no restrictions
- Put rights versus straight sell of interest
- Conditional distribution of retirement proceeds versus three-day trade public market

PUT OPTIONS AND THEIR IMPACT ON MARKETABILITY ADJUSTMENTS

In Chapter 12 of this text, there is a more in-depth discussion of what put options are and how they interact with other sections of plan design, sponsoring company financial condition, ESOP financial condition, and, ultimately, when and how participant accounts can realize their account balances by way of triggering events.

Assessing the existence and applicability of a discount for marketability was addressed in a Seventh Circuit decision in *Eyler v. Commissioner of Internal Revenue Service,* 88 F.3d 445 (7th Cir. 1996), which was an appeal from a federal tax court case 69 TCM 2200, 1995 WL 127907 1995.

The case centered on a good-faith determination of fair market value and its impact on adequate consideration to a leveraged ESOP. The court studied the valuation process and found that the plan trustee did not in good faith act on the merits of the transaction, as the fiduciary must understand the basis of the appraisal and spend some effort in reviewing the valuation. One key point was that the put option, although required by the regulations, does not eliminate the need for a lack of marketability adjustment.

LEVERAGE AND ITS IMPACT ON THE PUT OPTION

Chapter 10 of this text covers the effects of leverage in the ESOP and its unique exemption from prohibited transactions unique to the ESOP, as well as the pressures placed on the sponsoring company as it repays the principal and interest of the debt. These unique exemptions would ordinarily prohibit an ERISA plan from incurring debt. Special treatment, however, allows the sponsoring company and the ESOP to partner in acquiring shares of the company. One of the special features is the plan's ability to borrow money as a means to provide added benefit to the plan participants. When the ESOP uses debt, the repayment of the debt places additional cash requirements on the sponsoring company and often burdens the discretionary cash and borrowing capacity, thus increasing the entity's risk. When assessing the ability of the sponsoring company to make good on the put option for departing participants, the issue becomes one of ability to meet the cash demand of share distributions from qualified plan terminations.

When assessing the put rights with ESOPs that have leverage, the appraiser should inquire and analyze the plan documents. ERISA gives the authority in plan design to provide a stipulation that until all initial debt for the ESOP shares covered in a leveraged acquisition are paid in full, none of those shares are distributable until all ESOP debt is satisfied. If this feature is not part of the plan documents, the put rights fall as with any other distributable share to qualifying participants.

Substantially extending the required holding period postparticipant distribution event with usage of a promissory note of pending ESOP debt repayment impacts the liquidity of the shareholder. The further away the receipt of cash for tendered (put) shares, the larger the adjustment for its marketability.

TAX STATUS AND ITS IMPACT ON THE PUT OPTION

The validity of the put option and those considerations involved with leveraged plans has bearing in two very different areas, the S corporation or the C corporation, as covered in Chapter 15. Their impact on the size, probability, and availability of funding from the sponsoring company in the way of dividends and the size of the ownership interest can be significant, particularly if the ESOP sponsoring company has elected subchapter S status for tax treatment of federal income tax.

The tax structure of the ESOP corporation continues to be enhanced for the S corporation with the signing into law of The American Jobs Creation Act of 2004 on October 22, 2004. This act permits S corporation distributions on allocated shares held by an ESOP to be used to repay outstanding ESOP debt. This change allows the ESOP that holds S corporation shares, less restriction to reduce debt, allowing for the pay down of note principal more rapidly, provide a possible quicker building in the account balances of the participant and make available moneys to contribute to meet the obligations of a put option. As a broad generalization, market liquidity for the ESOP shares will be enhanced with an S tax status as compared to that of a C corporation tax status.

OBSERVATION OF QUANTIFYING MARKETABILITY ADJUSTMENTS

As an unscientific observation, appraisers may typically fall into one or more of the commonly used methods in developing an estimate of marketability adjustments:

- Providing a general, judgmental conclusion that the marketability discount is X percent

- Citing one or more tax court decisions as the basis for their conclusion that the marketability discount is X percent, whether there is any similarity between the subject company and the cited cases

- Citing some or all of the articles and studies discussed in the summary section, and then conclude that the marketability discount is X percent

- Attempting to analyze the specific facts of the case in relationship to the factors that are generally thought to influence marketability. Based on this nonquantitative analysis, appraisers then attempt to make an informed judgment and conclude that the marketability discount is X percent.[1]

For an in-depth review of the tax court analysis of several differing methods of determining marketability discounts, see *Estate of Mellinger v. Commissioner*, 112 T.C. 26 (1999).

SUMMARY

The proverbial "it depends on the facts and circumstances in each case" statement is applicable in assessing an adjustment for the lack of marketability. There does, however, emerge the duty for the trustee to the realities of a freely traded stock and thereby the likelihood of a discount for lack of marketability in most ESOP plans that hold sponsoring company shares as investments. It would appear that without compelling evidence to the contrary, ESOP shares will be subject to some form of adjustment for marketability as a discount.

The size of the adjustment is a subject of the two camps of thought discussed in this chapter, taken as a whole and assessing those features unique to ESOP shares when the assessment of discount is compared to that of the securities found in a freely traded marketplace.

18

Writing a
Valuation Conclusion*

"Put it before them briefly so they will read it, clearly so they will appreciate it, picturesquely so they will remember it and, above all, accurately so they will be guided by its light."

Joseph Pulitzer[1]

Although Mr. Pulitzer's quote was probably not written with a valuation in mind, it adequately describes the embodiment of what a valuation report should contain. The ESOP valuation process is not complete until a written document is furnished to the plan trustee(s). The most exceptional analysis may not be worthwhile if the results are not communicated in a well-drafted document.

Producing a written text featuring the appraiser's conclusion falls under the broad category of a *report*. In its purest form, a report is an account, story, tale, or description of an event, occurrence, or happening, as paraphrased from *Funk & Wagnall's Standard College Dictionary:* "An account of any occurrence prepared for publication through the press."

In the context of ESOP shares, the typical and varied assignments for valuation services have required that each engagement provides an appropriate written account for the conclusions of the appraiser. These written accounts generally fall under three broad categories:

1. Adequate consideration report
2. Summary (informal) report
3. Formal (self-contained) report

In ESOP valuations, the essence of an engagement is likened to what may be analytically and loosely weighed against a *special-purpose* property engagement.

---

*This chapter was contributed by Susan Parmlee.

All three written account categories have a proper place in the reporting of the appraiser's study findings and value indications.

REPORT WRITING AND THE HYPOTHESIS OF FAIRNESS

Drawing on the evolution of ERISA, much of the Department of Labor (DOL) compliance requirements for Esops are primarily directed to the employer/sponsoring company, its management, and trustees of qualified retirement plans, to ensure that the employee participant is fairly and similarly treated with all categories of employee status and that there are no discriminatory activities that would disadvantage the employee participant. The term *fair* has many connotations and definitions and depends on the context in which it is used. In some instances, fair may best be described as *ideal*. However, the hypothetical environment of the appraisal assignment is an observation from a universe of buyers and sellers and lacks the necessary specificity to quantify the term as *ideal*. The Internal Revenue Service (IRS) and the DOL consistently agree that the appraisal of a business interest is a range concept and is less precise than that of ideal.

Why the fascination with the word *fair?* That's a fair question. Much has been debated, written, and reported about appraisals and *fairness opinions*. The absence of DOL and IRS usage of the term *fairness opinion* is not an accident. The DOL chose to create new terminology for usage in an ESOP, namely that of *adequate consideration*. The IRS recognizes the usage of *fair market value* for much the same reason as DOL. There is no standard definition in appraisal of the word *fair* or *fairness* unless it is used in a narrowed context, under specific known conditions with specific and known circumstances. Thus, the appraiser who offers a fairness opinion in the text of an ESOP appraisal assignment may find it appropriate to include language specific to provisions of adequate consideration, as there might be difficulty in locating specific promulgations of DOL or IRS on fairness. In contrast, what is consistent and appears to comply is meeting the prescribed definitions of adequate consideration and fair market value.

GENERAL INFORMATION REGARDING VALUATION REPORTS

Requirement for Annual Reports

Are annual valuation reports required? A required annual valuation of the total ESOP participants' shares by a qualified, independent appraiser is mandatory under the Tax Reform Act of 1986 (TRA '86).[2] TRA '86 enacted IRC § 401(a) (28)(C), which provided that employer securities acquired by an ESOP after December 31, 1986, that are not readily tradable on an established securities market must be valued by an independent appraiser (within the meaning of IRC § 170(a)(1)).[3] In addition, a *qualified* appraiser is required, under IRS guidelines, inferring that the appraiser performs business valuations regularly and has knowledge of ESOP transactions.[4] Further, the Employee Retirement & Income Security Act of 1974 (ERISA) established regulatory requirements in which an ESOP can pay no more than adequate consideration in the purchase of employer securities.[5] Therefore, ESOP valuation reports should support the decisions of the trustees and must also withstand review by the Department of Labor and the Internal Revenue Service.

When Valuation Reports Are Required

When are valuation reports for ESOP purposes required?

- When the ESOP is originally created, the initial purchase from the owner must be reasonably priced.

- The shares owned must be revalued annually to determine the repurchase price in the event of employee retirement, death, or departure.

- When company stock may be transferred to the ESOP, valuation is required.

REGULATION OF THE VALUATION REPORTING PROCESS

Authoritative agencies such as the IRS and DOL direct the subject matter of ESOP business valuation reports. In addition, valuation standards from the Appraisal Standard Board of the Appraisal Foundation, authorized by the U.S. Congress that issues the Uniform Standards of Professional Appraisal Practice (USPAP), and professional organizations—including The Institute of Business Appraisers (IBA), American Society of Appraisers (ASA), Certified Valuation Analysts (CVA), and the International Valuation Standards Committee (IVSC)—greatly influence the content and organization of these valuation reports. These professional valuation associations propose standards of reporting which can be viewed as resourceful guidelines.

Purpose of ESOP Valuation Report

In order to comply with the requirements of the Department of Labor, the appraiser(s)' conclusion of fair market value, as defined previously in the text, must be reflected in a written document of valuation. In Revenue Ruling 59-60 § 3.01, the Internal Revenue Service enhances the definition with the following:

> [A] determination of Fair Market Value, being a question of fact, will depend upon the circumstances in each case . . . . Often, an appraiser will find a wide difference of opinion as to the Fair Market Value of a particular stock. In resolving such differences, (s)he should maintain a reasonable attitude in recognition of the fact that valuation is not an exact science. A sound valuation will be based upon all the relevant facts, but the elements of common sense, informed judgment and reasonableness must enter into the process of weighting those facts and determining their aggregate significance.[6]

The Revenue Rulings and Regulations emphasize that the valuation factors do not necessarily have equal weight.

Objective of Valuation Report

The IRS sheds light about "the primary objective of a valuation report is to provide convincing and compelling support for the conclusions reached. Valuation reports should contain all the information necessary to ensure a clear understanding of the valuation analyses and demonstrate how the conclusions were reached."[7]

Presentation of Written Documentation

How should the written documents be presented? All reports should be clearly written with every conclusion, statement, adjustment, approach, and method supported in the work papers and the report. The appraiser should use prudence and due care in researching and writing valuation reports.

TYPES OF REPORTS

As previously mentioned, written accounts generally fall under three broad report categories: adequate consideration, summary (informal), and formal (self-contained). These will be more fully described in the next three sections of this chapter.

Adequate Consideration Letter

In many appraisal assignments, the appraiser's work involves a valuation date that is generally at a point in time in the past. Although this might be the case for the routine annual appraisal assignment for an ESOP, it might not reflect initial or subsequent acquisitions and divestitures of shares with outside shareholders because the ESOP trustee is pledged to negotiate the sale of shares in real time, present mode. In these instances, providing a formal or summary appraisal report in advance of a transaction is usually not practical or feasible.

Generally, these appraisal projects require the appraiser to give some written declaration to the trustee that the price paid for the shares is within and, thereby, in compliance with the DOL provisions of adequate consideration of which a component is providing a fair market value range of values. This written document requirement can best be served in a written narrative of compliance with the adequate consideration provisions promulgated by the DOL. This written document does not have to be a written valuation report, in the strictest context, and compliance with the adequate consideration provisions letter is not to be considered synonymous with a fairness opinion of value.

Summary Valuation Report

Summary reports are an acceptable alternative to formal valuation reports, containing more information than an adequate consideration letter, and serving as a written document in compliance with requirements promulgated by the DOL.

Summary reports are usually utilized for annual updates, but not for significant transactions because they more resemble *Cliffs Notes,* as compared to a novel. In addition, the summary report format should not be used if there are extraordinary changes in economic conditions, financial statements, or operations of the subject company.

As with a formal report, the appraiser should have unfettered access to information, should perform all calculations to support the conclusions, and should include all approaches and methods in the work papers. While still meeting the compliance requirements discussed in this chapter, the advantage of a summary report over a formal valuation is its time-saving features and minimization of redundancy.

Formal Valuation Report

A formal valuation report is the most comprehensive written valuation report and is used for transactional reporting, post transactions, most tax-related issues, legal proceedings, and updates. A formal valuation report must comply with requirements promulgated by the DOL and the IRS. The formal valuation report minimally should contain an appraiser's statement signed by the appraiser, assumptions and limiting conditions, valuation approaches and methods, financial analysis, description of assets, a statement of the purpose of the appraisal and other DOL and IRS requirements described later in this chapter.

Required Contents of a Written Valuation Report

The DOL, with further explanations derived from Federal Deposit Insurance Corporation (FDIC) interpretations and the IRS, previously has stated or implied that a written documentation of valuation should contain these components as a minimum:[8]

- A summary of the qualifications of the person or persons making the valuation. The appraiser must be able to evaluate the specific type of equity stocks that are being valued in order to be considered qualified. The Internal Revenue Treasury Regulation § 54.4975-11(d)(5) expounds on the appraiser's qualifications, stating that "an independent appraisal will not in itself be a good faith determination of value in the case of a transaction between a plan and a disqualified person. However, in other cases, a determination of fair market value based on at least an annual appraisal independently arrived at by a person who customarily makes such appraisals and who is independent of any party to a transaction under Section 54.4975-7(b)(9) and (12) will be deemed to be a good faith determination of value."

- A statement of the asset's value, a statement of the methods used in determining that value, and the reasons for the valuation in light of those methods. For further explanation, Internal Revenue Treasury Regulation § 1.482-8 states that "in accordance with the best method rule of Section 1.482-1(c), a method may be applied in a particular case only if the comparability, quality of data, and reliability of assumptions under that method make it more reliable than any other available measure of the arm's length result."

- A full description of the asset being valued. The assets being valued are equity securities of a sponsoring corporation, often referred to as "Employer/Sponsoring" company securities that have been issued to and are currently held by an Employee Stock Ownership Plan.

- The factors taken into account in making the valuation, including any restrictions, understandings, agreements or obligations limiting the use or disposition of the property. Rev. Proc 66-49, issued by the Internal Revenue Service to provide information and guidelines for appraisals, stated that, in general, an appraisal report should contain "the bases upon which the appraisal was made, including any restrictions, understandings, or covenants limiting the use or disposition of the property."[9]

- The purpose for which the valuation was made. The intention of this DOL requirement is to evaluate the valuation in the appropriate context.

- The relevance or significance accorded to the valuation methodologies taken into account. Valuators utilize many different valuation methods. These methods are affected by changes in the treatments given and weight accorded to relevant information, which directly affects the result of the valuator's analysis. Therefore, a statement about the methods used might allow for a more accurate consideration of the validity of the valuation.

- The effective date of the valuation. This requirement in the Department of Labor proposed regulation § 2510.3-18(b)(ii) indicates that the fair market value must be determined as of the date of the transaction in question.

- A written assessment of all relevant factors, which must include those factors cited in Internal Revenue Service—Revenue Ruling No. 59-60:[10]

  1. The nature of the business and the history of the enterprise from its inception

  2. The economic outlook in general and the specific industry in particular

  3. The book value of the securities and the financial condition of the business

  4. The earnings capacity of the company

  5. The dividend-paying capacity of the company

  6. Whether the enterprise has goodwill or other intangible value

  7. The market price of securities of corporations engaged in the same or a similar line of business, which are actively traded in a free and open market, either on an exchange or over the counter

  8. The marketability, or lack thereof, of the securities

9. Whether the seller would be able to obtain a control premium from an unrelated third party with regard to the block of securities being valued, provided that in cases where a control premium is taken into account

- A written assessment of all relevant factors detailing any marketability adjustment(s) and that the put option rights were considered. Employer securities held by the ESOP may provide a put option whereby individual participants may, upon retirement, sell their shares back to the employer. Some kinds of put options may diminish the need to discount the value of the securities due to lack of marketability. Therefore, existence of the put option should be considered for valuation purposes only to the extent it is enforceable, and the employer has and may reasonably be expected to continue to have, adequate resources to meet its obligations.

- Statement of independence. Department of Labor proposed regulation § 2510.3-18(b)(3)(iii) defines the circumstances under which a fiduciary or an appraiser will be deemed to be independent. The fiduciary or appraiser must in fact be independent of all parties participating in the transaction other than the plan, and a determination of independence must be made in light of all relevant facts and circumstances, delineating certain circumstances under which this independence will be lacking. An appraiser will be considered independent of all parties to a transaction (other than the plan) only if a plan fiduciary has chosen the appraiser and has the right to terminate that appointment, and the plan is thereby established as the appraiser's client. Absent such circumstances, the appraiser may be unable to be completely neutral in the exercise of his or her function.[11]

- In cases where a valuation report has been prepared, the signature of the person making the valuation and the date the report was signed. If an appraiser considers that the written valuation report must be filed under USPAP, then the report must also contain a certification signed by the appraiser. 2004 USPAP Standards Rule 10-3 contains binding requirements from which departure is not permitted. Each written business or intangible asset appraisal report must contain a signed certification that is similar in content to the following form:[12]

I certify that, to the best of my knowledge and belief:

- The statements of fact contained in this report are true and correct.

- The reported analyses, opinions, and conclusions are limited only by the reported assumptions and limiting conditions and

(continues)

are my personal, impartial, and unbiased professional analyses, opinions, and conclusions.

- I have no (or the specified) present or prospective interest in the property that is the subject of this report, and I have no (or the specified) personal interest with respect to the parties involved.

- I have no bias with respect to the property that is the subject of this report or to the parties involved with this assignment.

- My engagement in this assignment was not contingent upon developing or reporting predetermined results.

- My compensation for completing this assignment is not contingent upon the development or reporting of a predetermined value or direction in value that favors the cause of the client, the amount of the value opinion, the attainment of a stipulated result, or the occurrence of a subsequent event directly related to the intended use of this appraisal.

- My analyses, opinions, and conclusions were developed, and this report has been prepared, in conformity with the *Uniform Standards of Professional Appraisal Practice.*

- No one provided significant business appraisal assistance to the person signing this certification. (If there are exceptions, the name of each individual providing significant business appraisal assistance must be stated.)

What is required for a conclusion in a valuation report? The American Society of Appraisers states:

[T]he conclusion of value reached by the appraiser shall be based upon the applicable standard of value, the purpose and intended use of the valuation, and all relevant information available as of the valuation date in carrying out the scope of the assignment. The conclusion of value reached by the appraiser will be based on value indications resulting from one or more methods performed under one or more appraisal approaches.[13]

CONCLUSION

In conclusion, as previously stated, a written valuation report is the part of the valuation process that records the assessment of how much a willing buyer would pay a willing seller for a business or business interest. The report contains and enumerates calculations performed by analyzing various ratios, such as price-to-earnings, discounted future cash flow and earnings, asset and liabilities value, and comparable companies and transactions, among other things. It provides a basis for adjustments that reflect whether the stock is for control or lack of control and marketability or lack of marketability.[14] A per-share value can be extracted by simply dividing the outstanding (considering unallocated and/or effects of dilution) shares of the company into the aggregate company value.

The plan administrator can determine the appropriate reporting of these shares and share values. The valuation report should be written to the plan trustee who generally retains the analyst. It does not matter whether the plan or the sponsoring company pays for the valuation services, and the trustee does not have to use the analyst's estimate. Rather, it is the plan trustee's responsibility to render the final conclusion. The analyst's task is to offer to the trustee a professional estimate of the fair market value of the ESOP shares and back it up with a suitable, supportive, compliant report.

Appendix A

Department of Labor

Proposed Regulation 2510.3-18(b)

Proposed 29 C.F.R. 2510.3-18

Definition of "Adequate Consideration"

Proposed Regulation Only
Published in the *Federal Register* on May 7, 1988 at 53 FR 17632.

Compliance with this regulation is *NOT* required, as it is still merely a proposal. It is reprinted to provide examiners with authoritative guidance as to approaches towards the valuation of securities when there is no organized market for them. While the specifics of the regulation do not apply, the general approach taken is valid and worthy of consideration. For this reason, the explanatory Preamble is also provided, in addition to the proposed regulation itself.

AGENCY: Pension and Welfare Benefits Administration, Department of Labor.

ACTION: Notice of proposed rulemaking.

SUMMARY: This document contains a notice of a proposed regulation under the Employee Retirement Income Security Act of 1974 (the Act or ERISA) and the Federal Employees' Retirement System Act of 1986 (FERSA). The proposal clarifies the definition of the term "adequate consideration" provided in section 3(18)(B) of the Act and section 8477(a)(2)(B) of FERSA for assets other than securities for which there is a generally recognized market. Section 3(18)(B) and section 8477(a)(2)(B) provide that the term "adequate consideration" for such assets means the fair market value of the asset as determined in good faith by the trustee or named fiduciary (or, in the case of FERSA, a fiduciary) pursuant to the terms of the plan and in accordance with regulations promulgated by the Secretary of Labor. Because valuation questions of this nature arise in a variety of contexts, the Department is proposing this regulation in order to provide the certainty necessary for plan fiduciaries to fulfill their statutory duties. If adopted, the regulation would affect plans investing in assets other than securities for which there is a generally recognized market.

DATES: Written comments on the proposed regulation must be received by July 18, 1988. If adopted, the regulation will be effective for transactions taking place after the date 30 days following publication of the regulation in final form.

Explanatory Preamble

(Proposed Regulation begins on page 181)

ADDRESS: Written comments on the proposed regulation (preferably three copies) should be submitted to: Office of Regulations and Interpretations, Pension and Welfare Benefits Administration, Room N-5671, U.S. Department of Labor, 200 Constitution Avenue NW., Washington, DC 20216, Attention: Adequate Consideration Proposal. All written comments will be available for public inspection at the Public Disclosure Room, Pension and Welfare Benefits Administration, U.S. Department of Labor, Room N-5507, 200 Constitution Avenue NW., Washington, DC.

FOR FURTHER INFORMATION CONTACT: Daniel J. Maguire, Esq., Plan Benefits Security Division, Office of the Solicitor, U.S. Department of Labor, Washington, DC 20210, (202) 523-9596 (not a toll-free number) or Mark A. Greenstein, Office of Regulations and Interpretations, Pension and Welfare Benefits Administration, (202) 523-7901 (not a toll-free number).

SUPPLEMENTARY INFORMATION:

A. Background

Notice is hereby given of a proposed regulation under section 3(18)(B) of the Act and section 8477(a)(2)(B) of FERSA. Section 3(18) of the Act provides the definition for the term "adequate consideration," and states: The term "adequate consideration" when used in part 4 of subtitle B means (A) in the case of a security for which there is a generally recognized market, either (i) the price of the security prevailing on a national securities exchange which is registered under section 6 of the Securities Exchange Act of 1934, or (ii) if the security is not traded on such a national securities exchange, a price not less favorable to the plan than the offering price for the security as established by the current bid and asked prices quoted by persons independent of the issuer and of any party in interest; and (B) in the case of an asset other than a security for which there is a generally recognized market, the fair market value of the asset as determined in good faith by the trustee or named fiduciary pursuant to the terms of the plan and in accordance with regulations promulgated by the Secretary.

The term "adequate consideration" appears four times in part 4 of subtitle B of Title I of the Act, and each time represents a central requirement for a statutory exemption from the prohibited transaction restrictions of the Act. Under section 408(b)(5), a plan may purchase insurance contracts from certain parties in interest if, among other conditions, the plan pays no more than adequate consideration. Section 408(b)(7) provides that the prohibited transaction provisions of section 406 shall not apply to the exercise of a privilege to convert securities, to the extent provided in regulations of the Secretary of Labor, only if the plan receives no less than adequate consideration pursuant to such conversion. Section 408(e) of the Act provides that the prohibitions in sections 406 and 407(a) of the Act shall not apply to the acquisition or sale by a plan of qualifying employer securities, or the acquisition, sale or lease by a plan of qualifying employer real property if, among other conditions, the acquisition, sale or lease is for adequate consideration. Section 414(c)(5) of the Act states that sections 406 and 407(a) of the Act shall not apply to the sale, exchange, or other disposition of property which is owned by a plan on June 30, 1974, and all times thereafter, to a party in interest, if such plan is required to dispose of the property in order to comply with the provisions of section 407(a) (relating to the prohibition against holding excess employer securities and employer real property), and if the plan receives not less than adequate consideration.

Public utilization of these statutory exemptions requires a determination of "adequate consideration" in accordance with the definition contained in section 3(18) of the Act. Guidance is especially important in this area because many of the transactions covered by these statutory exemptions involve plan dealings with the plan sponsor. A fiduciary's determination of the adequacy of consideration paid under such circumstances represents a major safeguard for plans against the potential for abuse inherent in such transactions. The Federal Employees' Retirement System Act of 1986 (FERSA) established the Federal Retirement Thrift Investment Board whose members act as fiduciaries with regard to the assets of the Thrift Savings Fund. In general, FERSA contains fiduciary obligation and prohibited transaction provisions similar to ERISA. However, unlike ERISA, FERSA prohibits party in interest transactions similar to those described in section 406(a) of ERISA only in those circumstances where adequate consideration is not exchanged between the Fund and the party in interest. Specifically, section 8477(c)(1) of FERSA provides that, except in exchange for adequate consideration, a fiduciary shall not permit the Thrift Savings Fund to engage in: transfers of its assets to, acquisition of property from or sales of property to, or transfers or exchanges of services with any person the fiduciary knows or should know to be a party in interest. Section 8477(a)(2) provides the FERSA definition for the term "adequate consideration" which is virtually identical to that contained in section 3(18) of ERISA. Thus, the proposal would apply to both section 3(18) of ERISA and section 8477(a)(2) of FERSA.

When the asset being valued is a security for which there is a generally recognized market, the plan fiduciary must determine "adequate consideration" by reference to the provisions of section 3(18)(A) of the Act (or with regard to FERSA, section 8477(a) (2)(A)). Section 3(18)(A) and section 8477(a)(2)(A) provide detailed reference points for the valuation of securities within its coverage, and in effect provides that adequate consideration for such securities is the prevailing market price. It is not the Department's intention to analyze the requirements of section 3(18)(A) or 8477(a)(2)(A) in this proposal. Fiduciaries must, however, determine whether a security is subject to the specific provisions of section 3(18)(A) (or section 8477(a)(2)(A) of FERSA) or the more general requirements of section 3(18)(B) (or section 8477(a)(2)(B)) as interpreted in this proposal. The question of whether a security is one for which there is a generally recognized market requires a factual determination in light of the character of the security and the nature and extent of market activity with regard to the security. Generally, the Department will examine whether a security is being actively traded so as to provide the benchmarks Congress intended. Isolated trading activity, or trades between related parties, generally will not be sufficient to show the existence of a generally recognized market for the purposes of section 3(18)(A) or section 8477(a)(2)(A).

In the case of all assets other than securities for which there is a generally recognized market, fiduciaries must determine adequate consideration pursuant to section 3(18)(B) of the Act (or, in the case of FERSA, section 8477(a)(2)(B)). Because it is designed to deal with all but a narrow class of assets, section 3(18)(B) and section 8477(a)(2)(B) are by their nature more general than section 3(18)(A) or section 8477(a)(2)(A). Although the Department has indicated that it will not issue advisory opinions stating whether certain stated consideration is "adequate consideration" for the purposes of section 3(18), ERISA Procedure 76-1, § 5.02(a) (41 FR 36281, 36282, August 27, 1976), the Department recognizes that plan fiduciaries have a need for guidance in valuing assets, and that standards to guide fiduciaries in this area may be particularly elusive with respect to assets other than securities for which there is a generally recognized market. See, for example, Donovan v. Cunningham, 716 F.2d 1455 (5th Cir. 1983) (court encourages the Department to adopt regulations under section 3(18)(B)). The Department has therefore determined to propose a regulation only under section 3(18)(B) and section 8477(a)(2)(B). This proposal is described more fully below.

It should be noted that it is not the Department's intention by this proposed regulation to relieve fiduciaries of the responsibility for making the required determinations of "adequate consideration" where applicable under the Act or FERSA. Nothing in the proposal should be construed as justifying a fiduciary's failure to take into account all relevant facts and circumstances in determining adequate consideration. Rather, the proposal is designed to provide a framework within which fiduciaries can fulfill their statutory duties. Further, fiduciaries should be aware that, even where a determination of adequate consideration comports with the requirements of section 3(18)(B) (or section 8477(a)(2)(B) of FERSA) and any regulation adopted thereunder, the investment of plan assets made pursuant to such determination will still be subject to the fiduciary requirements of Part 4 of Subtitle B of Title I of the Act, including the provisions of sections 403 and 404 of the Act, or the fiduciary responsibility provisions of FERSA.

B. Description of the Proposal

Proposed regulation 29 C.F.R. 2510.3-18(b) is divided into four major parts. Proposed § 2510.3-18(b)(1) states the general rule and delineates the scope of the regulation. Proposed § 2510.3-18(b)(2) addresses the concept of fair market value as it relates to a determination of "adequate consideration" under section 3(18)(B) of the Act.

Proposed § 2510.3-18(b)(3) deals with the requirement in section 3(18)(B) that valuing fiduciary act in good faith, and specifically discusses the use of an independent appraisal in connection with the determination of good faith. Proposed § 2510.3-18(b)(4) sets forth the content requirements for written valuations used as the basis for a determination of fair market value, with a special rule for the valuation of securities other than securities for which there is a generally recognized market. Each subsection is discussed in detail below.

1. *General Rule and Scope*

Proposed § 2510.3-18(b)(1)(i) essentially follows the language of section 3(18)(B) of the Act and section 8477(a)(2)(B) of FERSA and states that, in the case of a plan asset other than a security for which there is a generally recognized market, the term "adequate consideration" means the fair market value of the asset as determined in good faith by the trustee or named fiduciary (or, in the case of FERSA, a fiduciary) pursuant to the terms of the plan and in accordance with regulations promulgated by the Secretary of Labor.

Proposed § 2510.3-18(b)(1)(ii) delineates the scope of this regulation by establishing two criteria, both of which must be met for a valid determination of adequate consideration. First, the value assigned to an asset must reflect its fair market value as determined pursuant to proposed § 2510.3-18(b)(2). Second, the value assigned to an asset must be the product of a determination made by the fiduciary in good faith as defined in proposed § 2510.3-18(b)(3). The Department will consider that a fiduciary has determined adequate consideration in accordance with section 3(18)(B) of the Act or section 8477(a)(2)(B) of FERSA only if both of these requirements are satisfied.

The Department has proposed this two-part test for several reasons. First, Congress incorporated the concept of fair market value into the definition of adequate consideration. As explained more fully below, fair market value is an often used concept having an established meaning in the field of asset valuation. By reference to this term, it would appear that Congress did not intend to allow parties to a transaction to set an arbitrary value for the assets involved. Therefore, a valuation determination which fails to reflect the market forces embodied in the concept of fair market value would also fail to meet the requirements of section 3(18)(B) of the Act or section 8477(a)(2)(B) of FERSA.

Second, it would appear that Congress intended to allow a fiduciary a limited degree of latitude so long as that fiduciary acted in good faith. However, a fiduciary would clearly fail to fulfill the fiduciary duties delineated in Part 4 of Subtitle B of Title I of the Act if that fiduciary acted solely on the basis of naive or uninformed good intentions. See Donovan v. Cunningham, supra, 716 F.2d at 1467 ("[A] pure heart and an empty head are not enough.") The Department has therefore proposed standards for a determination of a fiduciary's good faith which must be satisfied in order to meet the requirements of section 3(18)(B) or section 8477(a)(2)(B) of FERSA.

Third, even if a fiduciary were to meet the good faith standards contained in this proposed regulation, there may be circumstances in which good faith alone fails to insure an equitable result. For example, errors in calculation or honest failure to consider certain information could produce valuation figures outside of the range of acceptable valuations of a given asset. Because the determination of adequate consideration is a central requirement of the statutory exemptions discussed above, the Department believes it must assure that such exemptions are made available only for those transactions possessing all the external safeguards envisioned by Congress. To achieve this end, the Department's proposed regulation links the fair market value and good faith requirements to assure that the resulting valuation reflects market considerations and is the product of a valuation process conducted in good faith.

2. Fair Market Value

The first part of the Department's proposed two part test under section 3(18)(B) and section 8477(a)(2)(B) requires that a determination of adequate consideration reflect the asset's fair market value. The term "fair market value" is defined in proposed § 2510.3-18(b)(2)(i) as the price at which an asset would change hands between a willing buyer and a willing seller when the former is not under any compulsion to buy and the latter is not under any compulsion to sell, and both parties are able, as well as willing, to trade and are well-informed about the asset and the market for that asset. This proposed definition essentially reflects the well-established meaning of this term in the area of asset valuation. See, for example, 26 C.F.R. 20.2031-1 (estate tax regulations); Rev. Rul. 59-60, 1959-1 Cum. Bull. 237; United States v. Cartwright, 411 U.S. 546, 551 (1973); Estate of Bright v. United States, 658 F.2d 999, 1005 (5th Cir. 1981). It should specifically be noted that comparable valuations reflecting transactions resulting from other than free and equal negotiations (e.g., a distress sale) will fail to establish fair market value. See Hooker Industries, Inc. v. Commissioner, 3 EBC 1849, 1854-55 (T.C. June 24, 1982). Similarly, the extent to which the Department will view a valuation as reflecting fair market value will be affected by an assessment of the level of expertise demonstrated by the parties making the valuation. See Donovan v. Cunningham, supra, 716 F.2d at 1468 (failure to apply sound business principles of evaluation, for whatever reason, may result in a valuation that does not reflect fair market value).[1]

---

1. Whether in any particular transaction a plan fiduciary is in fact well-informed about the asset in question and the market for that asset, including any specific circumstances which may affect the value of the asset, will be determined on a facts and circumstances basis. If, however, the fiduciary negotiating on behalf of the plan has or should have specific knowledge concerning either the particular asset or the market for that asset, it is the view of the Department that the fiduciary must take into account that specific knowledge in negotiating the price of the asset in order to meet the fair market value standard of this regulation. For example, a sale of plan-owned real estate at a negotiated price consistent with valuations of comparable property will not be a sale for adequate consideration if the negotiating fiduciary does not take into account any special knowledge which he has or should have about the asset or its market, e.g., that the property's value should reflect a premium due to a certain developer's specific land development plans.

The Department is aware that the fair market value of an asset will ordinarily be identified by a range of valuations rather than a specific, set figure. It is not the Department's intention that only one valuation figure will be acceptable as the fair market value of a specified asset. Rather, this proposal would require that the valuation assigned to an asset must reflect a figure within an acceptable range of valuations for that asset. In addition to this general formulation of the definition of fair market value, the Department is proposing two specific requirements for the determination of fair market value for the purposes of section 3(18)(B) and section 8477(a)(2)(B). First, proposed § 2510.3-18(b)(2)(ii) requires that fair market value must be determined as of the date of the transaction involving that asset. This requirement is designed to prevent situations such as arose in Donovan v. Cunningham, supra. In that case, the plan fiduciaries relied on a 1975 appraisal to set the value of employer securities purchased by an ESOP during 1976 and thereafter, and failed to take into account significant changes in the company's business condition in the interim. The court found that this reliance was unwarranted, and therefore the fiduciaries' valuation failed to reflect adequate consideration under section 3(18)(B). Id. at 1468-69.

Second, proposed § 2510.3-18(b)(2)(iii) states that the determination of fair market value must be reflected in written documentation of valuation[2] meeting the content requirements set forth in § 2510.3-18(b)(4). (The valuation content requirements are discussed below.) The Department has proposed this requirement in light of the role the adequate consideration requirement plays in a number of statutory exemptions from the prohibited transaction provisions of the Act. In determining whether a statutory exemption applies to a particular transaction, the burden of proof is upon the party seeking to make use of the statutory exemption to show that all the requirements of the provision are met. Donovan v. Cunningham, supra, 716 F.2d at 1467 n.27. In the Department's view, written documentation relating to the valuation is necessary for a determination of how, and on what basis, an asset was valued, and therefore whether that valuation reflected an asset's fair market value. In addition, the Department believes that it would be contrary to prudent business practices for a fiduciary to act in the absence of such written documentation of fair market value.

3. *Good Faith*

The second part of the Department's proposed two-part test under section 3(18)(B) and section 8477(a)(2)(B) requires that an assessment of adequate consideration be the product of a determination made in good faith by the plan trustee or named fiduciary

---

2. It should be noted that the written valuation required by this section of the proposal need not be a written report of an independent appraiser. Rather, it should be documentation sufficient to allow the Department to determine whether the content requirements of § 2510.3-18(b)(4) have been satisfied. The use of an independent appraiser may be relevant to a determination of good faith, as discussed with regard to proposed § 2510.3-18(b)(3), infra, but it is not required to satisfy the fair market value criterion in § 2510.3-18(b)(2)(i).

(or under FERSA, a fiduciary). Proposed § 2510.3-18(b)(3)(i) states that as a general matter this good faith requirement establishes an objective standard of conduct, rather than mandating an inquiry into the intent or state of mind of the plan trustee or named fiduciary. In this regard, the proposal is consistent with the opinion in Donovan v. Cunningham, supra, where the court stated that the good faith requirement in section 3(18)(B): is not a search for subjective good faith * * * The statutory reference to good faith in Section 3(18) must be read in light of the overriding duties of Section 404. 716 F.2d at 1467. The inquiry into good faith under the proposal therefore focuses on the fiduciary's conduct in determining fair market value. An examination of all relevant facts and circumstances is necessary for a determination of whether a fiduciary has met this objective good faith standard.

Proposed § 2510.3-18(b)(3)(ii) focuses on two factors which must be present in order for the Department to be satisfied that the fiduciary has acted in good faith. First, this section would require a fiduciary to apply sound business principles of evaluation and to conduct a prudent investigation of the circumstances prevailing at the time of the valuation. This requirement reflects the Cunningham court's emphasis on the use of prudent business practices in valuing plan assets.

Second, this section states that either the fiduciary making the valuation must itself be independent of all the parties to the transaction (other than the plan), or the fiduciary must rely on the report of an appraiser who is independent of all the parties to the transaction (other than the plan). (The criteria for determining independence are discussed below.) As noted above, under ERISA, the determination of adequate consideration is a central safeguard in many statutory exemptions applicable to plan transactions with the plan sponsor. The close relationship between the plan and the plan sponsor in such situations raises a significant potential for conflicts of interest as the fiduciary values assets which are the subject of transactions between the plan and the plan sponsor. In light of this possibility, the Department believes that good faith may only be demonstrated when the valuation is made by persons independent of the parties to the transaction (other than the plan), for example, a valuation made by an independent fiduciary or by a fiduciary acting pursuant to the report of an independent appraiser.

The Department emphasizes that the two requirements of proposed § 2510.3-18(b)(3)(ii) are designed to work in concert. For example, a plan fiduciary charged with valuation may be independent of all the parties to a transaction and may, in light of the requirement of proposed § 2510.3-18(b)(3)(ii)(B), decide to undertake the valuation process itself. However, if the independent fiduciary has neither the experience, facilities nor expertise to make the type of valuation under consideration, the decision by that fiduciary to make the valuation would fail to meet the prudent investigation and sound business principles requirement of proposed § 2510.3-18(b)(3)(ii)(A).

Proposed § 2510.3-18(b)(3)(iii) defines the circumstances under which a fiduciary or an appraiser will be deemed to be independent for the purposes of subparagraph (3)(ii)(B), above. The proposal notes that the fiduciary or the appraiser must in fact be independent of all parties participating in the transaction other than the plan. The proposal also notes that a determination of independence must be made in light of all relevant facts and circumstances, and then delineates certain circumstances under which this independence will be lacking. These circumstances reflect the definitions of the terms "affiliate" and "control" in Departmental regulation 29 C.F.R. 2510.3-21(e) (defining the circumstances under which an investment adviser is a fiduciary). It should be noted that, under these proposed provisions, an appraiser will be considered independent of all parties to a transaction (other than the plan) only if a plan fiduciary has chosen the appraiser and has the right to terminate that appointment, and the plan is thereby established as the appraiser's client.[3] Absent such circumstances, the appraiser may be unable to be completely neutral in the exercise of his function.[4]

4. Valuation Content—General

Proposed § 2510.3-18(b)(4)(i) sets the content requirements for the written documentation of valuation required for a determination of fair market value under proposed § 2510.3-18(b)(2)(iii). The proposal follows to a large extent the requirements of Rev. Proc. 66-49, 1966-2 C.B. 1257, which sets forth the format required by the IRS for the valuation of donated property. The Department believes that this format is a familiar one, and will therefore facilitate compliance. Several additions to the IRS requirements merit brief explanation.

First, proposed paragraph (b)(4)(i)(E) requires a statement of the purpose for which the valuation was made. A valuation undertaken, for example, for a yearly financial report may prove an inadequate basis for any sale of the asset in question. This requirement is intended to facilitate review of the valuation in the correct context.

Second, proposed paragraph (b)(4)(i)(F) requires a statement as to the relative weight accorded to relevant valuation methodologies. The Department's experience in this area indicates that there are a number of different methodologies used within the appraisal industry. By varying the treatment given and emphasis accorded relevant information, these methodologies directly affect the result of the appraiser's analysis.

---

3. The independence of an appraiser will not be affected solely because the plan sponsor pays the appraiser's fee.

4. With regard to this independence requirement the Department notes that new section 401(a)(28) of the Code (added by section 1175(a) of the Tax Reform Act of 1986) requires that, in the case of an employee stock ownership plan, employer securities which are not readily tradable on established securities markets must be valued by an independent appraiser. New section 401(a)(28)(C) states that the term "independent appraiser" means an appraiser meeting requirements similar to the requirements of regulations under section 170(a)(1) of the Code (relating to IRS verification of the value assigned for deduction purposes to assets donated to charitable organizations). The Department notes that the requirements of proposed regulation § 2510.3-18(b)(3)(iii) are not the same as the requirements of the regulations issued by the IRS under section 170(a)(1) of the Code. The IRS has not yet promulgated rules under Code section 401(a)(28).

It is the Department's understanding that appraisers will often use different methodologies to cross-check their results. A statement of the method or methods used would allow for a more accurate assessment of the validity of the valuation.

Finally, proposed subparagraph (b)(4)(i)(G) requires a statement of the valuation's effective date. This reflects the requirement in proposed § 2510.3-18(b)(ii) that fair market value must be determined as of the date of the transaction in question.

5. Valuation Content—Special Rule

Proposed § 2510.3-18(b)(4)(ii) establishes additional content requirements for written documentation of valuation when the asset being appraised is a security other than a security for which there is a generally recognized market. In other words, the requirements of the proposed special rule supplement, rather than supplant, the requirements of paragraph (b)(4)(i). The proposed special rule establishes a nonexclusive list of factors to be considered when the asset being valued is a security not covered by section 3(18)(A) of the Act or section 8477(a)(2)(A) of FERSA. Such securities pose special valuation problems because they are not traded or are so thinly traded that it is difficult to assess the effect on such securities of the market forces usually considered in determining fair market value. The Internal Revenue Service has had occasion to address the valuation problems posed by one type of such securities—securities issued by closely held corporations. Rev. Rul. 59-60, 1959-1 Cum. Bull. 237, lists a variety of factors to be considered when valuing securities of closely held corporations for tax purposes.[5] The Department's experience indicates that Rev. Rul. 59-60 is familiar to plan fiduciaries, plan sponsors and the corporate community in general. The Department has, therefore, modeled this proposed special rule after Rev. Rul. 59-60 with certain additions and changes discussed below. It should be emphasized, however, that this is a nonexclusive list of factors to be considered. Certain of the factors listed may not be relevant to every valuation inquiry, although the fiduciary will bear the burden of demonstrating such irrelevance. Similarly, reliance on this list will not relieve fiduciaries from the duty to consider all relevant facts and circumstances when valuing such securities. The purpose of the proposed list is to guide fiduciaries in the course of their inquiry.

Several of the factors listed in proposed § 2510.3-18(b)(4)(ii) merit special comment and explanation. Proposed subparagraph (G) states that the fair market value of securities other than those for which there is a generally recognized market may be established by reference to the market price of similar securities of corporations

---

5. Rev. Rul. 59-60 was modified by Rev. Rul. 65-193 (1965-2 C.B. 370) regarding the valuation of tangible and intangible corporate assets. The provisions of Rev. Rul. 59-60, as modified, were extended to the valuation of corporate securities for income and other tax purposes by Rev. Rul. 68-609 (1968-2 C.B. 327). In addition, Rev. Rul. 77-287 (1977-2 C.B. 319). amplified. Rev. Rul. 59-60 by indicating the ways in which the factors listed in Rev. Rul. 59-60 should be applied when valuing restricted securities.

engaged in the same or a similar line of business whose securities are actively traded in a free and open market, either on an exchange or over the counter. The Department intends that the degree of comparability must be assessed in order to approximate as closely as possible the market forces at work with regard to the corporation issuing the securities in question.

Proposed subparagraph (H) requires an assessment of the effect of the securities' marketability or lack thereof. Rev. Rul. 59-60 does not explicitly require such an assessment, but the Department believes that the marketability of these types of securities will directly affect their price. In this regard, the Department is aware that, especially in situations involving employee stock ownership plans (ESOPs),[6] the employer securities held by the ESOP will provide a "put" option whereby individual participants may upon retirement sell their shares back to the employer.[7] It has been argued that some kinds of "put" options may diminish the need to discount the value of the securities due to lack of marketability. The Department believes that the existence of the "put" option should be considered for valuation purposes only to the extent it is enforceable and the employer has and may reasonably be expected to continue to have, adequate resources to meet its obligations. Thus, the Department proposes to require that the plan fiduciary assess whether these "put" rights are actually enforceable, and whether the employer will be able to pay for the securities when and if the "put" is exercised.

Finally, proposed subparagraph (I) deals with the role of control premiums in valuing securities other than those for which there is a generally recognized market. The Department proposes that a plan purchasing control may pay a control premium, and a plan selling control should receive a control premium. Specifically, the Department proposes that a plan may pay such a premium only to the extent a third party would pay a control premium. In this regard, the Department's position is that the payment of a control premium is unwarranted unless the plan obtains both voting control and control in fact. The Department will therefore carefully scrutinize situations to ascertain whether the transaction involving payment of such a premium actually results in the passing of control to the plan. For example, it may be difficult to determine that a plan paying a control premium has received control in fact where it is reasonable to assume at the time of acquisition that distribution of shares to plan participants will cause the plan's control of the company to be dissipated within a short period of time

---

6. The definition of the term "adequate consideration" under ERISA is of particular importance to the establishment and maintenance of ESOPs because, pursuant to section 408(e) of the Act, an ESOP may acquire employer securities from a party in interest only under certain conditions, including that the plan pay no more than adequate consideration for the securities.

7. Regulation 29 C.F.R. 2550.408b-(j) requires such a put option in order for a loan from a party in interest to the ESOP to qualify for the statutory exemption in section 408(b)(3) of ERISA from the prohibited transactions provisions of ERISA.

subsequent to acquisition.[8] In the Department's view, however, a plan would not fail to receive control merely because individuals who were previously officers, directors or shareholders of the corporation continue as plan fiduciaries or corporate officials after the plan has acquired the securities. Nonetheless, the retention of management and the utilization of corporate officials as plan fiduciaries, when viewed in conjunction with other facts, may indicate that actual control has not passed to the plan within the meaning of paragraph (b)(4)(ii)(I) of the proposed regulation. Similarly, if the plan purchases employer securities in small increments pursuant to an understanding with the employer that the employer will eventually sell a controlling portion of shares to the plan, a control premium would be warranted only to the extent that the understanding with the employer was actually a binding agreement obligating the employer to pass control within a reasonable time. See Donovan v. Cunningham, supra, 716 F.2d at 1472-74 (mere intention to transfer control not sufficient).

6. Service Arrangements Subject to FERSA

Section 8477(c)(1)(C) of FERSA permits the exchange of services between the Thrift Savings Fund and a party in interest only in exchange for adequate consideration. In this context, the proposal defines the term "adequate consideration as "reasonable compensation", as that term is described in sections 408(b)(2) and 408(c)(2) of ERISA and the regulations promulgated thereunder. By so doing, the proposal would establish a consistent standard of exemptive relief for both ERISA and FERSA with regard to what otherwise would be prohibited service arrangements.

Regulatory Flexibility Act

The Department has determined that this regulation would not have a significant economic effect on small plans. In conducting the analysis required under the Regulatory Flexibility Act, it was estimated that approximately 6,250 small plans may be affected by the regulation. The total additional cost to these plans, over and above the costs already being incurred under established valuation practices, are estimated not to exceed $875,000 per year, or $140 per plan for small plans choosing to engage in otherwise prohibited transactions that are exempted under the statute conditioned on a finding of adequate consideration.

Executive Order 12291

The Department has determined that the proposed regulatory action would not constitute a "major rule" as that term is used in Executive Order 12291 because the action would not result in: an annual effect on the economy of $100 million; a major increase

---

8. However, the Department notes that the mere pass-through of voting rights to participants would not in itself affect a determination that a plan has received control in fact, notwithstanding the existence of participant voting rights, if the plan fiduciaries having control over plan assets ordinarily may resell the shares to a third party and command a control premium, without the need to secure the approval of the plan participants.

in costs of prices for consumers, individual industries, government agencies, or geographical regions; or significant adverse effects on competition, employment, investment, productivity, innovation, or on the ability of United States based enterprises to compete with foreign based enterprises in domestic or export markets.

Paperwork Reduction Act

This proposed regulation contains several paperwork requirements. The regulation has been forwarded for approval to the Office of Management and Budget under the provisions of the Paperwork Reduction Act of 1980 (Pub. L. 96-511). A control number has not yet been assigned.

Statutory Authority

This regulation is proposed under section 3(18) and 505 of the Act (29 USC 1003(18) and 1135); Secretary of Labor's Order No. 1-87; and sections 8477(a)(2)(B) and 8477(f) of FERSA.

For the reasons set out in the preamble, the Department proposes to amend Part 2510 of Chapter XXV of Title 29 of the Code of Federal Regulations as follows:

Draft Regulation

PART 2510—[AMENDED]

1. The authority for Part 2510 is revised to read as follows:

   Authority: Sec. 3(2), 111(c), 505, Pub. L. 93-406, 88 Stat. 852, 894, (29 USC 1002(2), 1031, 1135); Secretary of Labor's Order No. 27-74, 1-86, 1-87, and Labor Management Services Administration Order No. 2-6.

   Section 2510.3-18 is also issued under sec. 3(18) of the Act (29 USC 1003(18)) and Sections 8477(a)(2)(B) and (f) of FERSA (5 USC 8477)

   Section 2510.3-101 is also issued under sec. 102 of Reorganization Plan No. 4 of 1978 (43 FR 47713, October 17, 1978), effective December 31, 1978 (44 FR 1065, January 3, 1978); 3 C.F.R. 1978 Comp. 332, and sec. 11018(d) of Pub. L. 99-272, 100 Stat. 82.

   Section 2510.3-102 is also issued under sec. 102 of Reorganization Plan No. 4 of 1978 (43 FR 47713, October 17, 1978), effective December 31, 1978 (44 FR 1065, January 3, 1978), and 3 C.F.R. 1978 Comp. 332.

2. Section 2510.3-18 is added to read as follows:

   Section 2510.3-18: Adequate Consideration

   (a) [Reserved]

   (b)(1)(i) General.

   (A) Section 3(18)(B) of the Employee Retirement Income Security Act of 1974 (the Act) provides that, in the case of a plan asset other than a security for which there is a generally recognized market, the term "adequate consideration" when used in Part 4 of Subtitle B of Title I of the Act means the fair market value of the asset as determined in good faith by the trustee or named fiduciary pursuant to the terms of the plan and in accordance with regulations promulgated by the Secretary of Labor.

  (B) Section 8477(a)(2)(B) of the Federal Employees' Retirement System Act of 1986 (FERSA) provides that, in the case of an asset other than a security for which there is a generally recognized market, the term "adequate consideration" means the fair market value of the asset as determined in good faith by a fiduciary or fiduciaries in accordance with regulations prescribed by the Secretary of Labor.

  (ii) Scope. The requirements of section 3(18)(B) of the Act and section 8477 (a)(2)(B) of FERSA will not be met unless the value assigned to a plan asset both reflects the asset's fair market value as defined in paragraph (b)(2) of this section and results from a determination made by the plan trustee or named fiduciary (or, in the case of FERSA, a fiduciary) in good faith as described in paragraph (b)(3) of this section. Paragraph (b)(5) of this section contains a special rule for service contracts subject to FERSA.

(2) Fair Market Value

  (i) Except as otherwise specified in this section, the term "fair market value" as used in section 3(18)(B) of the Act and section 8477(a)(2)(B) of FERSA means the price at which an asset would change hands between a willing buyer and a willing seller when the former is not under any compulsion to buy and the latter is not under any compulsion to sell, and both parties are able, as well as willing, to trade and are well informed about the asset and the market for such asset.

  (ii) The fair market value of an asset for the purposes of section 3(18)(B) of the Act and section 8477(a)(2)(B) of FERSA must be determined as of the date of the transaction involving that asset.

  (iii) The fair market value of an asset for the purposes of section 3(18)(B) of the Act and section 8477(a)(2)(B) of FERSA must be reflected in written documentation of valuation meeting the requirements set forth in paragraph (b)(4), of this section.

(3) Good Faith

  (i) General Rule. The requirement in section 3(18)(B) of the Act and section 8477(a)(2)(B) of FERSA that the fiduciary must determine fair market value in good faith establishes an objective, rather than a subjective, standard of conduct. Subject to the conditions in paragraphs (b)(3)(ii) and (iii) of this section, an assessment of whether the fiduciary has acted in good faith will be made in light of all relevant facts and circumstances.

  (ii) In considering all relevant facts and circumstances, the Department will not view a fiduciary as having acted in good faith unless

(A) The fiduciary has arrived at a determination of fair market value by way of a prudent investigation of circumstances prevailing at the time of the valuation, and the application of sound business principles of evaluation; and

(B) The fiduciary making the valuation either,

(1) Is independent of all parties to the transaction (other than the plan)

(2) Relies on the report of an appraiser who is independent of all parties to the transaction (other than the plan).

(iii) In order to satisfy the independence requirement of paragraph (b)(3) (ii) (B), of this section, a person must in fact be independent of all parties (other than the plan) participating in the transaction. For the purposes of this section, an assessment of independence will be made in light of all relevant facts and circumstances. However, a person will not be considered to be independent of all parties to the transaction if that person:

(1) Is directly or indirectly, through one or more intermediaries, controlling, controlled by, or under common control with any of the parties to the transaction (other than the plan);

(2) Is an officer, director, partner, employee, employer or relative (as defined in section 3(15) of the Act, and including siblings) of any such parties (other than the plan);

(3) Is a corporation or partnership of which any such party (other than the plan) is an officer, director or partner.

For the purposes of this subparagraph, the term "control," in connection with a person other than an individual, means the power to exercise a controlling influence over the management or policies of that person.

(4) Valuation Content

(i) In order to comply with the requirement in paragraph (b)(2)(iii), of this section, that the determination of fair market value be reflected in written documentation of valuation, such written documentation must contain, at a minimum, the following information:

(A) A summary of the qualifications to evaluate assets of the type being valued of the person or persons making the valuation;

(B) A statement of the asset's value, a statement of the methods used in determining that value, and the reasons for the valuation in light of those methods;

(C) A full description of the asset being valued;

(D) The factors taken into account in making the valuation, including any restrictions, understandings, agreements or obligations limiting the use or disposition of the property;

(E) The purpose for which the valuation was made;

(F) The relevance or significance accorded to the valuation methodologies taken into account;

(G) The effective date of the valuation; and

(H) In cases where a valuation report has been prepared, the signature of the person making the valuation and the date the report was signed.

(ii) Special Rule. When the asset being valued is a security other than a security covered by section 3(18)(A) of the Act or section 8477(a)(2)(A) of FERSA, the written valuation required by paragraph (b)(2)(iii) of this section, must contain the information required in paragraph (b)(4)(i) of this section, and must include, in addition to an assessment of all other relevant factors, an assessment of the factors listed below:

(A) The nature of the business and the history of the enterprise from its inception;

(B) The economic outlook in general, and the condition and outlook of the specific industry in particular;

(C) The book value of the securities and the financial condition of the business;

(D) The earning capacity of the company;

(E) The dividend-paying capacity of the company;

(F) Whether or not the enterprise has goodwill or other intangible value;

(G) The market price of securities of corporations engaged in the same or a similar line of business, which are actively traded in a free and open market, either on an exchange or over-the-counter;

(H) The marketability, or lack thereof, of the securities. Where the plan is the purchaser of securities that are subject to "put" rights and such rights are taken into account in reducing the discount for lack of marketability, such assessment shall include consideration of the extent to which such rights are enforceable, as well as the company's ability to meet its obligations with respect to the "put" rights (taking into account the company's financial strength and liquidity);

(I) Whether or not the seller would be able to obtain a control premium from an unrelated third party with regard to the block of securities being valued, provided that in cases where a control premium is taken into account:

(1) Actual control (both in form and in substance) is passed to the purchaser with the sale, or will be passed to the purchaser within a reasonable time pursuant to a binding agreement in effect at the time of the sale, and

(2) It is reasonable to assume that the purchaser's control will not be dissipated within a short period of time subsequent to acquisition.

Service Arrangements Subject to FERSA. For purposes of determinations pursuant to section 8477(c)(1)(C) of FERSA (relating to the provision of services) the term "adequate consideration" under section 8477(a)(2)(B) of FERSA means "reasonable compensation" as defined in sections 408(b)(2) and 408(c)(2) of the Act and §§ 2550.408 b-2(d) and 2550.408c-2 of this chapter.

Effective Date. This section will be effective for transactions taking place after the date 30 days following publication of the final regulation in the Federal Register.

Signed in Washington, D.C., this 11th day of May 1988.

David M. Walker,
Assistant Secretary, Pension and Welfare
Benefits Administration
U.S. Department of Labor

Appendix B

IRS Training Class Regarding Examination of ESOPs

CPE for FY 2003

This appendix contains a series of articles published in April 2003 as the *Employee Plans Continuing Professional Education (CPE) Technical Instruction Program for Fiscal Year 2003*. These materials were designed specifically for training purposes only. Under no circumstances should the contents of these articles be used or cited as authority for setting or sustaining a technical position.

CHAPTER 8

Examining Employee Stock Ownership Plans (ESOPs), Including New Developments

By Steven James (Gulf Coast)
and Jerry Livingston (Special Review)
and Steve Linder (R&A), Reviewers

INTERNAL REVENUE SERVICE

TAX EXEMPT AND GOVERNMENT ENTITIES

Table of Contents

Objectives

ESOP Requirements—Definition of an ESOP
Definition of ESOP
Example

Prohibited Transaction Exemption
Introduction
4975(d)(13)
ERISA 408(e) and 408(b)(12)

Operational Aspects and Advantages of ESOPs
Introduction: ESOP Distinguished with Other Plans
ESOP Used as a Financing Tool
ESOPs Uses Exempt Loans and Suspense Accounts
ESOPs Can Invest in Employer Securities
Special Tax Rules for ESOPs
Example of an Exempt Loan
Examination Steps

Qualifying Employer Securities
Introduction
Definition of Qualifying Employer Security Under Section 4975(e)(8)
Qualifying Security Definition for an ESOP Is Different than for Plans
Special Definition of Controlled Group for ESOPs
Special Circumstances for a First-tier Subsidiary under Section 409(l)
Special Circumstances for a Second-tier Subsidiary
Example

Examination Steps
Examine ESOP Investment Accounts
For ESOPs with Closely Held Stock
For ESOPs with Preferred Stock
Special Rule under Section 409(l)(4)
Determine Whether the Stock Is Readily Tradable
Common Stock
Verify Types of Shares Held by ESOP

If Plan Fails to Satisfy ESOP Requirements

Participation, Coverage and Nondiscrimination
Introduction
ESOP May Not Be Aggregated with Another Plan
ESOP Cannot Satisfy 401(a)(4) with a Nondesign-based Safe Harbor
ESOP Cannot Be Aggregated unless a Special Rule Is Met
   Example: Plan with ESOP and Non-ESOP Components
   Example: ESOP Fails Coverage
Examination Steps

Permitted Disparity and Right to Demand Qualified Employer Securities
Permitted Disparity
Distributions: Right to Demand QES
Exceptions to Right to Demand Distribution

Distributions, Timing and Payment Requirements
Section 409(o)
When Section 409(o) Applies
Form of Distribution
If ESOPs Acquires More than One Class of Employer Securities
Assets Released from a Suspense Account
Examination Steps: Distributions

Put Option
Introduction
Publicly Traded Defined
If Employer Violates Federal Law by Honoring Put Option
When Put Option Is Exercisable
Other Requirements
Examination Steps: Put Options

Joint and Survivor Rules
Introduction Certain ESOP Benefits Not Subject to QJSA
Rationale for This Exception
When Exception Is Applicable
Examination Steps: QJSA

Floor Offset Arrangements

ESOP Cannot Be Used to Offset Benefits under a DB Plan

Examination Steps: Floor Offset

Valuation and Independent Appraiser

Valuation and Independent Appraiser

Valuation Must Be Made in Good Faith

Examination Steps: Valuation

Effect of Improper Valuation

Fiduciary Is Responsible for Proper Valuation

A PT Occurs if an ESOP Pays a Disqualified Person Too Much

If Stock Is Overvalued

   Example

   Example

Unless Exception Applies, PT Occurs for Transaction
between a Plan and a DP

Exception Adequate Consideration

Potential Exclusive Benefit Violation: RR 69-494

Examination Steps: Valuation

Determine Whether Fair Market Value Was Used

Review Valuation Report

Check Employer's Audit Report and Documentation

Determine Whether Stock Appraisal Reflects Certain Factors

Evaluate Stock Purchases for Exclusive Benefit Violation

If Stock Purchased at FMV, but Later Declines in Value

Ask for Engineering Assistance

Voting Rights

If Employer Has Registration Type Class of Securities

If Employer Does Not Have Registration Type Class Securities

Right to Direct Plan as to Voting Depends on Applicable State Law

Voting Rights and Unallocated Shares

If Plan Trustee Does Not Receive Voting Instructions

Examination Steps

Repaying an Exempt Loan from the Proceeds of the Sale of Unallocated Employer Securities

Introduction

Exempt Loan Must be Primarily for the Benefit of ESOP Participants

Whether the Primary Benefit Is Violated Depends on Facts and Circumstances

Analysis of Published Guidance—ESOP Did Not Fail as a Result of Using Proceeds to Repay Loan

Analysis of Published Guidance in which ESOP Did Fail Due to Proceeds Used to Repay Exempt Loan

Unallocated Employer Securities Used to Repay Loan—Possible 415(c) Violation

Rationale of Current Position Regarding 415 and Analysis if this Issue Is Discovered upon Examination

Example: Using Proceeds of Sale of Stock to Repay an Exempt Loan

Examination Steps

When Qualifying Securities Can Be Forfeited

Forfeiture Allocation

Example

Examination Steps

Right of First Refusal

Right of First Refusal

Examination Steps

Special ESOP Transactions: Section 1042 Transfers

Introduction

Definitions

Taxpayer's Basis in Qualified Replacement Property

Manner of Election

Statement of Election

Statement of Election Must Be Verified by Consent of Corporation

IRC Section 1042—Prohibited Allocation

Example: Prohibited Allocation

Excise Tax on Prohibited Allocations of IRC Section 1042 Employer Securities

OVERVIEW

Introduction

This lesson provides guidance pertaining to the examination of both leveraged and nonleveraged employee stock ownership plans. This chapter describes the qualification requirements under IRC sections 401(a) and 409, as well as the additional requirements for ESOPs under IRC section 4975(e)(7) and the applicable regulations, related to both leveraged and nonleveraged ESOPs. This chapter also covers other issues pertinent to ESOPs, such as the IRC section 404(k) deduction rules, IRC section 1042 transfers, the partial interest exclusion and special rules pertaining to Sub S ESOPs. Finally, this chapter discusses recent changes made by EGTRRA.

OBJECTIVES

At the end of this lesson, you will be able to:

1) Determine whether the ESOP is operated in a qualified manner.

2) Determine that the ESOP is properly invested in qualifying employer securities (QES), as defined by IRC section 409(l).

3) Determine that distribution requirements are properly satisfied (timeliness and form).

4) Determine that the applicable put options are properly applied.

5) Determine that the QES is properly valued.

6) Determine whether the employer's contributions, including dividends, are deductible.

7) Determine if the premature repayment of an exempt loan by selling the QES in the suspense account is appropriate.

8) Determine whether allocations in the ESOP are valid for a S Corp.

ESOP REQUIREMENTS—DEFINITION OF AN ESOP

Definition of ESOP

An Employee Stock Ownership Plan, by definition, is a qualified retirement plan consisting of either a stock bonus or a stock bonus/money purchase combination plan, which is designed to invest primarily in qualifying employer securities. See IRC section 4975(e)(7)(A). An ESOP must satisfy the requirements of IRC section 4975(e)(7) and Reg. § 54.4975-11, certain portions of Code section 409 and the plan as a whole must meet Code section 401(a). Further, any use of exempt loans with respect to an ESOP, generally referred to as a leveraged ESOP, must comply with the rules relating to exempt loans contained in Regulation § 54.4975-7.

To qualify as an ESOP, the plan must be formally designated as such within the plan document. See Reg. § 54.4975-11(a)(2). Normally, the entire plan is formally designated as an ESOP. However, it is permissible for a plan to provide that only a portion of a qualified plan is an ESOP. As such, an ESOP may form a portion of a plan, the balance of which includes a qualified pension, profit sharing, or stock bonus plan, which is not an ESOP. See Reg. § 54.4975-11(a)(5). Plan terms should clearly state if an ESOP only pertains to a portion of the plan, and clearly identify that portion of the plan that is intended to comprise the ESOP. This portion of the plan is subject to all ESOP requirements, both in form and operation.

If a plan fails to qualify as an ESOP under IRC section 4975(e)(7), it may still be a qualified plan (such as a stock bonus plan) under IRC section 401(a).

See Reg. § 54.4975-7(b)(1)(i).

Example The following is an example where only a portion of the plan constitutes an ESOP. The preamble to this plan provides that the plan is intended to be a stock bonus ESOP with a 401(k) feature. Plan terms provide that the matching and discretionary contributions constitute the ESOP portion of the plan, whereas the 401(k) contributions constitute the non-ESOP portion of the plan. Plan terms clearly provide for separate ESOP accounts for the matching and discretionary contributions and a separate 401(k) account (to hold non-ESOP elective contributions and earnings and losses thereon).

In this instance the ESOP accounts are, per plan terms, designed to invest primarily in QES, while the 401(k) accounts are not subject to such investment requirements. The plan provides that participants have the right to elect the form of investment with respect to their own elective contributions contained in their 401(k) accounts (in various designated investment vehicles). Finally, the ESOP requirements (and special rules), including the right to demand distribution in QES, apply only to the ESOP portion of the plan, not to the 401(k) accounts.

PROHIBITED TRANSACTION EXEMPTION

Introduction

The use of loans to acquire qualifying employer securities would be a prohibited transaction if the plan were not an ESOP. This is because the general rule provides that the direct or indirect lending of money or other extension of credit between a plan and a disqualified person, such as the employer, is a prohibited transaction under IRC section 4975(c)(1)(B). In addition, the general prohibition would result in an improper extension of credit to the plan as a result of the employer's guarantee to the lender that a plan would repay the loan. See Reg. § 54.4975-7(b)(1)(ii). There is a statutory exemption to the prohibited transactions for loans to a leveraged ESOP. See IRC sections 4975(d)(3) and 4975(e)(7). The loan to the ESOP is not a prohibited transaction if the loan is:

1) Primarily for the benefit of plan participants, and

2) At a reasonable interest rate, with any collateral which is given to a disqualified person by the plan consisting only of qualifying employer securities.

4975(d)(13)

IRC section 4975(d)(13) provides a statutory exemption from the prohibited transactions with respect to any transaction which is exempt from section 406 of such Act by reason of section 408(e) of such Act (or which would be so exempt if such section 406 applied to such transaction) or which is exempt from section 406 of such Act by reason of section 408(b)(12).

ERISA 408(e) and 408(b)(12)

ERISA Act section 408(e) provides for a statutory exemption relating to the acquisition or sale by the plan of qualifying employer securities provided that such acquisition or sale by the plan:

1) Is for adequate consideration, at a price not less favorable to the plan than the price determined under ERISA Act section 407(e)(1),

2) No commission is charged with respect thereto, and

3) The plan is an eligible account plan.

ERISA Act section 408(b)(12) is a rule allowing for the disposition of certain stock that at the time of acquisition constituted qualifying employer securities under Title I, but due to a change in definition are no longer qualifying employer securities.

OPERATIONAL ASPECTS AND ADVANTAGES OF ESOPs

Introduction: ESOP Distinguished with Other Plans

Like other qualified plans, ESOPs enjoy the normal tax advantages available to qualified plans. However, ESOPs also enjoy other tax advantages peculiar to ESOPs, such as increased deduction limits, deduction of IRC section 404(k) dividends, expanded IRC section 415 annual additions, and other special tax advantages.

For the plan sponsor, ESOPs provide a method of corporate financing not available to other qualified plans through the use of exempt loans. For participants, ESOPs provide a retirement vehicle that confers an increased level of corporate ownership through investment of qualified employer securities by the plan.

ESOP Used as a Financing Tool

Leveraged ESOPs provide the employer with a vehicle as a financing tool, through the borrowing of money involving the ESOP. This leveraged transaction involves the acquisition of qualifying employer securities (QES) from the employer or other shareholders, using debt-financing to acquire the employer securities.

ESOPs Uses Exempt Loans and Suspense Accounts

This use of exempt loans and the suspense account is another advantage of ESOPs. It permits a larger amount of stock to be acquired initially by the ESOP from the employer or disqualified person than the amount that could be acquired by other types of plans (due to contribution and 415 restrictions). Stock acquired by an ESOP though the use of an exempt loan is initially not allocated, but placed in a suspense account.

This permits the employer to spread out deductible contributions over a period of years as contributions are made to service the debt, with a delayed allocation through release of the stock from such suspense account in subsequent years as payments are made on the exempt loan. This is one of few permitted uses of suspense accounts permitted in defined contribution plans.

ESOPs Can Invest in Employer Securities

Generally, qualified plans are not permitted to acquire or hold employer securities or employer real property with a fair market value in excess of 10% of plan assets. See ERISA Act sections 406(a)(1)(E), 406(a)(2) and 407(a)(2). Eligible individual account plans are specifically exempted from the 10% limitation and the investment diversification rules. See ERISA Act sections 407(b)(1), 404(a)(1)(C), and 404(a)(2). Because Esops are eligible individual account plans under ERISA Act section 407(d)(3), ESOPs can invest in employer securities without regard to the 10% limitation. An ESOP must provide, by its terms, that the ESOP is designed to invest primarily in qualifying employer securities.

Special Tax Rules for ESOPs

In addition, special tax rules, such as qualifying IRC section 1042 transfers, permit nonrecognition of gain by the seller of qualifying employer securities sold to the ESOP, while at the same time transferring substantial ownership interests in stock of the company to the plan.

Example of an Exempt Loan

Assume an employer has need for $10,000,000 in corporate financing. The ESOP can be used to acquire such funds through the use of an exempt loan. The ESOP secures a loan for such amount from an outside lender, such as a bank. The ESOP signs a promissory note for the amount of the loan, with such loan then guaranteed by a third party (generally the employer). (In a back-to-back loan, the employer receives the loan and then loans the proceeds to the ESOP to acquire employer securities for the ESOP).

The ESOP would then purchase $10,000,000 in qualifying employer securities from employer (or from another shareholder). The result is that the employer (or shareholder) receives $10,000,000 in cash, and the ESOP receives the equivalent value in qualifying employer securities, with an equal amount of debt owed to the outside lender (i.e., bank). The loan can be and is generally secured by a pledge of the stock acquired by the ESOP. The stock is then held unallocated in a suspense account, until contributions are made to release the shares.

Under the prohibited transaction exemption involving the use of exempt loans, the employer is now obligated to make sufficient contributions to the ESOP in order for the ESOP to make timely payment to the bank on the debt. See GCM 39747, March 14, 1986, S. Rep. No. 94-36, 94th Cong., lst Sess., 58-59 (1975). Each year, the employer makes a tax-deductible payment to the ESOP sufficient to enable the ESOP to make its annual debt payments to the bank. The ESOP is also permitted to repay the acquisition indebtedness from earnings on contributions received, as well as dividends received on the stock. However, pre-existing plan assets should not be used to service the debt. Since the employer's contributions to the ESOP are deductible within the IRC section 404(a)(9) limits, a leveraged ESOP allows the company to repay the entire loan on a tax-favored basis.

The stock is initially held unallocated by the ESOP in the suspense account (encumbered stock). As payments are made on the debt, a proportional amount of stock is released from the suspense account pursuant to one of two specific release formulas (provided for in the plan) and the released stock is then allocated to participants in a nondiscriminatory manner.

Examination Steps

The basic preexamination planning instructions are contained in IRM section 4.71.1. As part of the preexamination planning:

1) Analyze the return to determine if the plan is designated as an ESOP. Often, the plan name includes a specific reference to the plan as an ESOP.

2) Review the Form 5500 Pension Benefit Codes. These codes include separate designations for leveraged ESOPs, nonleveraged ESOPs and Sub S ESOPs.

3) Review the Form 5500, Schedule H (Financial Information) and/or Schedule I (Financial Information — Small Plan) for identified investment in employer securities. Also, review the answers on these forms to any questions relating to investment in excess of certain percentages in any one type of investment.

4) Review the Form 5500, Schedule H (Financial Information) for liabilities that could reveal the existence of an exempt loan, in conjunction with the investment in employer securities. The amount of the exempt loan liability would normally be entered under Liabilities as Acquisition Indebtedness or as Other Liabilities.

5) Review Schedule I (Financial Information — Small Plan) for disclosure of a substantial amount for liabilities in relation to plan assets.

6) Review the prior favorable determination letter for any reference to a ruling on the ESOP (i.e., an IRC section 4975(e)(7) or IRC section 409 caveat).

7) If the prior determination file or application can be secured, review the application to determine if a Form 5309 (Application for Determination of Employee Stock Ownership Plan), an attached schedule to the Form 5300 application, was filed. This Form 5309 is used to request a determination with respect to either a tax credit ESOP under IRC section 409 and/or a leveraged or nonleveraged ESOP under IRC section 4975(e)(7). This Form 5309 should result in the applicable IRC section 409 or IRC section 4975(e)(7) caveat on the favorable determination letter.

QUALIFYING EMPLOYER SECURITIES

Introduction

An ESOP must invest primarily in qualifying employer securities. See IRC section 4975(e)(7). There is no specific percentage that defines the term "primarily," however, the term generally would require at least 50% of the ESOP assets to be invested in qualifying employer securities. In actuality, it is a flexible term that takes into account facts and circumstances such as the investment performance of the qualifying employer securities.

An ESOP can sell qualifying employer securities or refrain from purchasing additional securities based on the investment performance of the securities. This would be consistent with the fiduciary duties under Title I of ERISA. The Department of Labor (DOL) stated in Advisory Opinion 83-6A (1/24/83) that there may be instances where the investment of more than 50% of plan assets in qualifying employer securities would not satisfy the fiduciary responsibility requirements of Title I. The DOL Advisory Opinion concluded that the "primarily" requirement must be satisfied over the life of the ESOP.

Definition of Qualifying Employer Security Under Section 4975(e)(8)

IRC section 4975(e)(8) defines a "qualifying employer security" as an employer security within the meaning of IRC section 409(l). IRC section 409(l) provides that qualifying employer securities consist of the following:

1) Common stock issued by the employer, or by a corporation within the same controlled group, which is readily tradable on an established securities market.

2) If there is no readily tradable common stock, closely held common stock of the employer (or by a corporation which is a member of the same controlled group) which has a combination of voting power and dividend rights equal to or in excess of the class of common stock of the employer (or of any other such corporation) having the greatest voting rights and the greatest dividend rights.

3) Noncallable preferred stock if the stock is convertible at any time into stock which meets the requirements of a) or b) above (whichever is applicable), and if the conversion price is reasonable as of the date the ESOP acquired the preferred stock.

Qualifying Security Definition for an ESOP Is Different than for Plans

Note that the statutory definition of qualifying employer securities with respect to an ESOP is more stringent than the definition of qualifying employer securities used for non-ESOP plans. Refer to ERISA Act section 407(d)(5). For example, the definition of qualifying employer securities for non-ESOPs under ERISA Act section 407(d)(5) would include any stock, including nonvoting stock, and other marketable obligations.

Special Definition of Controlled Group for ESOPs

For purposes of IRC section 409(l), a "controlled group of corporations" is defined at IRC section 1563(a), but without regard to the insurance company rule at IRC section 1563(a)(4) and without regard to the exception to the attribution from trusts rule at IRC section 1563(e)(3)(C).

This special rule applies to the determination of the definition of qualified employer securities under Code section 409(l). This special rule does not extend the definition of the determination of the controlled group for qualification purposes, such as coverage and nondiscrimination testing.

Special Circumstances for a First-tier Subsidiary under Section 409(l)

IRC section 409(l)(4) provides special circumstances in which a first tier subsidiary may be considered to be includable in a controlled group of corporations for purposes of IRC section 409(l), even where the parent owns less than 80% of the first tier subsidiary. The effect of this provision is to permit the acquisition of the controlling corporation's stock by an ESOP maintained by the first tier subsidiary (or vice versa). If a corporation owns directly stock possessing 50% of the voting power in all classes of stock and at least 50% of each class of nonvoting stock in the first tier subsidiary, then the first tier subsidiary (and all other corporations below it in the chain which would meet the 80% test of IRC 1563(a) if the first tier subsidiary were the parent) is considered to be an "includable corporation" for IRC section 409(l) purposes.

Special Circumstances for a Second-Tier Subsidiary

IRC section 409(l)(4) provides special circumstances in which a second-tier subsidiary may be considered to be includable in a controlled group of corporations for purposes of IRC section 409. The effect of this provision is to permit the acquisition of the controlling corporation's stock by an ESOP maintained by the second-tier subsidiary (or vice versa).

If a corporation owns directly stock possessing all of the voting power in all classes of stock and all of the nonvoting stock of a first-tier subsidiary, and if the first-tier subsidiary owns stock possessing at least 50% of the voting power of all classes of stock and at least 50% of each class of nonvoting stock of the second-tier subsidiary (and all other corporations below it in the chain which would meet the 80% test of IRC section 1563(a) if the second-tier subsidiary were the common parent) is considered to be an "includable corporation" for purposes of IRC section 409(l).

Example An ESOP under examination was reviewed with respect to its investment in QES. The preamble to the plan designated the entire plan as the ESOP and provided that the plan was designed to invest primarily in QES. The trust document provided that the plan trustee was responsible for the investment of trust funds. The plan had been in existence for ten years, and the trust assets were currently invested in 8 distinct investment funds, one of which was a fund investing in QES. The breakdown of the investments revealed that the largest single investment was 20% (of total assets) invested in the QES fund, with the remaining seven funds invested between 10% to 15% (of total assets) each.

Upon further investigation, the agent determined that the ESOP had been invested in QES over the ten year life of the ESOP for each year since inception at around the 20% level and that the employer and fiduciary could not provide an adequate explanation as to the failure to invest a larger percentage of plan assets in QES.

In this instant case, consideration should be given to addressing the failure of the ESOP to comply with IRC section 4975(e)(7) as the plan has operationally failed to meet the requirement that the ESOP is designed to invest primarily in QES.

EXAMINATION STEPS

Examine ESOP Investment Accounts

Examine the ESOP's investment accounts to verify it is investing primarily in qualifying employer securities, as defined in IRC section 409(l).

For ESOPs with Closely Held Stock

If the ESOP holds closely held common stock of the employer, check that neither the employer (nor any member of the controlled group) has readily tradable common stock. This information may have to be requested from the employer. If there is readily tradable common stock, then the ESOP cannot hold the closely held stock.

For ESOPs with Preferred Stock

If the ESOP holds preferred stock, determine whether the conversion price is reasonable. Look at the conversion formula in the corporate charter documents. Also look at the answer to the question concerning the conversion formula on Schedule E, ESOP Annual Information. If the conversion formula does not allow participants to share in any appreciation in the value of the common stock, the conversion price is not reasonable.

Note: A conversion price that is based on the common stock's fair market value as of the date the ESOP acquired the preferred stock is reasonable because it permits participants to share in all of the appreciation in the value of the common stock. A formula that includes a conversion premium is permitted if the conversion premium is reasonable.

The reasonableness of a conversion premium is determined on its facts and circumstances. Generally, a reasonable conversion premium will be in the 20% to 30% range.

Special Rule under Section 409(l)(4)

The special rule under IRC section 409(l)(4) which expands the definition of a controlled group of corporations, as applied to the determination of qualifying employer securities, applies to controlled corporations, but does not apply to partnerships or sole proprietorship. See PLR 9236042 and GCM 39880.

Determine Whether the Stock Is Readily Tradable

Determination of whether the stock is "readily tradable on an established securities market" should have the same meaning as the term "publicly traded" as defined in Regulation § 54.4975-7(b)(1)(iv). This regulation provides that a security listed on a national securities exchange registered under section 6 of the Securities Exchange Act of 1934 or quoted on a system sponsored by a national securities association registered under section 15A(b) of the Securities Exchange Act is "publicly traded." Refer to PLR 9529043 for an example of this interpretation.

Common Stock

Common Stock quoted on the NASDAQ SmallCap Market, a separate market on the NASDAQ system, is classified as an established security system, making common stock traded on it as IRC section 409(l) stock. Refer to PLR 9529043.

Verify Types of Shares Held by ESOP

It is permissible for an ESOP to hold and acquire qualifying employer securities (as more liberally defined under Title I of ERISA per Act sections 407(a)(1) and 407(d)

(5)). For example, in addition to investing primarily in IRC section 409(l) qualifying employer securities, the plan could also invest in stock as defined under ERISA Act section 407(d)(5), such as in nonvoting class B stock.

However, notwithstanding other plan investments, the examiner should verify, for example, that the ESOP was investing primarily in IRC section 409(l) shares, that participants were given the right to demand distribution entirely in IRC section 409(l) stock, and that all stock acquired with exempt loan proceeds was IRC section 409(l) stock.

If Plan Fails to Satisfy ESOP Requirements

If a plan fails to qualify as an ESOP under IRC section 4975(e)(7), it may still be a qualified plan (such as a stock bonus plan) under Code section 401(a). However, consideration should be given to any plan operation that is limited to ESOPs, such as use of exempt loans, 404(k) dividend deductions, and expanded IRC section 415 rules, among others. If any of these apply, then failure to comply with IRC section 409(l) could result in prohibited transactions, deduction and/or qualification issues, depending on the specific statutory violations.

PARTICIPATION, COVERAGE AND NONDISCRIMINATION

Introduction

The participation (IRC section 401(a)(26) for years beginning before January 1, 1997), coverage (IRC section 410(b)), and nondiscrimination (IRC section 401(a)(4)) requirements are applicable to an ESOP. These requirements must be satisfied separately by an ESOP.

An ESOP may not be considered together with another plan in order to meet the participation, coverage or nondiscrimination requirements. See Regs. §§ 54.4975-11 (e)(1), 1.401(a)(26)-2(d)(1)(i), 1.410(b)-7(c)(2) and 1.401(a)(4)-1(c)(4).

IRC section 401(a)(26) is inapplicable to defined contribution plans for years beginning after December 31, 1996.

ESOP May Not Be Aggregated with Another Plan

An ESOP cannot be aggregated with another plan. For example, the use of matching employer contributions to an ESOP to satisfy the nondiscrimination requirements relating to qualified cash or deferred arrangements (CODAs) (including a cash or deferred arrangement which forms a portion of the ESOP) is not permitted. See Reg. § 1.401(k)-1(g)(11), Reg. § 1.401(k)-1(g)(1)(ii)(B), IRC 401(k)(3) and the Technical Guidance on CODAs in IRM 4.72.2.6.

ESOP Cannot Satisfy 401(a)(4) with a Nondesign-based Safe Harbor

An ESOP cannot satisfy the IRC 401(a)(4) nondiscrimination requirements through the use of a nondesign-based safe harbor formula under Reg. § 1.401(a)(4)-2(b)(3), nor through the use of a cross-testing formula under Reg. § 1.401(a)(4)-8(b).

ESOP Cannot Be Aggregated unless a Special Rule Is Met

In addition, an ESOP cannot be aggregated with another ESOP to satisfy coverage or nondiscrimination requirements unless the special rule of Reg. § 54.4975-11(e)(2) is met.

This special rule provides that two or more Esops can be aggregated for purposes of IRC sections 410(b) or 401(a)(4) and (5), only if the proportion of qualifying employer securities (QES) to total plan assets is substantially the same for each ESOP and (i) the QES held by all Esops are of the same class or (ii) the ratios of each class held to all such securities is substantially the same for each plan.

Refer also to Beals Bros. Management Corp v. Comm., U.S. Court of Appeals, 8th Circuit, 300 F.3d 963, 2002 U.S. App., which held that the aggregation of two Esops (of related employers in a controlled group) was improper and that the ESOP for management employees failed to satisfy the coverage requirements of IRC section 410(b). The ESOP maintained for the nonmanagement employees received almost no contributions, whereas the ESOP set up for the management employees received more significant contributions.

Example: Plan with ESOP and Non-ESOP Components   A plan provides for both ESOP and non-ESOP components within the plan, along with separate accounting. The plan provides for discretionary contributions only, but provides that the employer will designate such contributions when made as either ESOP or non-ESOP contributions. The plan allocation formula for the non-ESOP contributions provides for a safe harbor formula utilizing permitted disparity under IRC section 401(I). The plan allocation formula for the ESOP contributions provides for a safe harbor formula (compensation to total compensation), that does not utilize permitted disparity.

A review of the determination application and exhibits reflect a Demo 4, which reflects satisfaction of coverage for each separately disaggregated plan per Reg. § 1.410(b)-7(c)(2) and satisfaction of the nondiscrimination in amount requirements by each disaggregated ESOP and non-ESOP plan components per 1.401(a)(4)-1(b)(2).

Besides testing each allocation formula separately, the examiner should verify that the designated ESOP contributions are allocated pursuant to the safe harbor formula without permitted disparity. If eligibility requirements are different for the ESOP and non-ESOP components of the plan, the workpapers should reflect separate analyses for each component with respect to IRC section 410(b).

Example: ESOP Fails Coverage   An agent is assigned an ESOP for examination. During the course of the examination, the agent determines that the plan benefits only highly compensated employees and does not benefit certain statutorily eligible nonhighly compensated employees.

As such, this ESOP appears to fail to satisfy the coverage requirement of IRC section 410(b). Subsequent discussions with the taxpayer's representative reveal that the employer also maintains a profit sharing plan that provides comparable benefits to all nonhighly compensated employees. The representative submits documentation that supports that the contributions for the year under examination are nondiscriminatory when these plans are aggregated. The agent properly concludes that the ESOP is not qualified. The reason is that an ESOP cannot be aggregated with other plans in order to satisfy IRC section 410(b).

Examination Steps

1) Check that the ESOP satisfies the participation, coverage and nondiscrimination requirements without being aggregated with any other plan. This disaggregation also applies to any non-ESOP portion of the plan of which it is a part.

2) In the case of an ESOP that is part of a CODA, check the terms of the ESOP to ensure that if the employer matches the employees' elective deferrals under the CODA by making contributions to the ESOP, the matching contributions to the ESOP are not taken into account for purposes of meeting the nondiscrimination rules of IRC 401(k). Also, check the CODA's terms. Ensure also that the ESOP matching contributions satisfy IRC section 401(m). See the Technical Guidance on Matching Contributions in IRM 4.72.3.

3) In the case of an ESOP that contains provisions for CODAs and matching contributions, ensure that the ADP and ACP tests are run separately with respect to the ESOP and non-ESOP plans or portions of the plan.

PERMITTED DISPARITY AND RIGHT TO DEMAND QUALIFIED EMPLOYER SECURITIES

Permitted Disparity

An ESOP established after 11/1/77, cannot be integrated with Social Security benefits. ESOPs established and integrated before such date may remain integrated. However, such plans must not be amended to increase the integration level or the integration percentage. See Reg. § 54.4975-11(a)(7)(ii). Such plans may in operation continue to increase the level of integration if under the plan such increase is limited by reference to a criterion existing apart from the plan. Similarly, the permitted disparity rules of IRC section 401(l) do not apply to ESOPs, except for ESOPs which were in existence on 11/1/77, which were integrated. See Reg. § 1.401(l)-1(a)(4).

Distributions: Right to Demand QES

Distributions from an ESOP may be made entirely in qualifying employer securities or may be made in cash, or a combination of cash and stock. However, any distribution from an ESOP is subject to the participant's right to demand that their entire distribution be in the form of qualifying employer securities. See IRC section 409(h).

An employee also has the right to require the employer to repurchase certain employer securities that the employee receives in a distribution (i.e., put option).

Exceptions to Right to Demand Distribution

Exceptions to the right to demand distribution in the form of qualifying employer securities include:

1) If the employer's corporate charter (or bylaws) restricts the ownership of substantially all outstanding employer securities to employees or to a trust under a qualified plan, the participant may be precluded from demanding a distribution in the form of employer securities. See IRC section 409(h)(2)(B).

2) TRA '97 provides that an ESOP maintained by an S corporation can preclude the distribution of employer securities to a participant. See IRC section 409(h)(2)(B).

3) Employer stock that was subject to the right of diversification and that the participant had previously elected to diversify per IRC section 401(a)(28)(B) is not subject to the right to demand distribution in the form of qualifying employer securities. See IRC section 409(h)(7) and Notice 88-56, Q&A 11.

If stock distributed to the participant is not readily tradable on established security market, then a put option is required subsequent to distribution.

DISTRIBUTIONS, TIMING, AND PAYMENT REQUIREMENTS

Section 409(o)

IRC section 409(o) provides that an ESOP participant who is entitled to receive a distribution can elect to commence distributions sooner than the periods described under IRC sections 401(a)(14) and IRC 401(a)(9). A participant can elect (if applicable, with the consent of his/her spouse per IRC section 401(a)(11) and IRC 417), to commence the distribution of his/her account balance not later than one year after the close of the plan year (1) which the participant separates from service by reason of normal retirement age, disability, or death, or (2) which is the 5th plan year following the plan year in which the participant otherwise separates from service, as long as the participant is not reemployed by the employer before this distribution is required to begin.

When Section 409(o) Applies

IRC section 409(o) applies only to stock acquired after December 31, 1986. However, the election with respect to this right to elect an accelerated distribution does not apply to any employer securities acquired with the proceeds of an ESOP loan until the close of the plan year in which the loan is repaid in full.

Form of Distribution

Unless the participant elects otherwise, the account balance must be distributed in substantially equal periodic payments (at least annually) over a period not to exceed

5 years. If the participant's account balance exceeds $500,000 (adjusted for cost-of-living increases), the distribution period is increased to 5 years plus one additional year (up to 5 additional years) for each $100,000 (adjusted for cost-of-living increases), or fraction thereof, by which the balance exceeds $500,000 (as adjusted). See Notice 2001-84, I.R.B. 2001-53.

If ESOPs Acquires More than One Class of Employer Securities

If an ESOP acquires more than one class of employer securities available for distribution with the proceeds of the loan, the distributee must receive substantially the same proportion of each class. Thus, a distributee may not receive only preferred stock if the loan proceeds were also used to acquire voting common stock. See Reg. § 54.4975-11(f)(2).

1) The above distribution is based on shares allocated to a participant's account and such allocation is proportionate (as to separate classes of stock) with respect to shares acquired with each loan.

2) This rule does not apply when separate loans at separate times are used to buy different classes of stock.

Assets Released from a Suspense Account

Assets:

- Released from the ESOP suspense account (related to leveraged ESOPs with exempt loans), and

- Allocated to a participant's account can be forfeited only after other assets have been forfeited. See Reg. § 54.4975-11(d)(4).

Examination Steps: Distributions

1) Make sure the plan gives employees the right to receive their distribution in the form of qualifying employer securities, unless the corporate charter or by-laws restricts stock ownership to employees or to a qualified plan, or unless the ESOP is maintained by an S corporation that precludes the distribution of employer securities to participants.

2) Check the plan to make sure that participants can elect an accelerated distribution under IRC 409(o).

3) Look at the assets allocated to a participant from the suspense account. If securities available for distribution consist of more than one class, check that the participant received substantially the same proportion of each class as reflected in the suspense account assets available for distribution.

4) Check that the released suspense account assets allocated to a participant's account were forfeited after other assets were forfeited. If more than one class

of qualifying employer securities has been allocated to a participant's account, make sure the participant forfeits the same proportion of each class.

5) If an ESOP provides for both a Stock Account and an Other Investments Account, ensure that the right to demand qualifying employer securities applies to the entire ESOP plan (all accounts constituting the ESOP), not just the Stock Account, with the exception of stock diversified as required by IRC section 409(h)(7) diversification. See Notice 88-56, Q&A-11. Note that if a plan permits more liberal diversification rights that those required under IRC section 401(a)(28)(B), the right to demand distribution in the form of QES applies to all amounts in excess of the minimum amount required to be diversified under IRC section 401 (a)(28)(B).

6) Any delayed distribution attempting to utilize the IRC section 409(o)(1)(B) exception for timing of distributions (i.e., delay distribution until the exempt loan is paid off) does not override the requirement to distribute per IRC sections 401(a)(9) or 401(a)(14). If this rule is utilized, scrutinize terminated participants with deferred distributions to verify compliance with IRC sections 401(a)(9) and (14).

PUT OPTION

Introduction

IRC section 409(h) and Reg. § 54.4975-7(b)(10) require an employer security to be subject to a put option if it is not readily tradable on an established market when distributed or if it is subject to a trading limitation when distributed. See also IRC section 401(a)(23).

The put option is a post-distribution right that permits the participant or beneficiary to require the employer to repurchase such distributed stock where there is no ready market in which to sell such stock.

Publicly Traded Defined

Employer securities are "readily tradable on an established securities market" if they are "publicly traded" as defined under Reg. § 54.4975-7(b)(1)(iv). Refer also to PLR 9529043. "Publicly traded" includes securities that are:

1) Listed on a national securities exchange registered under section 6 of the Securities Exchange Act of 1934, or

2) Quoted on a system sponsored by a national securities association registered under section 15A(b) of the Securities Exchange Act. The National Association of Securities Dealers (NASD) is a national securities association registered under section 15A(b). It runs the National Association of Securities Dealers Automatic Quotation System (NASDAQ). Therefore, over-the-counter stocks traded on NASDAQ are publicly traded. Note: Stocks listed on the "pink sheets" are not

publicly traded because the "pink sheets" are not a system sponsored by the NASD. See PLR 9036039.

If Employer Violates Federal Law by Honoring Put Option

The put option must permit a participant to "put" stock that is not a readily tradable security or is subject to a trading limitation to the employer. However, if the employer will violate Federal or state law by honoring such put option, the put option must permit the security to be put, in a manner consistent with such law, to a third party (other than the ESOP) that has substantial net worth at the time the loan is made and whose net worth is reasonably expected to remain substantial. An ESOP cannot be required to honor a put option, but it can have the right to assume the obligations of the put option.

When Put Option Is Exercisable

The put option must be exercisable for at least 60 days following the date of the distribution and for at least an additional 60-day period in the following plan year. See IRC section 409(h)(4).

If the participant receives a total distribution which is required to be repurchased by the employer, the employer must make payments at least as rapid as substantially equal periodic payments (at least annually) over a period beginning not later than 30 days after exercise of the put option and not exceeding 5 years. In addition, the employer must provide adequate security and pay reasonable interest on the unpaid amounts of the total distribution. See IRC section 409(h)(5).

Other Requirements

If the participant receives ESOP distributions in the form of installments that are required to be repurchased by the employer, the employer must make full payment for the securities no later than 30 days after the put option is exercised. See IRC section 409(h)(6).

In the case of an ESOP established and maintained by a bank or similar financial institution, which is prohibited by law from redeeming or purchasing its own securities, a special exception applies. For this exception, even where securities are not readily tradable, no put option is required if the participants had the right to elect to receive distributions in cash.

Examination Steps: Put Options

1) Check that employer securities not readily tradable on an established market can be put to the employer. Note that if the ESOP itself is honoring the put option, check that there is an appropriate fiduciary decision involved with respect to this decision to reacquire the stock, in lieu of the taxpayer making the repurchase.

2) Make sure the put is exercisable for two 60-day periods: This would include 60 days following the date the employer securities were distributed and 60 days in the following plan year.

3) If the employee "puts" the shares to the employer that were received in a total distribution, make sure the employer provides adequate security and pays reasonable interest on the unpaid portion. A put option is not adequately secured if it is not secured by any tangible assets. For example, adequate security may be an irrevocable letter of credit, a surety bond issued by a third party insurance company rated "A" or better by a recognized insurance rating agency, or by a first priority perfected security interest against company assets capable of being sold, foreclosed upon or otherwise disposed of in case of default. Promissory notes, secured by a company's full faith and credit, are not adequate security. See PLR 9438002. In addition, the employer securities themselves that were repurchased cannot be treated as adequate security.

JOINT AND SURVIVOR RULES

Introduction Certain ESOP Benefits Not Subject to QJSA

IRC section 401(a)(11)(C) provides an exception to the qualified joint and survivor annuity (QJSA) and qualified pre-retirement survivor annuity (QPSA) requirements for certain ESOP benefits. The statute provides that the QJSA and QPSA rules do not apply to that portion of a participant's accrued benefit in an ESOP to which the IRC 409(h) rules apply. Remember that IRC section 4975(e)(7) requires an ESOP to satisfy IRC section 409(h). Therefore, this exception applies not only to a stock bonus ESOP, but also a stock bonus/money purchase combination ESOP, as defined in IRC section 4975(e)(7).

Rationale for This Exception

The reason for this exception is that an ESOP's primary purpose is to enable a participant to share in the growth of the employer through ownership in the company, which includes the ability to demand distribution in the form of qualifying employer securities.

When Exception Is Applicable

This exception is applicable where the plan provides that the ESOP participant's vested benefits are payable to the spouse on death, where the participant does not elect a life annuity, and where the ESOP is not a transferee plan of assets from a defined benefit plan or a defined contribution plan subject to IRC 412 minimum funding standards. See also Reg. 1.401(a)-20, Q&A 3(c).

Examination Steps: QJSA

1) Verify that the ESOP complies with Code section 409(h), with respect to the participant's right to demand distribution in the form of qualifying employer securities. Unless an exception applies under IRC section 409(h) with respect to the right of the participant to demand qualifying employer securities, this right should override the QJSA and QPSA requirements. For example, the participant

should not be precluded from electing a distribution in the form of qualifying employer securities, merely because consent of the participant's spouse has not been secured.

2) Verify that the ESOP satisfies the conditions contained in the IRC section 401 (a)(11)(C) exception to the QPJA or QJSA language, both in form and operation.

3) If the ESOP permits a participant to elect a life annuity, ensure the QJSA and QPSA requirements are satisfied, in form and operation (again, this language should not override the 409(h) right of a participant to demand distribution in the form of qualifying employer securities).

4) If only a portion of a plan is designated as an ESOP, ensure that the non-ESOP portion of the plan satisfies the QJSA and QPSA requirements, if applicable.

FLOOR OFFSET ARRANGEMENTS

ESOP Cannot Be Used to Offset Benefits under a DB Plan

Generally, under the prohibited transaction rules of ERISA, a plan may not invest more than 10% of its assets in qualifying employer securities. However, this limitation does not apply to eligible individual account plans. See ERISA Act sections 407(a) and (b).

An ESOP is an eligible individual account plan, unless its benefits are taken into account in determining the benefits payable to a participant under any defined benefit plan. See ERISA 407(d)(3)(C). This means an ESOP cannot be used to offset the benefits under a defined benefit plan in a floor-offset arrangement, effective with respect to arrangements established after 12/17/87. After that effective date, a floor-offset arrangement is treated as a single plan for purposes of the 10% limit. Where the 10% limit is exceeded, a prohibited transaction has taken place under IRC 4975 (c)(1)(A) due to the sale or exchange of employer securities between a plan and a disqualified person which is not exempt under IRC 4975(d)(13), if there is a transaction with a disqualified person.

In addition, Regulation § 1.401(a)-20, Q&A 5 provides that any plan that would not otherwise be subject to the survivor annuity requirements of sections 401(a)(11) and 417 whose benefits are used to offset benefits in a plan subject to such requirements is subject to the survivor annuity requirements with respect to those participants whose benefits are offset. Thus, there is a question as to whether any benefit provided by an ESOP can be used to offset a defined benefit without violating either IRC section 401(a)(11) or 409(h) requirements, due to QJSA and QPSA requirements of the offset portion in the ESOP in contravention of the ESOP requirement to permit the participant to be able to demand their distribution entirely in qualifying employer securities.

Examination Steps: Floor Offset

1) Determine whether the employer maintains any defined benefit plans.

2) If yes, determine whether the benefits provided by the defined benefit plan are reduced by benefits under the ESOP in an arrangement established after 12/17/87.

3) Determine whether the value of the employer securities exceeds 10% of the combined assets of the ESOP and the defined benefit plan.

4) If yes, impose the prohibited transaction tax on the fair market value of the employer securities that exceeds 10% of the assets of the combined plans, if there is a transaction with a disqualified person.

5) If yes, also consider the potential qualification issues under IRC sections 401 (a)(11), 417 and 409, based on the QJSA/QPSA requirements of Regulation § 1.401(a)-20, Q&A 5 and the conflicting ESOP requirements contained in IRC section 409(h).

VALUATION AND INDEPENDENT APPRAISER

Valuation and Independent Appraiser

Since ESOPs are designed to invest primarily in employer securities, the examination of this type of plan necessitates that you be able to determine the fair market value of qualified employer securities. TRA '86 enacted IRC section 401(a)(28)(C) which provides that employer securities acquired by an ESOP (whether by contribution or purchase) after 12/31/86 that are not readily tradable on an established securities market must be valued by an independent appraiser (within the meaning of IRC section 170(a)(1)). Valuation by an independent appraiser is not required in the case of employer securities that are readily tradable on an established securities market. See IRM 4.72.8, Technical Guidance on Valuation Assets for a detailed discussion of the independent appraiser rules for nonpublicly traded shares held by an ESOP.

Valuation Must Be Made in Good Faith

Regulation § 54.4975-11(d)(5), *Valuation,* provides that the valuation must be made in good faith and based on all relevant factors for determining the fair market value. In the case of a transaction involving the plan and a disqualified person, the value must be determined as of the date of the transaction. For all other purposes, the fair market value must be determined as of the most recent valuation date under the plan.

Examination Steps: Valuation

1) The balance sheet on Form 5500 provides information such as whether investments are in employer securities, acquisition indebtedness, other liabilities (indicates leverage), and/or party-in-interest transactions.

   In smaller plans, determine whether a valuation was made by adding the assets at the beginning of the year to the contributions and receipts less the disbursements during the year and comparing the total to the assets at the end of the year. If the total equals the assets at the end of the year, a valuation probably has not been made because the total only reflects the receipts and disbursements.

2) When reviewing the income statement, note any noncash contributions as these may also indicate the acquisition of employer securities.

3) Where stock is publicly traded, examine stock confirmation slips, trust receipt and disbursement accounts, and market records to verify the fair market value of security transactions.

4) Review the applicable question on the Form 5500 series return concerning independent appraisers to determine whether employer securities held in an ESOP that are not readily tradable on an established securities market were valued by an independent appraiser. Secure and analyze the appraisal report.

5) Where stock is not publicly traded, ensure that for stock acquired after 12/31/86 that such stock is valued by an independent appraiser, as required by IRC section 401(a)(28)(C). If the transaction does not involve a disqualified person, the fair market value must be determined as of the plan's most recent valuation date. Examine the records used to value the stock at the last valuation date in order to determine whether the assigned value is comparable to the value of comparable nonpublicly traded companies. See Reg. § 54.4975-11(d)(5). The stock held by the plan should be valued at least annually, as required for qualified plans. See Rev. Rul. 80-155.

6) Where stock is not publicly traded and the transaction involves a disqualified person, the fair market value must be determined as of the transaction date. Secure the appraisal report, if any, and use it as a basis for verifying the adequate consideration rules. If possible, request both the prior and subsequent appraisals for comparison purposes.

If the appraisal method is not consistently applied, inquire as to the reason for the change. In addition, determine whether any projections used were reasonable estimates of what has actually occurred. In addition, consider the presence and/or absence of assumptions used in the appraisal such as discounts due to lack of marketability and/or minority ownership. Note: Particular attention should be given to subsequent events that could have been foreseen and have an impact on value. See Rev. Rul. 59-60, 1959-1 C.B. 237. The independent appraisal will not in itself be a good faith determination.

Also, examine the capital stock accounts of the employer to substantiate transactions of similar stock. Another source of information related to stock sales might include a review of corporate minutes. If there is a problem with the stock valuation, use Form 5202, "Request for Engineering Service" to request assistance from the Examination engineer.

EFFECT OF IMPROPER VALUATION

Fiduciary Is Responsible for Proper Valuation

The fiduciary is responsible for determining that employer securities are properly valued. It is not enough for a fiduciary to rely in good faith on a third party valuation to establish that adequate consideration was paid. A fiduciary must make his/her own prudent investigation of value and determine that the underlying assumptions on which the valuation was made have not changed at the time the ESOP purchases the shares. See Donovan v. Cunningham, 716 F.2d 1455 (5th Cir. 1983) and Revenue Ruling 59-60.

A PT Occurs if an ESOP Pays a Disqualified Person Too Much

There is a prohibited transaction if an ESOP pays a disqualified person too much for employer securities. This may occur due to an improper valuation of employer stock that is closely-held. See Eyler v. Commissioner, No. 95-2482, U.S. Court of Appeals, 7th Circuit, 88 F.3d 445.

If Stock Is Overvalued

Where stock contributed to the plan is overvalued at time of contribution, the result could be a partial disallowance of the deduction taken. If the stock contributed is undervalued, the effect could be a potential violation under IRC section 415 (depending on the amount of stock contributed and allocated).

Example For the plan year ended December 31, 1999, the plan sponsor contributed 10,000 shares of employer securities to their plan, valued at $15 per share. A deduction of $150,000 was taken on the Form 1120 for the tax year ended December 31, 1999 with respect to such contribution.

Upon examination, the agent determined that no independent appraisal had been performed and that the value was an estimate made by the CEO. Subsequent development in the case resulted in a determination that the fair market value of the shares contributed was actually closer to $10 per share. The result was a disallowance of $50,000 for the Form 1120 for the tax year ended December 31, 1999.

Example Same facts as previous example, except that the fair market value of shares contributed was subsequently determined to equal $30 per share. Note that the employer still only deducted $150,000 based on their valuation. In addition, based on a fair market value of $30 per share, one HCE received an allocation for 1999 of $60,000.

The maximum deductible limit under IRC section 404 (taking into consideration IRC section 404(j)) was determined to be $200,000 for the tax year ended December 31, 1999. The result is that a nondeductible contribution of $100,000 was made ($200,000 − (10,000 shares × $30/share)). As a result, a Form 5330 with excise tax of $10,000 is due under IRC section 4972 (10% of $100,000). In addition, as one participant's allocation exceeded the IRC section 415 limits by an amount of $30,000, this operational failure affecting plan qualification should also be addressed and corrected. Finally, based on the revised valuation, the employer is entitled to an additional deduction of $50,000 for the tax year ended December 31, 1999 (assuming plan retains qualified status).

Unless Exception Applies, PT Occurs for Transaction between a Plan and a DP

There is a prohibited transaction if there is a sale of any property between a plan and a disqualified person (e.g., an employer) unless the prohibited transaction exception below applies. See IRC sections 4975(e)(2)(C) and 4975(c)(1)(A).

Exception Adequate Consideration

The prohibited transaction exception applies where the sale is for "adequate consideration." See IRC section 4975(d)(13) and ERISA Act section 408(e). Adequate consideration is defined as the fair market value of the security as determined in good faith by the plan trustee or named fiduciary. See ERISA Act section 3(18).

Potential Exclusive Benefit Violation: RR 69-494

In addition to a prohibited transaction occurring due to an improper valuation of stock acquired or sold, an exclusive benefit violation may occur if an ESOP acquires stock *for more* than its fair market value, (e.g., the stock is acquired from a shareholder). A decision to pursue an exclusive benefit violation, in addition to prohibited transactions, should be considered only when the scope of the transactions are substantial in relation to total plan assets and should be determined based on the relevant facts and circumstances.

Revenue Ruling 69-494, 1969-2 C.B. 88, provides guidelines for determining whether a plan investment is consistent with the exclusive benefit rule. These guidelines, as applied to ESOPs, require a determination of whether the amount paid for the stock exceeds its fair market value at the time of acquisition. (All requirements of Rev. Rul. 69-494 do not apply to stock bonus plans and ESOPs.) An exclusive benefit violation should be considered only where there is a significant depletion of plan assets.

EXAMINATION STEPS: VALUATION

Determine Whether Fair Market Value Was Used

Determine whether fair market value was utilized in the acquisition, sale or noncash contribution of employer stock.

If the stock is not publicly traded, request copies of the most recent independent appraisals of employer securities. Consideration should also be given to requesting prior and subsequent years' appraisals for comparison purposes.

Failure to value nonpublicly traded stock by utilizing an independent appraiser is a qualification failure under IRC section 401(a)(28)(C) that should be pursued. Corrective options include requiring the taxpayer to secure the services of an independent appraiser to make the appropriate appraisals for the pertinent periods or dates of transactions.

Review Valuation Report

Look at the valuation report on the company's shares. See if the company that makes products has share prices that rise and fall with its earnings. If the company's earnings have fallen but the report says the price per share has risen, it may indicate an incorrect valuation. Also check the correlation between earnings and stock price if there is no valuation report.

Check Employer's Audit Report and Documentation

Check the employer's audit report to see if the company's earnings have fallen after the valuation report was written. If they have, it is likely the shares' value should also have fallen. The plan fiduciary can no longer rely on the price per share from the valuation report because the facts on which it was based have changed.

Ask to see documentation of the fiduciary's prudent investigation to ensure the underlying assumptions have not changed since the last valuation.

Determine Whether Stock Appraisal Reflects Certain Factors

Determine whether the stock appraisal reflects the appropriate factors for determining value contained in Rev. Rul. 59-60, including an adjustment to the stock value due to lack of marketability and/or minority ownership (by the ESOP), if applicable.

Evaluate Stock Purchases for Exclusive Benefit Violation

Evaluate stock purchases for exclusive benefit violations by applying the fair market value rules of Rev. Rul. 69-494 at the time of the initial purchase and again at the time of any subsequent purchase. Even if the initial purchase did not violate the exclusive benefit rule, a subsequent purchase may have resulted in a violation.

Although technically an exclusive benefit violation, a violation of the exclusive benefit rule generally should not be pursued where it appears employer securities were acquired at an inflated price but the stock subsequently increased in value with the result that a benefit to plan participants has occurred.

If such stock was acquired from a disqualified person, imposing the excise tax under IRC section 4975 would still be appropriate.

If Stock Purchased at FMV, but Later Declines in Value

Note that neither a prohibited transaction nor a violation of the exclusive benefit rule will occur merely because employer securities acquired at fair market value later decline in value.

Ask for Engineering Assistance

If you have concerns about the validity of a stock appraisal, consideration should be given to requesting Engineering Assistance.

VOTING RIGHTS

If Employer Has Registration Type Class of Securities

Employer securities held by an ESOP must meet the IRC section 409(e) requirements pertaining to voting rights.

If the employer has a "registration-type class of securities," each participant must be entitled to direct the plan as to the manner in which employer securities, allocated to the account of such participant, are to be voted. A registration-type class of securities means a class of securities required to be registered under section 12 of the Securities Exchange Act of 1934.

If Employer Does Not Have Registration Type Class Securities

If the employer does not have a registration-type class of securities, each participant must be entitled to direct the plan as to the manner in which voting rights under employer securities, allocated to the account of such participant, are to be exercised with respect to any corporate matter which involves the voting of such shares with respect to the:

- Approval or disapproval of a corporate merger or consolidation,
- Recapitalization,
- Reclassification,
- Liquidation,
- Dissolution, or
- Sale of substantially all assets of a trade or business.

Right to Direct Plan as to Voting Depends on Applicable State Law

The right to direct the plan as to the voting of allocated securities in the above instances exists only if the applicable state law also provides for shareholder voting in those instances. IRC section 409(e)(5) also provides for a special "1 vote participant' rule for nonregistration-type class of securities. This special rule permits the voting of an issue with each participant allowed 1 vote with respect to the issue, with the trustee voting the shares held by the plan in proportion to the votes received.

Voting Rights and Unallocated Shares

The voting rights above do not have to be passed through to the participant with respect to unallocated shares. It is not uncommon for plan provisions to provide for the voting of unallocated shares in the same proportional manner as the directions received by the fiduciary for the voting of the allocated shares. However, the Department of Labor has held that the responsibility for voting unallocated shares should rest with the plan trustee. The plan trustee may follow plan provisions only to the extent permitted by ERISA Act section 404(a)(1)(D), i.e., insofar as such plan provisions are consistent with the provisions of Titles I and IV of ERISA. See DOL Advisory Opinion Letter (unnumbered) dated 2/23/89.

If Plan Trustee Does Not Receive Voting Instructions

If a plan trustee does not receive voting instructions on employer securities allocated to a participant's account, the plan can provide that the trustee will vote those shares. See Rev. Rul. 95-57, 1995-35 I.R.B. 5.

Examination Steps

1) Check the plan terms to make sure participants are entitled to vote employer securities allocated to their accounts.

2) Check the summary plan description to make sure participants are aware of their right to vote allocated employer securities in accordance with IRC section 409(e).

3) Check the corporate minutes to determine whether any events occurred that entitle participants to pass-through voting. If yes, then verify that the participants were given the right to the vote on the applicable issue.

DIVERSIFICATION

Introduction

For employer securities acquired after 12/31/86, IRC section 401(a)(28)(B) provides that each qualified participant in a plan may elect, within 90 days after the close of each plan year in the qualified election period, to direct the plan with regard to the investment of at least 25% of the participant's plan account.

The account balance subject to the diversification election increases to 50% in the final year of the election period.

Determining the Number of Shares Subject to Diversification

Q&A 9 of Notice 88-56, 1988-1 C.B. 540, provides that the portion of a qualified participant's account subject to the diversification election in all years of the qualified election period (other than the final year) is equal to (1) 25% of the number of shares of employer securities acquired by the plan after 12/31/86, that have ever been allocated to a qualified participant's account, less (2) the number of shares of employer securities previously diversified pursuant to a diversification election made after 12/31/86.

Defining Qualified Participant, Years of Participation and Qualified Election Period

A "qualified participant" is any employee who has completed at least 10 years of participation in the plan and has attained age 55.

In determining years of participation in the plan, include years the employee participated in a predecessor plan.

The "qualified election period" is the 6 plan year period beginning with the later of the first plan year (1) in which the individual first becomes a qualified participant, or (2) beginning after 12/31/86.

Three Methods to Satisfy Diversification

There are three methods by which a plan can satisfy the diversification requirement. The first two are statutory and appear in IRC section 401(a)(28)(B)(ii).

204 | Appendix B

- First, the plan can provide that the portion of the participant's account subject to the diversification election is distributed within 90 days after the period in which the election can be made.

- Second, the plan can offer at least three investment options to each participant making the diversification election, and within 90 days after the election period ends, the plan invests the portion of the amount in accordance with the diversification election.

- Third, the plan can offer a participant the option to direct the plan to transfer the portion of the account subject to the diversification election to another qualified defined contribution plan of the employer that offers at least three investment options. This transfer must be made no later than 90 days after the end of the election period. See Notice 88-56, Q&A 13.

Example Participant A, who participates in the ABC Corp ESOP, attains age 55 with 10 years of participation in the plan year ended December 31, 1999. Participant A has 200 shares of stock, valued at $25 per share, which were contributed after December 31, 1986, as of the end of this plan year. Participant A is a qualified participant entitled to elect diversification of up to 50 shares in the 90-day election period beginning January 1, 2000 (25% of 200 shares).

In addition, Participant A will be eligible to elect diversification during the subsequent election periods in 2001, 2002, 2003, 2004 and 2005 (50% in the election period in 2005).

Example Same facts as previous example. For the plan year ended December 31, 2000, an additional allocation of 40 shares of stock is allocated to Participant A's account.

Assuming that Participant A only elected diversification of 20 shares in the 1st election period, Participant A would be eligible to elect diversification of an additional 40 shares in the 2nd 90-day election period beginning January 1, 2001 (25% of 240 cumulative shares minus 20 shares previously diversified).

Examination Steps

1) Determine which plan participants meet the age (55) and service (10 years of participation) requirements to qualify as "qualified participants," if any.

2) Inquire about any potential predecessor plans, to determine if additional years of participation should be considered in the determination of the "qualified participants."

3) Check that the plan provides a diversification election for employer securities acquired after 12/31/86. Ensure that all qualified participants were given the right to diversify, and that such right was handled within the prescribed time frames.

NONTERMINABLE ESOP PROVISIONS AND 411(D)(6)

Introduction

After an ESOP ceases to be an ESOP (such as when the plan is amended and converted into a non-ESOP plan), an employee's right to put nonreadily tradable employer securities to the employer must continue to apply. It is a nonterminable right described at Reg. § 54.4975-11(a)(3)(ii). However, a plan that is no longer an ESOP is not required to be primarily invested in employer securities because the right to a particular form of investment is not an IRC section 411(d)(6) protected benefit.

Section 411(d)(6)

IRC section 411(d)(6) and the regulations thereunder provide that a plan will not satisfy the requirements of IRC 411 if the accrued benefit, early retirement benefit, retirement-type subsidy or optional forms of benefits of participants are eliminated or reduced by a plan amendment. IRC section 411(d)(6)(C) provides an exception to the IRC section 411(d)(6) prohibitions for ESOPs with respect to modifying distribution options (provided the modification is made in a nondiscriminatory manner per the regulations). Reg. § 1.411(d)-4, A-2(d) provides guidance on the elimination, with respect to all participants, of IRC section 411(d)(6) protected optional forms of benefits applicable to ESOPs. It is not an impermissible cutback if the employer eliminates, or retains the discretion to eliminate, the lump sum or installment option with respect to all participants, provided such elimination is consistent with the distribution and payment requirements applicable to such plans (e.g., those required by IRC section 409).

Right to Employer Stock Can Be Eliminated in Certain Situations

If the employer becomes substantially employee-owned, or the employer is an S corporation (for taxable years of the employer beginning after December 31, 1997), the right to demand a distribution in employer stock, with respect to all participants, can be eliminated and cash can be substituted instead. Where employer securities become readily tradable, the employer can eliminate the right to demand a distribution in cash and instead provide that the distribution will be made in the form of employer securities. Where employer securities cease to be readily tradable, a distribution in the form of employer securities can be eliminated and cash can be substituted instead.

If the employer securities continue to be readily tradable, but substantially all of the employer stock or assets of the employer's business are sold, a distribution in the form of employer securities can be eliminated and cash can be substituted instead. Although the Commissioner can provide additional rules and exceptions in revenue rulings, notices and other documents of general applicability, this has not been done at this time.

Examination Steps

1) In an ESOP amended to become a non-ESOP, make sure the right to put non-readily tradable employer securities to the employer is not eliminated.

2) Determine whether optional forms of benefits that have been eliminated comply with the exceptions for ESOPs under Reg. § 1.411(d)-4, Q&A 2(d).

3) If during the year of examination, a plan eliminates the right to receive lump sum distributions and instead just provides for installment distributions, please review the plan operation to ensure that the criteria in Reg. § 1.411(d)-4, Q&A 2(d)(i) is satisfied. Such elimination of the lump sum distribution must result in plan terms and operation providing that the remaining distribution options are consistent with ESOP requirements (such as the right to demand QES and the IRC section 409(o) rights). In addition, the elimination of the lump sum option should apply to all participants, not just a certain group.

SECTION 415 LIMITS

Stock Acquired in an Exempt Loan—How Annual Additions Are Calculated

An ESOP may be funded through an exempt loan (a leveraged ESOP) or may be funded directly by employer contributions (nonleveraged ESOP). Employer securities held by a leveraged ESOP are released from the suspense account and allocated to participants' accounts by reason of employer contributions to the ESOP to repay the loan and by reason of the use of dividends on employer securities in the ESOP to repay the loan. If stock has been acquired in an exempt loan, annual additions under IRC section 415(c) can be calculated under either of two methods. The annual additions can be determined either with respect to (1) the amount of the employer contributions to the ESOP used to repay a loan, or (2) the value of the employer securities allocated to participants. Plan terms should specify the method used. See Reg. § 1.415-6(g)(4) and Notice 87-21, Q&A 11.

If the annual additions are calculated with respect to employer contributions, appreciation in the stock's value from the time it entered the suspense account will not be counted for IRC section 415 purposes. See Regs. §§ 1.415-6(g)(4), 54.4975-11(a)(8)(ii) and 54.4975-7(b)(8)(iii).

If ESOP Not Funded by an Exempt Loan

If an ESOP is not funded by an exempt loan, the fair market value of the employer securities on the date they were contributed to the ESOP is treated as an annual addition. See Reg. § 1.415-6(b)(4).

Special Rule for Determining Annual Additions—415(c)(6)

IRC section 415(c)(6) provides for a special rule in determining annual additions made to an ESOP. If not more than one-third of the employer contributions to an ESOP for a plan year are allocated to the accounts of participants who are highly compensated employees, within the meaning of IRC 414(q), then all forfeitures of leveraged stock and all employer contributions used to pay interest on a leveraged loan which are charged against the participant's account are eliminated from the computation of the annual addition. This should be stated in plan. This is called a broad-based ESOP.

Court Cases that have sustained the Service's position with respect to excess annual additions made to ESOPs include Steel Balls, Inc. v. Commissioner, Docket No. 13492-93R, U.S. Tax Court, T.C. Memo 1995-266, Howard E. Clendenen, Inc. v. Commissioner, No. 98-4183, U.S. Court of Appeals, 8th Circuit, 207 F.3d 1071 and Roblene v. Commissioner, No 21576-95R, U.S. Tax Court, T.C. Memo 1999-161.

Examination Steps

1) Determine whether the ESOP is funded by an exempt loan or by direct employer contributions.

2) If the ESOP is not funded by an exempt loan, ensure the fair market value of stock on the date it was contributed to the ESOP is treated as an annual addition.

3) If the ESOP is funded by an exempt loan, determine whether annual additions are calculated based on employer contributions to repay the loan, or based on the fair market value of the employer securities when allocated to participant accounts. Review the terms of the plan to determine the method used when testing for the IRC section 415 limits.

4) If annual additions are calculated based on employer contributions to repay an exempt loan, a separate computation will be necessary to arrive at each participant's share of the contribution used by the ESOP to repay the loan.

   Analyze the encumbered stock account and the liability accounts of the trust to determine the number of shares released from encumbrance and the employer contribution, so that a contribution per released share can be determined. Then, multiply the number of released encumbered shares allocated to a participant's account by the cost per released share in order to arrive at an amount to be used to verify compliance with IRC section 415. Do not include shares released due to the payment of dividends. Also, if you are examining a broad-based ESOP, do not include shares released due to the payment of loan interest. The formula is:

TOTAL CONTRIBUTION TO PAY LOAN TOTAL NUMBER OF RELEASED SHARES = COST PER RELEASED SHARE

5) Determine whether more than $1/3$ of employer contributions to a leveraged ESOP were allocated to the accounts of highly compensated employees. If yes, check that annual additions include forfeitures of employer securities and employer contributions used by the ESOP to pay interest on loans to acquire employer securities.

6) Check the plan document to see if it permits the plan to use the special ESOP rules under IRC section 415(c)(6).

TAX CREDIT ESOPs

Tax Credit ESOPs

Prior to 1987, the statutes provided for two other types of ESOPs. Taxpayers were allowed tax credits, as well as deductions, for contributions made to Tax Reduction

Act Stock Ownership Plans (TRASOPS), which were subsequently replaced by the Payroll Based Stock Ownership Plans (PAYSOPS). However, as both the PAYSOP and TRASOP rules have been repealed for several years, they will not be covered by this chapter. If you need information relating to these types of Esops, refer to IRM 4.72.4.1.3.

DEDUCTION LIMITS

Deduction Limits: Leveraged ESOP Deductions

There are special deduction rules for contributions to an ESOP used to repay principal and interest on a loan to an ESOP. See IRC section 404(a)(9). Under the general rule of IRC section 404(a)(3), an employer's deduction for contributions to a stock bonus or profit-sharing plan is limited to 15% of the participants' compensation. Under the general rule of IRC 404(a)(7), where an employer maintains one or more defined contribution plans and one or more defined benefit plans, an employer's deduction for contributions for all plans is the greater of 25% of compensation or the amount necessary to meet the minimum funding standards of IRC section 412. See IRC section 404(a)(7).

Exception to Use to Pay Back ESOP Loan

IRC section 404(a)(9)(A) provides that notwithstanding the provisions of IRC sections 404(a)(3) and (a)(7), an employer's deduction for contributions paid to an ESOP to repay the principal on a loan used to acquire qualifying employer securities can be as high as 25% of the ESOP participants' compensation.

In addition, there is no limit on the employer's deduction with respect to contributions to an ESOP applied toward the payment of interest on the exempt loan. The ESOP must actually use the employer contributions to repay the exempt loan by the due date of the employer's return (including extensions) to take advantage of these increased limits.

Company M maintains a leveraged ESOP. For the 1997 plan year, Company M makes a contribution of 30% of the participants' compensation to repay principal and interest on the ESOP loan: 25% of compensation was used to repay the principal on the loan and 5% of compensation was used to repay the interest on the loan. The entire 1997 contribution is deductible under IRC section 404(a)(9).

Deduction Limits: IRC Section 404(k) (Dividend Deduction) — Pre-EGTRRA (Prior to 2002)

In addition to the deduction permitted under IRC sections 404(a)(3) or 404(a)(9), a C Corporation may deduct dividends (called applicable dividends) under IRC section 404(k) paid on employer securities held by an ESOP if such dividends are (i) paid in cash to the participants or their beneficiaries, (ii) paid to the plan and distributed in cash to the participants or their beneficiaries within 90 days after the close of the plan year in which the dividends are paid to the plan, or (iii) used to repay an ESOP loan. Note that this deduction for dividends is not allowed for S Corporations.

If Dividends Used to Repay Loans

If dividends on allocated stock are used to repay a loan, the fair market value of employer securities released from suspense and allocated to participants' accounts must equal or exceed the amount of such dividends. This allocation due to the use of dividends is in addition to the allocation due to the loan repayment. [Note: The stock released due to use of dividends on allocated shares should be allocated to the respective participant's stock account associated with the applicable dividend].

If Employer Securities Paying Dividends Were Acquired after 8/4/89

If the employer securities paying the dividends were acquired after 8/4/89, such dividends are deductible under IRC section 404(k)(2)(A)(iii) only if they are used to repay a loan the proceeds of which were used to acquire the employer securities that are paying the dividends.

However, dividends on employer securities that were not acquired in an exempt loan, but were acquired by an ESOP before 8/5/89, can be used to repay a loan the proceeds of which were used to acquire employer securities and deducted under IRC section 404(k).

Example: Facts Company M maintains an ESOP that acquired qualified employer securities in an exempt loan in 1994. Also in 1994, Employer M terminated a profitsharing plan and permitted participants to have a direct transfer of their profit sharing plan accounts to the ESOP. The cash transferred from the profitsharing plan to the ESOP is reinvested in employer securities. The exempt loan obtained by the ESOP is repaid with contributions made by Company M and with cash dividends paid on the qualified employer securities held by the ESOP which were purchased with the exempt loan proceeds.

Example: Analysis Company M can claim a dividend deduction under IRC section 404(k) for the dividends paid on the securities acquired in the exempt loan that are used to repay the loan.

Company M cannot claim a dividend deduction under IRC section 404(k) to the extent the exempt loan was repaid with cash dividends paid on employer securities purchased with the funds transferred from the terminated profitsharing plan. This is because, although these employer securities were acquired by the ESOP after 8/4/89, they do not relate to employer securities acquired with the proceeds of the exempt loan.

Disallowing a Deduction

Disallow an IRC section 404(k) dividend deduction if the dividend constitutes, in substance, an evasion of taxation or is not a dividend as defined in IRC section 316. See

IRC section 404(k)(5)(A). This determination will depend on the facts and circumstances relating to the declaration and issuance of dividends.

Example Amounts paid that exceed accumulated and current earnings and profits may not constitute a dividend. Amounts that constitute the payment of unreasonable compensation, or are not reasonable dividends, are an evasion of taxation and cannot be deducted as dividends under IRC section 404(k). An example of a reasonable dividend is one that is at a rate normally paid by the employer in the ordinary course of business.

Example Company M repays an exempt loan with dividends on employer securities acquired with exempt loan proceeds. Company M claims a dividend deduction under IRC section 404(k). You ascertain the dividend rate is 70%, and that this is an extraordinary dividend that is greatly in excess of the dividend Company M can reasonably be expected to pay on a recurring basis. These dividends are not reasonable and are not deductible under IRC section 404(k).

Redemptions of Stock Are Not Dividends

Corporate payments in redemption of stock held by an ESOP that are used to make distributions to terminating ESOP participants do not constitute "applicable dividends" under IRC section 404(k)(5)(A) and are not deductible. See Rev. Rul. 2001-6, 2001-6 I.R.B. 491. Moreover, any deduction for such payments in redemption of stock is barred under section 162(k).

Examination Steps

1) Cancelled checks, payroll records, trust receipts and disbursement records, and participant's accounts should be examined to determine whether the IRC section 404 limits have been exceeded. Problems could also arise if the number of participants decreased so as to lower the deductible limits.

2) Look at the applicable question on Schedule E, ESOP Annual Information, of Form 5500, to find out whether the employer repaid the exempt loan using dividends on employer securities.

3) Look at the question on Schedule E with regard to whether any dividends used to repay an exempt loan were not generated by employer securities acquired in that exempt loan. If the answer is yes, find out if the employer securities paying those dividends were acquired after 8/4/89. If yes, disallow the deduction.

4) Determine whether the amount of dividends paid exceed the employer's current or accumulated earnings or profits under IRC section 316. Review the question on Schedule E of Form 5500 for this information. If yes, disallow the deduction.

5) Check whether the dividends paid on employer securities held by the ESOP are reasonable. A reasonable dividend does not include an unusually large dividend used to repay ESOP debt, which is greatly in excess of the dividend the ESOP

sponsor can reasonably be expected to pay on a recurring basis. A reasonable dividend is one that is at a rate normally paid by the sponsor in the ordinary course of business.

6) Determine whether any corporate redemptions of ESOP stock were deducted under IRC section 404(k). If yes, disallow the deduction. Refer to Rev. Rul. 2001-6, I.R.B. 2001-6 for an example and description of an improper deduction of a corporate redemption of stock from the ESOP.

DEDUCTION LIMITS: EGTRRA (POST 2001)

Change by EGTRRA

IRC section 404(k)(2), relating to the deduction of applicable dividends to an ESOP, was expanded by EGTRRA, effective for tax years beginning after 12/31/01. The law was liberalized to permit the deduction of applicable dividends of an ESOP, where the applicable dividends, in accordance with plan terms, are either:

1) Paid in cash directly to the participant or beneficiary,

2) Paid to the plan and later distributed in cash to either the participant or beneficiary no later than 90 days after the close of the plan year in which paid,

3) At the election of the participant or beneficiary, the dividends are paid to the ESOP and reinvested in employer securities. This preceding election is only permitted where the plan also provides that the participant can alternatively elect that the dividends be paid in cash as described in (1) or (2) above (plan can offer one or both options, as described in Notice 2002-2, Q&A 2), or

4) Used to make payment on an exempt loan, the proceeds of which were used to acquire employer securities (whether or not allocated to participants) with respect to which the dividend is paid. Note that this rule is still subject to the IRC 404(k)(2)(B) limitation if the dividends arise from allocated shares (i.e., employer securities released and allocated to the participant must have FMV no less than amount of dividends used).

Applicable Dividends Must Be Fully Vested, 404(k)(7) if Election to Pay Dividends to ESOP

Applicable dividends that are deducted by the corporation must be fully vested if the participant makes the election to pay such dividends to the ESOP and reinvest them in employer securities. See Notice 2002-2, Q&A 9 and IRC section 404(k)(7).

Therefore, an ESOP must provide that a participant is fully vested in any dividend with respect to which the participant is offered the election under IRC section 404(k)(2)(A)(iii).

Under prior law, with respect to dividends retained by the plan, these dividends constituted applicable dividends under IRC section 404(k) only if used to make payments on an exempt loan.

The EGTRRA law change will now permit the deduction of dividends paid to the ESOP, even if not used to service the exempt loan, if the plan also permits the participant the option to elect to have the dividends paid in cash pursuant to either election (1) or (2) above.

Timing of Deduction

For the rules relating to the timing of the deduction, refer to Notice 2002-2, I.R.B. 2002-2, 285 (January 14, 2002). In general, the new deduction rules permit a deduction for the dividend for taxable years beginning on or after 1/1/02. With respect to dividends that are reinvested in the ESOP, the deduction is allowed under the new rules if the later of the date on which the dividend is reinvested in employer securities or the date on which the participant's election becomes irrevocable occurs in 2002.

The timing of the deduction is such that the applicable dividend becomes deductible in the later of the taxable year of the corporation in which the dividend is reinvested in employer securities or the date on which the participant's election becomes irrevocable. Dividends paid to the plan and distributed to participants within 90 days after the end of the plan year are deductible in the taxable year of the corporation in which the dividend is paid or distributed to the participant. See Q&A 4 of Notice 2002-2.

Refer to Notice 2002-2 for additional guidance, such as conditions related to the manner of election by the participant, the impermissible designation of a plan as an ESOP (must be an ESOP as of the record date for the dividend), and examples of the new deduction rules.

Secretary May Disallow Deduction if Dividend Constitutes an Avoidance of Taxation, etc.

EGTRRA also amended IRC section 404(k)(5)(A) to provide that the Secretary may disallow the deduction for any dividend under IRC section 404(k)(1) if the Secretary determines that the dividend constitutes, in substance, an avoidance or evasion of taxation. This includes the authority to disallow a deduction for unreasonable dividends.

With respect to dividends reinvested under § 404(k)(2)(A)(iii), a dividend paid on common stock that is primarily and regularly traded on an established securities market (within the meaning of § 54.4975-7(b)(1)(iv) of the Excise Tax Regulations) is presumed to be a reasonable dividend.

In the case of a corporation with no outstanding common stock (determined on a controlled group basis) that is primarily and regularly traded on an established securities market, a determination regarding whether the dividend is reasonable is made by comparing the dividend rate on the stock held by the ESOP with the dividend rate for common stock of comparable corporations whose stock is primarily and regularly traded on an established securities market.

Whether a closely held corporation is comparable to a corporation whose stock is primarily and regularly traded on an established securities market is determined by comparing relevant corporate characteristics such as industry, size of the corporation, earnings, debt-equity structure, and dividend history. See Notice 2002-2, I.R.B. 2002-2, Q&A 11.

EXEMPT LOANS

Definition of Exempt Loan

This section describes the requirements for an exempt loan. The failure of a plan to follow these rules will result in the loan failing to be exempt under Code section 4975 and subject to the prohibited transaction excise tax. Failure to follow these rules does not cause the plan to become nonqualified. An exempt loan is a loan that meets the requirements of Reg. § 54.4975-7(b). A nonexempt loan is a loan that fails to satisfy the requirements of Reg. § 54.4975-7(b).

An exempt loan is a loan made to an ESOP by a disqualified person or a loan to an ESOP from a third party that is guaranteed by a disqualified person. See Reg. § 54.4975-7(b)(1)(ii). Generally, these kinds of loans are prohibited transactions under IRC section 4975(c)(1)(B) because they constitute the direct or indirect lending of money or other extension of credit between a plan and a disqualified person. IRC section 4975(d)(3) provides that if the requirements for that section are met, such loans to an ESOP are exempt from the prohibited transaction rules.

The failure of a plan to follow the exempt loan rules results in the loan being non-exempt and subject to the prohibited transaction tax. Such failure to follow the rules does not cause the plan to be disqualified or lose its status as an ESOP.

Examination Steps

If during the course of an examination of an ESOP with exempt loan provisions, you determine that the loan is nonexempt, treat as a prohibited transaction under IRM 4.72.11, Prohibited Transactions. The effect is that the direct or indirect extension of credit applicable to the exempt loan would no longer be exempt.

Other issues that may arise include the loss of certain special deduction rules for leveraged ESOPs, as well as the loss of the certain interest and forfeitures applicable to the exempt loan that would now be considered annual additions under IRC section 415(c)(6).

Primary Benefit Requirement

An exempt loan must be primarily for the benefit of the ESOP participant and their beneficiaries. All the surrounding facts and circumstances should be considered in determining this requirement.

At the time an exempt loan is made, the interest rate for the loan and the price of securities acquired with the loan proceeds should not be such that the plan assets might be drained off.

The terms of the loan must be at least as favorable as the terms of a comparable loan resulting from an arm's-length negotiated transaction between independent parties.

The loan should be for a specific term and not payable on demand. See IRC section 4975(d)(3) and Reg. § 54.4975-7(b)(3), (b) (7) and (b)(13).

Examination Steps

1) Secure a copy of the loan documents related to the existing exempt loan. The loan document should be scrutinized to determine whether the terms of the loan

were reasonable as of the date the loan was made and of the date that the qualified employer securities were purchased. Determine whether the interest rate for the loan and the price paid for the securities would have had the effect of draining off plan assets. The prime interest rate, rates for similar transactions, rates charged by banks, and rates charged by other financial institutions should be used as a measuring device to determine an acceptable interest rate.

2) Scrutinize the loan against prior loans of the same nature and loans to other entities to determine whether arms-length dealing existed. Items to be compared are interest, cost of assets purchased, collateral, prepayment penalties, and any other provisions or restriction in the terms of the loan.

3) For purposes of determining whether fair market value was paid for the securities, refer to the earlier chapter segments, relating to valuation of employer securities.

4) Any other facts and circumstances relating to the loan can be used to substantiate compliance with or violation of the primary benefit requirement.

Use of Loan Proceeds

Exempt loan proceeds must be used by an ESOP within a reasonable amount of time after their acquisition by the ESOP:

1) To acquire qualifying employer securities;

2) To repay the loan; or

3) To repay a prior exempt loan. Securities acquired with exempt loan proceeds may not be subject to a put, call, or other option, or buy-sell or similar arrangement while held by the ESOP or when distributed from the ESOP, other than the right of first refusal and the IRC section 409(h) put option. See Reg. § 54.4975-7(b)(4).

Examination Steps

1) Examine the buy and sell slips, receipt records, and loan contracts to determine the exempt loan proceeds were used to:

   a) Purchase qualifying employer securities;

   b) Repay such loans; or

   c) Repay a prior exempt loan.

2) Examine the securities to ensure there is no call, put, other option, buy-sell arrangement or any other restriction on the securities while in the trust or upon distribution, other than those provided in Regs. § 54.4975-7(b)(9) and (10).

Collateral for Exempt Loans

The collateral pledged by the ESOP with respect to any exempt loan must be limited to the qualifying employer securities purchased with such exempt loan or the qualifying employer securities that were used as collateral on a prior exempt loan repaid with the proceeds of the current exempt loan. See Reg. § 54.4975-7(b)(5).

Liability of ESOP for Exempt Loan

An exempt loan should be without recourse against the ESOP. A lender can seek repayment of an ESOP loan only out of the following plan assets:

1) Assets acquired with exempt loan proceeds that are collateral for the loan;

2) Collateral used in a prior exempt loan repaid with exempt loan proceeds;

3) Contributions made to the ESOP to meet plan exempt loan obligations;

4) Earnings on collateral or the contributions noted in 3) above. The payments made with respect to an exempt loan by the ESOP during the year must not exceed an amount equal to the sum of contributions and earnings received during or prior to the year less payments in prior years. The purpose of the preceding requirement is that pre-existing plan assets prior to the exempt loan should not be used to service the debt. Also, these contributions and earnings must be accounted for separately on the books of accounts of the ESOP until the loan is repaid. See Reg. § 54.4975-7(b)(5).

Examination Steps

1) Examine the ESOP, the assets and the exempt loan contract to ensure that any recourse by the lender does not exceed the assets of the ESOP as stated above.

2) Request an accounting that supports that the exempt loan is not repaid with any pre-existing plan assets.

Default

If the loan is secured by the employer securities held in the suspense account and there is a default on the loan, a lender who is a third party and not a disqualified person can have suspense account assets transferred to the extent of the remaining loan amount.

If the lender is a disqualified person (e.g., the employer), then the amount that can be transferred on default is the amount of the missed payment. This prevents an employer from manipulating the default mechanism in order to use plan assets to repay an exempt loan.

A default can cause a loan to be a nonexempt loan. See Reg. 54.4975-7(b)(5) and (6). The use of exempt loans to acquire QES creates an obligation by the employer to make sufficient contributions to service the debt and release the shares for allocations to participants.

The failure to make sufficient contributions to pay the debt could cause the loan to be nonexempt and thus subject the taxpayer to prohibited transaction liability.

Examination Steps

1) Determine whether there has been a default in repaying the loan.

2) If there has been a default, check whether the shares in the suspense account are collateral for the loan. Ensure that the plan does not transfer any plan assets in the event of default to any third party in excess of the lesser of the 1) the amount of the default or the 2) the collateralized stock.

3) If the stock in the suspense account is collateral for the loan and the employer is the lender, ensure that the employer does not use suspense account assets greater in value than the missed payment to repay the loan.

4) Determine whether the default has caused the loan to become nonexempt. The agent should review all the facts and circumstances relating to the default to determine whether to pursue such default as a prohibited transaction.

Release of Stock from Suspense Account

Employer securities acquired with exempt loan proceeds are required to be placed in a suspense account to be allocated to participants' accounts as the loan is paid off by employer contributions.

Methods by which Exempt Loans Are Paid

An exempt loan is repaid and qualifying employer securities are released from the suspense account based on one of two methods.

The first and most common method is based on principal and interest payments.

The second method (special rule) permits the release of qualifying employer securities from a suspense account based solely on principal payments, if certain conditions are met. See Reg. § 54.4975-7(b)(8). This second method results in low allocations of securities in the early years of the loan, when mainly interest is being paid off. Sometimes employers will renew loans in which securities are released based only on principal payments in order to keep allocations low.

Requirements to Use the Principal Only Method

However, in order to utilize the principal only method, the exempt loan must provide:

- For level annual payments over 10 years or less,
- With interest disregarded only to extent that it would be determined to be interest under standard loan amortization tables, and
- That by reason of renewal, extension or refinancing, the sum of the expired duration of the exempt loan, the renewal period, the extension period, and the duration of the new exempt loan can not extend over 10 years.

Stock Released from a Suspense Account

Stock released from the suspense account must be allocated to participants' accounts in shares of stock or other nonmonetary units, rather than by dollar amounts. Reg. § 54.4975-11(d)(2).

Example XYZ Corporation establishes an ESOP that borrows $10,000,000 from a bank, which it uses to acquire 200,000 shares of XYZ stock (QES). XYZ guarantees the exempt loan, which is for 10 years at 7% and is payable in level annual payments of $1,423,775. Total payments on the loan equal $14,237,750.

The plan uses the first method to release shares from suspense (i.e., the principal and interest method), with the number of shares to be released the first year equaling 20,000 shares. This is based on calculation of $1,423,775/$14,237,750 × 200,000 shares.

If all loan payments are made as originally scheduled, the number of securities released each year will also equal 20,000.

Example Same facts as above, except that the release from suspense is based on the special rule (release based on principal payments only). The level annual payments are $1,423,775. Total payments on the loan over the 10-year term equal $14,237,750.

In the first year, the annual payment of $1,423,775 involves a $723,775 principal payment and a $700,000 interest payment. The number of shares to be released the first year is equal to 14,476 shares. This is based on a calculation of $723,775 ÷ $10,000,000 × 200,000 shares.

If loan payments are made as originally scheduled, the number of securities released in subsequent years will increase, as the portion of the loan payment representing the principal payments increases.

EXAMINATION STEPS-EXEMPT LOANS

Refer to Schedule E, ESOP Annual Information

Refer to the question on Schedule E, ESOP Annual Information, which determines the method the employer uses to repay the loan.

Analyze Loan Contract and Other Information

Analyze the loan contract and its repayment provisions to verify that as the loan is repaid, stock is released from the suspense account and allocated to participant accounts.

Analyze the loan contract, the encumbrance account, the allocation schedule, and the receipts and disbursements accounts to substantiate compliance with the regulations.

Also, if you encounter a situation where contributions have been missed for a period of years, or where there are large repayments to the lender, additional analysis should be undertaken to determine if the effect of such nonpayment or large payments proves to be a violation of the exclusive benefit requirement or the antidiscrimination provisions of the Code.

Failure to make sufficient contributions to make timely payments on the debt could also, based on the facts and circumstances, cause the loan to be nonexempt.

Example Assume an employer originally entered into an exempt loan and acquired qualified employer securities with an exempt loan that required substantially level annual payments over 10 years. The necessary contributions were made the first two years to make the required loan payments due and the requisite shares were released for allocation. However, no contributions were made the next four years, with no action taken by the fiduciary with respect to such nonpayment. If no valid business reason exists to support nonpayment of contributions necessary to service the debt, considerations should be given to treating the exempt loan as nonexempt under IRC 4975(c)(1)(B).

Determine Method of Repayment Principal and Interest, or Principal Only

Determine whether the loan is structured so that securities are being released from the suspense account based on principal and interest or by reference to principal payments only.

If the principal only method is used, ensure the plan document permits the release of shares from the suspense account based on the principal only method. If so, determine whether the loan period, and any renewal, extension, or refinancing period exceeds 10 years. The release of employer securities from a suspense account must revert to the principal and interest method when the loan period (including extensions) exceeds 10 years. See Reg. § 54.4975-7(b)(8)(ii).

Verify that one of the two release formulas are properly applied to release shares from the suspense account as contributions are made and payments are made on the exempt loan. Recommend that the agent request a copy of the workpapers for the plan year under audit related to the release formula that was used by the plan administrator. The agent should determine that the proper amount of shares were released from the suspense account as a result of the loan repayment.

REPAYING AN EXEMPT LOAN FROM THE PROCEEDS OF THE SALE OF UNALLOCATED EMPLOYER SECURITIES

Introduction

Employer securities acquired with exempt loan proceeds are placed in a suspense account to be allocated to participants' accounts as the loan is paid off by employer contributions. If unallocated employer securities are used to repay the loan, they will not be available for allocation to participants' accounts.

Exempt Loan Must be Primarily for the Benefit of ESOP Participants

IRC section 4975(d)(3) and Reg. § 54.4975-7(b)(3) provide that an exempt loan must be primarily for the benefit of the ESOP participants. Thus, neither plan terms nor operation should provide for the sale of qualifying employer securities in the suspense account with the resultant proceeds derived from the sale of the unallocated employer securities to repay the loan.

Whether the Primary Benefit Is Violated Depends on Facts and Circumstances

Whether an ESOP in operation violates the primary benefit requirement by repaying an exempt loan with the proceeds from the sale of unallocated securities will be determined based on all the surrounding facts and circumstances. Among the facts relevant to the primary benefit requirement are whether:

- The transaction promotes employee ownership of employer stock,
- Contributions to an ESOP that is part of a stock bonus plan are recurring and substantial, and
- The extent to which the method of repayment of the exempt loan benefits the employees.

All aspects of the loan transaction, including the method of repayment, will be scrutinized to see whether the primary benefit requirement is satisfied.

Analysis of Published Guidance—ESOP Did Not Fail as a Result of Using Proceeds to Repay Loan

Essentially, employer securities acquired with an exempt loan create an obligation by the employer to make annual contributions to the plan sufficient to meet the plan's obligation of paying interest and principal on the debt. S. Rep. No. 94-36, 94th Cong., 1st session, 58-59 (1975).

If unallocated employer securities are used to repay the loan, they will not be available for allocation to the participants' accounts. IRC section 4975(d)(3) and Reg. § 54.4975-7(b)(3) provide that an exempt loan must be primarily for the benefit of the ESOP participants.

Thus, a plan that repaid an exempt loan using proceeds derived from the sale of unallocated employer securities held in suspense could cause the exempt loan to become a nonexempt loan.

Although not cited as authority, refer to Private Letter Rulings 8231043, 8231039 and 8044074 for an explanation of scenarios where the Service determined that the use of the proceeds from the sale of unallocated employer securities held in a suspense account to repay the loan did not cause the ESOP to fail to satisfy IRC section 4975(d)(3).

In these particular cases, the Service held that the proceeds from the sale of unallocated employer may be used to repay the exempt loan where:

- A tender offer has been made that may result in employer securities no longer being available and
- The price fixed during the tender offer would produce a financial gain to the plan participants.

However, these determinations were based on the relevant facts and circumstances involved.

Analysis of Published Guidance in which ESOP Did Fail Due to Proceeds Used to Repay Exempt Loan

Conversely, other PLRs, such as PLR 8828009, have held that, based on a particular set of facts and circumstances, the use the proceeds from the sale of unallocated employer securities held in a suspense account to repay the loan caused the ESOP to fail to satisfy IRC section 4975(d)(3). GCM 39747, issued 3/14/86, explained, in part, that an ESOP is a technique of corporate finance designed to build beneficial equity ownership of shares in the employer corporation into its employees, without requiring any cash outlays on their part, any reduction in pay or other employee benefits, or the surrender of any rights on the part of the employees. S. Rep. No. 94-938, 94th Cong., 2d Sess., 180 (1976).

The Service has noted that both the securing of capital funds for necessary capital growth and the bringing about of stock ownership by all corporate employees are to be considered part of a leveraged ESOP's exempt functions under section 401(a). See Rev. Rul. 79-122, 1979-1 CB 204.

GCM 39747 went on to provide that while an arrangement whereby securities acquired are thereafter sold for loan repayment may further the corporate finance objective, it does not further the stock ownership objective.

This GCM concluded that a plan that contained blanket language to permit a sale of unallocated shares in suspense to make payments on the loan **was not** an arrangement that is "primarily for the benefit of participants and beneficiaries of the plan" as required by section 4975(d)(3)(A).

Unallocated Employer Securities Used to Repay Loan—Possible 415(c) Violation

In addition to considerations of the exempt loan requirements of IRC section 4975(e) (7) and applicable regulations, another issue to consider is the potential of an IRC section 415(c) violation.

Earlier positions contained in PLRs issued by the IRS provided that the use of unallocated shares to make repayments on the exempt loan also constituted IRC 415 annual additions, based on a formula that considered the ratio of the cost basis in the stock in relation to the final selling price. See PLRs 9507031, 9417033, 9417032 and 9416043.

However, upon further consideration, the current position is contained in the May 18, 1998 memo from Carol Gold, Director Employee Plans, Subject: Technical Advice Request Concerning Annual Additions under Section 415 of the Internal Revenue Code.

The determination as to whether the proceeds from the sale of unallocated shares constitute earnings or annual additions is now based on:

- The specific facts and circumstances surrounding the sale, and
- Whether this sale satisfies the primary benefit requirement of Reg. § 54.4975-7 (b)(3).

Rationale of Current Position Regarding 415 and Analysis if this Issue Is Discovered upon Examination

This position is based, in part, on Reg. § 1.415-6(b)(2)(i), which provides that the Commissioner may, in appropriate cases, considering all the facts and circumstances, treat certain allocations to participant accounts as giving rise to annual additions.

If this issue is discovered on examination, the examiner should

- Analyze the facts and circumstances surrounding the sale (of employer stock in the suspense account), and

- Determine whether such sale represents a bona fide sale and whether it satisfies the primary benefit requirement.

If is determined that the sale was not a bona fide sale or that the sale did not satisfy the primary benefit requirement, consideration should be given to recharacterizing those amounts released from the suspense/encumbrance account into annual additions in accordance with Reg. § 1.415-6(b)(2)(i).

Example: Using Proceeds of Sale of Stock to Repay an Exempt Loan An ESOP was established in 1997 and contributions sufficient to make payments on the exempt loan were made in 1997, 1998 and 1999. In 2000, an unrelated third party made a tender offer to purchase all employer stock at a premium. In late 2000, pursuant to a vote of all the shareholders of the employer, all outstanding shares were sold to the unrelated third party. The plan was terminated, with the proceeds from the sale of employer stock previously held in the ESOP's suspense account used to pay off the exempt loan, and the remaining balance of the proceeds allocated as gain among all the eligible participants.

In the instant case, the examiner determined that based on the facts and circumstances surrounding the transactions:

- The premature sale of employer stock did not violate the primary benefit and exempt loan rules of IRC section 4975(e)(7),

- Nor did the remaining proceeds allocated as earnings constitute annual additions under IRC section 415(c).

Examination Steps

1) During pre-planning, refer to Schedule E to the question that inquires as to whether unallocated securities or proceeds from the sale of unallocated shares were utilized to repay any exempt loan. If yes, an explanation of the transaction should be attached to the Schedule E.

2) Request a detailed explanation from the plan sponsor and plan trustee as to the circumstances and decision making that went into the decision to sell unallocated shares in the suspense account to make payments on the exempt loan.

3) The agent should analyze the reasons behind the premature sale of unallocated stock and make a determination as to whether the facts and circumstances support a finding that the primary benefit requirement has or has not been violated. If it is determined that such sale was not for the primary benefit of participants, the loan would be nonexempt.

WHEN QUALIFYING SECURITIES CAN BE FORFEITED

Forfeiture Allocation

Plan terms should provide (and plan operation reflect) that qualifying employer securities are forfeited only after other assets. Reg. § 54.4975-11(d)(4).

If more than one class of qualifying employer securities subject to exempt loan provisions have been allocated to a participant's account, the plan must forfeit the same proportion of each such class. Reg. § 54.4975-11(d)(4).

> **Example** A participant was 80% vested in their account balance upon termination. Just prior to date of distribution, the participant's Stock Account was valued at $5,100 and the Other Investment Account was valued at $4,900. The plan administrator made a lump sum distribution to the participant in the form of $4,100 in QES and $3,900 in cash. The allocation schedules reflected forfeiture from the Stock Account of $1,000 and a forfeiture from the Other Investment Account of $1,000. This was improper. Even though the participant was only 80% vested, the entire $2,000 forfeiture should have emanated from the Other Investment Account pursuant to Reg. § 54.4975-11(d)(4), with the participant receiving their distribution in the form of $5,100 in QES and $2,900 in cash.

Examination Steps

1) The analysis of distributions made to terminated participants should include not only a determination that the proper vested amount was paid, but should also include a determination that any forfeitures comply with Reg. § 54.4975-11(d)(4).

2) Review the participant's allocation statements immediately preceding the date of plan distribution. Ensure that no forfeitures from a participant's account relate to the stock account until assets from other assets have been forfeited. If the participant's account holds more than one class of IRC section 409(l) shares, please ensure that the plan administrator applies the vesting schedule in such a manner that the same proportionate percentage of forfeiture apply to each such class of stock.

RIGHT OF FIRST REFUSAL

Right of First Refusal

Qualifying employer securities acquired with exempt loan proceeds may be, but need not be, subject to a right of first refusal. This is a post-distribution right in favor of the employer or ESOP, or both, that enables an employer to keep shares of closely-held stock which have been distributed to a participant in friendly hands and out of the hands of third parties.

When a participant receives an offer by a third party to buy nonpublicly traded securities, the participant must notify the employer or ESOP (whichever holds the right of first refusal) of the written offer by the third party to purchase the securities.

The employer, or ESOP, has 14 days to match the good faith offer (selling price and other terms) by the third party or to pay, if greater, the fair market value of the securities (and match other terms). The right of first refusal should lapse after the 14-day period. See Reg. § 54.4975-7(b)(9).

Examination Steps

1) Examine the receipt and disbursement records of the ESOP securities and the employer securities accounts to determine if either the trust or the employer has purchased securities which had previously been distributed to a participant and then reacquired from the participant under a right of first refusal provided in the plan. If the securities in question were purchased originally with the proceeds of an exempt loan, then scrutinize the transaction to ensure:

   a) The stock is not publicly traded at the time the right is exercised;

   b) The right only applies to the employer or the trust (ESOP) or both;

   c) The right was only enforceable within 14 days from the date written notice was given to the holder of the right of an offer by a third party; and

   d) The selling price and other terms are the greater of—(i) the fair market value per Reg. 54.4975-11(d)(5), or (ii) the price and terms offered by a buyer, excluding the employer and the trust (ESOP), making a good faith offer to purchase the security.

2) Secure copies of the good faith offer and, if necessary, contact third parties and the former participants to verify the above requirements. Care should be taken to comply with disclosure requirements.

SPECIAL ESOP TRANSACTIONS: SECTION 1042 TRANSFERS

Introduction

IRC section 1042 provides for nonrecognition of gain where an individual shareholder elects to sell qualified securities to an ESOP and defer any gain on such sale by reinvesting the proceeds in another domestic operating corporation. Under IRC section 1042, if a taxpayer or executor elects to sell qualified securities to an ESOP, and the taxpayer purchases qualified replacement property within the replacement period, then any long-term capital gain will be recognized only to the extent the amount realized on the sale exceeds the cost to the taxpayer of the qualified replacement property. After the sale, the ESOP must own at least 30% of:

1) Each class of outstanding stock of the corporation which issued the qualified securities, or

2) The total value of all outstanding stock of the corporation.

The taxpayer must have held the qualified securities for at least 3 years as of the time of the sale. The replacement period is the period that begins 3 months before and ends 12 months after the date of the sale of the qualified securities.

Definitions

"Qualified replacement property" is any security issued by a domestic operating corporation which:

1) Did not, for the taxable year preceding the taxable year in which such security was purchased, have passive investment income in excess of 25% of the gross receipts of the corporation, and

2) Is not the corporation which issued the qualified securities.

"Qualified securities" are employer securities, defined in IRC section 409(l), issued by a domestic corporation that has no stock readily tradable on an established securities market, and not received by the taxpayer from a qualified plan or pursuant to the exercise of a stock option.

Taxpayer's Basis in Qualified Replacement Property

The taxpayer's basis in the qualified replacement property is reduced by the amount of the gain not recognized by reason of the purchase. When the taxpayer disposes of any qualified replacement property, any gain is to be recognized to the extent of the gain that was not recognized due to the purchase of the qualified replacement property. But see the exception at IRC section 1042(e)(3).

Manner of Election

An IRC section 1042 election is not available to a C Corporation or to a shareholder of an S Corporation. See IRC section 1042(c)(1)(A) and 1042(c)(7). In addition, an IRC section 1042 election requires certain written elections to be made by the individual shareholder.

The selling shareholder's election must be made in a "statement of election" attached to the taxpayer's income tax return filed on or before the due date (including extensions) for the taxable year in which the sale occurs. This election, once made, is irrevocable.

Statement of Election

The "statement of election" shall provide that the taxpayer elects to treat such sale of securities as a sale of qualified securities under IRC section 1042. In addition, the statement should contain the following information:

1) A description of the qualified securities sold, including the type and number of shares;

2) The date of the sale of qualified securities;

3) The adjusted basis of the qualified securities;

4) The amount realized upon the sale of the qualified securities;

5) The ESOP to which the qualified securities were sold;

6) If the sale is part of a single, interrelated sale involving other taxpayers, include the name, TIN, and number of shares sold by other taxpayers; and

7) If qualified replacement property was purchased at the time of the election, attach a "statement of purchase" describing the qualified replacement property, date of purchase, cost, and declaration such property is to be the qualified replacement property. This statement must be notarized by the later of 30 days after the purchase or March 6, 1986. If the qualified replacement property was not purchased at the time of the election, this notarized statement with the required information noted above must be attached to the subsequent income tax return.

Statement of Election Must Be Verified by Consent of Corporation

In addition to the above, the taxpayer's "statement of election" must be accompanied by the verified written statement of consent of the corporation (or corporations) whose employees are covered by the ESOP (or authorized officer of the eligible worker cooperative), consenting to the application of IRC section 4978(a) (relating to excise tax on certain dispositions of employer securities prior to expiration of the three year holding period). Refer to Reg. § 1.1042-1T, Q&A 3.

IRC Section 1042—Prohibited Allocation

IRC section 409(n) states a plan must provide that the assets of an ESOP attributable to employer securities acquired by the ESOP in a sale to which IRC section 1042 applies (IRC section 1042 securities) cannot accrue for the benefit of the persons specified in IRC section 409(n). Also, the IRC section 1042 securities acquired by the ESOP cannot be allocated to the accounts of the persons specified in IRC section 409(n) directly or indirectly under any qualified plan of the employer. Any stock acquired in a sale to an ESOP will be subject to the restrictions of IRC section 409(n) if any of the sellers elect IRC section 1042 treatment with respect to their sale of employer securities. Allocations of IRC section 1042 securities cannot be made during the nonallocation period to any taxpayer who makes an IRC section 1042 election, or to anyone who is related to the taxpayer within the meaning of IRC section 267(b), unless the lineal descendant exception of IRC section 409(n)(3)(A) applies. This exception provides that an allocation of IRC section 1042 shares to a relative of the taxpayer who made the IRC section 1042 election is not prohibited if he/she is a lineal descendant of the taxpayer, and the amount allocated to all such lineal descendants during the nonallocation period does not exceed 5% of the employer securities held by the plan attributable to a sale under IRC section 1042 by a person related to such descendants (within the meaning of IRC section 267(c)(4)). The lineal descendant exception does not apply to persons prohibited from allocations because they are treated as 25% shareholders, described below.

The nonallocation period is the period beginning when the securities are sold to the plan pursuant to IRC section 1042, and ends on the later of 1) 10 years after the date of the sale, or 2) the date this indebtedness is repaid, if the plan borrowed money to purchase the IRC section 1042 securities. Allocations of IRC section 1042 securities also cannot be made, at any time, to a person who owns, after the application of IRC section 318(a), more than 25% of 1) any class of outstanding stock of the corporation which issued the employer securities or of any corporation which is a member of the same controlled group, or 2) the total value of any class of outstanding stock of such a corporation. IRC section 318(a) is applied to the "25% ownership of any class of stock" test without regard to the employee trust exception in IRC section 318(a)(2)(B)(i).

Therefore, stock owned by a qualified plan is attributed to a participant or beneficiary for purposes of (1) above. A person is treated as a 25% shareholder if he/she has the requisite ownership interest at any time in the one-year period ending on the date of the sale to the plan, or the date the securities are allocated to participants in the plan.

Example: Prohibited Allocation Individual A of ABC Corporation makes the appropriate IRC section 1042 election and sells his 15% ownership in the company to the ABC ESOP. Assume all conditions for an IRC section 1042 nonrecognition of gain are satisfied with respect to such sale, including proper elections and the acquisition of qualified replacement property. Immediately after the sale, the ESOP owns 75% of the sole outstanding stock of the corporation. In addition, Individual B owns 20% of all outstanding shares outside of the plan and owns an additional 10% of stock (allocated to his ESOP stock account). The plan contains necessary language permitting an IRC section 1042 transfer and contains the required language precluding allocation of such securities during the nonallocation period to persons as described in IRC section 409(n).

Based on the terms of the plan and the allocation restrictions of IRC 409(n), neither Individual A (i.e., the person who made the 1042 election) nor Individual B (i.e., the more than 25% shareholder) should receive any allocation of stock pertaining to the IRC section 1042 transfer. With respect to Individual B, note that Code section 409(n) requires the determination of ownership through application of IRC section 318, without regard to the employee trust exception in paragraph (2)(B)(i).

Excise Tax on Prohibited Allocations of IRC section 1042 Employer Securities

If there is a prohibited allocation in violation of IRC section 409(n) of qualified securities acquired in an IRC section 1042 sale, the securities are treated as though they have been distributed to the participant. See IRC section 409(n)(2).

An excise tax under IRC section 4979A is imposed if there is a prohibited allocation of qualified securities acquired in an IRC section 1042 sale. The tax is equal to 50% of the amount involved and is to be paid by the employer sponsoring the plan.

Early Disposition of IRC Section 1042 Employer Securities

IRC Section 4978 Excise Tax—An excise tax under IRC section 4978 can be imposed if, during the 3-year period after the date on which an ESOP acquired any qualified securities in a nonrecognition sale under IRC section 1042, the plan disposes any of the securities and:

1) The total number of shares held by the plan after the disposition is less than the total number of employer securities held immediately after the sale, or

2) Except to the extent provided in regulations, the value of qualified securities held by the plan after the disposition is less than 30% of the total value of all employer securities as of the disposition.

Determining the Amount of the Excise Tax

The excise tax will be 10% of the amount realized on the disposition if either 1) or 2). above apply. However, the amount realized for this purpose will not exceed that portion allocable to qualified securities acquired in the sale to which the nonrecognition of gain provisions applied, determined as if such securities were disposed of:

• First, from IRC section 133 securities acquired during the 3-year period ending on the date of such disposition;

• Second, from IRC section 133 securities acquired before such 3-year period unless such securities have been allocated to accounts of participants;

• Third, from IRC section 1042 securities acquired during the 3-year period ending on the date of disposition;

• Fourth, from any other employer securities.

The 3-year holding period and excise tax do not apply to any distribution of qualified securities (or sale of such securities) which is made by reason of a participant's:

1) Death or disability,

2) Separation from service for any period which results in a one-year break in service, or

3) Retirement after attaining $59\frac{1}{2}$ years of age.

EXCISE TAX NOT IMPOSED ON FOLLOWING EXCHANGES OR DISPOSITIONS

The following are exchanges or dispositions on which the excise tax is not imposed.

1) An exchange of qualified securities in an IRC section 368(a)(1) reorganization for stock of another corporation.

2) An exchange of qualified securities in an IRC section 332 liquidation into an eligible worker-owned cooperative (determined by substituting 100% for 80% everyplace it appears in IRC section 332(b)(1)).

3) The disposition of shares pursuant to a diversification election under IRC section 401(a)(28).

Examination Steps

1) Review plan terms to determine if the plan is designed to permit the purchase of employer securities under IRC section 1042 and that the plan contains the prohibited nonallocation language with respect to persons described in IRC section 409(n).

2) Verify that after the acquisition of the employer securities, the ESOP owned at least 30% of 1) each class of outstanding stock of the employer corporation, or 2) the total value of all outstanding stock of the corporation.

3) Inspect the taxpayer's income tax return for the year that the sale of the IRC section 1042 shares to the ESOP occurred. Ensure that the proper "statement of election" and notarized "statement of purchase" were attached to the taxpayer's income tax return ("statement of purchase" could be attached to either this or the subsequent income tax return). Scrutinize the particulars with respect to the shares involved in the sale and the identification of the replacement properties. In addition, review the attached verified written statement of consent of the corporation (or corporations) whose employees are covered by the ESOP (or authorized officer of the eligible worker cooperative), consenting to the application of IRC section 4978(a).

4) Check that the employer securities sold to the ESOP were held for at least 3 years by the taxpayer prior to the sale. Refer to the taxpayer's individual or corporate return, if necessary.

5) Determine whether "qualified replacement property" was purchased within the replacement period by the taxpayer. Refer to the taxpayer's individual tax return, if necessary.

6) Determine whether any IRC section 1042 securities are allocated to the persons specified in IRC section 409(n) and whether the allocations occurred during the nonallocation period. If yes, determine if the prohibited allocation is treated as a taxable distribution to the participant. See IRC section 409(n)(2). In addition, request a copy of the Form 5330 to verify that the excise tax under IRC section 4979A is properly reported (equal to 50% of the amount involved and paid by the employer sponsoring the plan).

7) Check whether any IRC section 1042 securities were disposed of within 3 years after the plan acquired them. If they were disposed of within the 3-year period, determine if an exception applies. If not, address the excise tax reportable on Form 5330 under IRC section 4978.

8) If it is determined that the conditions of IRC section 1042 were not satisfied, consideration should be given to making a referral to the appropriate exam function for the income tax adjustment.

SPECIAL ESOP TRANSACTIONS, PARTIAL INTEREST EXCLUSION

Partial Interest Exclusion

A bank, insurance company, corporation actively engaged in the business of lending money, or a regulated investment company may exclude 50% of the interest received from a securities acquisition loan. See IRC section 133(a). A securities acquisition loan may result in a lower interest rate on a loan to an ESOP.

Note: IRC section 133 was repealed by the SBJPA effective with respect to loans made after 8/20/96, (other than loans made pursuant to a written binding contract in effect before 6/10/96).

Defining a Security Acquisition Loan

A "securities acquisition loan" is:

1) A loan to a corporation (back to back loan) or ESOP (direct loan) to the extent the proceeds are used to acquire employer securities for the ESOP (see IRC section 133(b)(1)(A)), or

2) A loan to a corporation to the extent that, within 30 days, employer securities are transferred to the plan in an amount equal to the loan proceeds, provided the securities are allocable to participant accounts within one year of the loan (an immediate allocation loan). See IRC section 133(b)(1)(B).

Loan May Be Treated as a Security Acquisition Loan

A loan to a corporation which is lent to an ESOP is treated as a securities acquisition loan if:

1) The repayment terms are substantially similar to the loans terms to the corporation from the lender (a mirror loan), or

2) The loan from the corporation to the ESOP requires a more rapid repayment of interest or principal (a rapid payment loan), and allocations under the ESOP attributable to this repayment do not discriminate in favor of highly compensated employees (within the meaning of IRC section 414(q)). See IRC section 133(b)(3).

If Security Acquisition Loan Is Made after 7/10/89

If a securities acquisition loan is made after 7/10/89:

- The term of the securities acquisition loan cannot be greater than 15 years, and

- The plan must hold more than 50% of each class of outstanding stock of the employer corporation, or more than 50% of the value of all outstanding stock of the corporation. See IRC section 133(b)(6).

In addition, if the loan is made after 7/10/89, ESOP participants must be able to direct the voting of all allocated securities in the ESOP acquired through a securities acquisition loan in accordance with IRC section 409 (e)(2). The full pass-through of voting rights applies even if the securities are not a registration-type class of securities (i.e., are closely held). See IRC section 133(b)(7).

Excludable Period during which the Partial Interest Exclusion Is Available

The excludable period during which the partial interest exclusion is available is, in general, the 7-year period beginning on the date of the loan for any original securities acquisition loan (i.e., the direct loan or back to back loan described at IRC section 133(b)(1)(A) or immediate allocation loan described at IRC section 133(b)(1)(B)).

However, if the term of an original acquisition loan described at IRC section 133 (b)(1)(A) is greater than 7 years, the excludable period is the term of the loan (which cannot be greater than 15 years).

The excludable period for a rapid payment loan described at IRC section 133(b) (3)(B) or an immediate allocation loan described at IRC section 133(b)(1)(B) cannot be greater than 7 years.

SPECIAL ESOP TRANSACTION, SECTION 133 EXCISE TAX

IRC Section 133 Excise Tax

An excise tax is imposed if a taxable event occurs with respect to securities acquired by an ESOP in an IRC 133 transaction. See IRC section 4978B. A taxable event subject to the excise tax occurs where there is any disposition of employer securities acquired in a IRC section 133 transaction within 3 years of their acquisition if:

1) The total number of employer securities held by the plan after the disposition is less than the total number of employer securities held after the acquisition, or

2) Except to the extent provided in regulations, the value of the employer securities held by the plan after the disposition is 50% or less of the total value of all employer securities at the time of the disposition. A taxable event subject to the excise tax also occurs if there is a disposition of employer securities acquired in an IRC section 133 transaction to which a. and b. above do not apply if the disposition occurs before the securities are allocated to participant accounts, and the proceeds of the disposition are not allocated.

Determining the Excise Tax

The excise tax is equal to 10% of the amount realized on the disposition to the extent allocable to IRC 133 securities, determined as if such securities were disposed of:

- First, from IRC section 133 securities acquired during the 3-year period ending with disposition, beginning with the securities first so acquired;

- Second, from IRC section 133 securities acquired prior to the 3-year period, unless such securities (or proceeds from their disposition) have been allocated to participant accounts;

- Third, from IRC section 1042 securities acquired during the 3 year period ending on the date of the disposition, beginning with the securities first so acquired; and

- Fourth, from any other employer securities.

Section 133 Excise Tax Does Not Apply to the Following

- The excise tax does not apply to a distribution of IRC section 133 securities which is made due to a participant's:

    1) Death or disability,

    2) Separation from service for a period which results in a one-year break in service, or

    3) Retirement after attaining $59^1/_2$ years of age.

- The excise tax does not apply to an exchange of IRC section 133 securities in a corporate liquidation under IRC section 4978(d)(3) involving an eligible worker-owned cooperative.

- The disposition of IRC section 133 securities pursuant to a diversification election under IRC section 401(a)(28) will also not be treated as a disposition.

- An exchange of IRC section 133 securities for employer securities of another corporation pursuant to an IRC section 368(a)(1) reorganization will not be treated as a disposition.

- A forced disposition of IRC section 133 securities due to operation of a State law will not be treated as a disposition if the securities were regularly traded on an established securities market at the time they were acquired by the plan.

Examination Steps

1) Look at the applicable questions on Schedule E of Form 5500, ESOP Annual Information, to determine whether the plan has engaged in a securities acquisition loan under IRC section 133. If yes, complete the remaining examination steps in this section.

2) Determine whether the loan is from a qualified lender.

3) Check that the loan qualifies as a securities acquisition loan.

4) For post 7/10/89 loans, determine whether the ESOP held 50% of the stock, or 50% of the value of the stock, after the securities acquisition loan.

5) For post 7/10/89 loans, make sure full pass-through voting rights apply to IRC section 133 securities that have been allocated.

6) Determine whether the partial interest rate exclusion of the lender is available for a period not in excess of the excludable period. This is an item for referral to a corporate tax examiner.

7) Determine whether any IRC section 133 securities were disposed of in a taxable event. If yes, find out whether any of the exceptions to the excise tax apply.

SPECIAL ESOP TRANSACTION—SECTION 4980 EXCEPTION

IRC Section 4980 Exception

There was an exception to the tax on the amount of any employer reversion from a qualified plan to the extent any of the reversion is transferred to an ESOP. IRC section 4980(c)(3). This exception applied to any amount transferred:

1) After 3/31/85, and before 1/1/89, or

2) After 12/31/88, pursuant to a termination which occurs after 3/31/85, and before 1/1/89.

Within 90 days after the transfer (or longer period as the Secretary may prescribe), the amount transferred, and the income therein, must be invested in employer securities or used to repay an ESOP loan that was used to purchase employer securities.

The amount allocated to participant accounts in the year of the transfer cannot be less than the lesser of the maximum allowable under IRC section 415 or 1/8 of the amount attributable to the securities acquired.

Any portion of the transferred amount which is not allocated to participant accounts in the year of the transfer must be credited to a suspense account (IRC section 4980 suspense account) and allocated from that account to the accounts of participants ratably over a period not greater than seven years. Additional employer contributions to an ESOP cannot be made until the allocation of such amount. When amounts are allocated to participant accounts from the IRC 4980 suspense account, they are treated as employer contributions for IRC section 415 purposes, except the annual addition will not exceed the value of the securities when they were placed in the IRC section 4980 suspense account.

At least half of the participants in the qualified plan from which the reversion is being transferred must be ESOP participants as of the close of the first plan year in which the allocation is required.

Examination Steps

1) Check whether the ESOP contains an IRC section 4980 suspense account. If yes, go on to the other examination steps in this section.

2) Make sure the transfer of assets to the IRC section 4980 suspense account took place: a) After 3/31/85, and before 1/1/89; or b) After 12/31/88, due to a plan termination after 3/31/85 and before 1/1/89. There is no exception to the reversion tax for amounts transferred to an ESOP after these dates.

3) Check that the transferred assets were used within 90 days (or longer, if an extension was granted) to purchase employer securities or to repay a loan.

4) Make sure amounts in the IRC section 4980 suspense account are allocated over a period not greater than seven years.

5) If (2), (3) or (4) are not met, impose the excise tax under IRC section 4980(a) on the amount transferred to the ESOP.

SPECIAL ESOP TRANSACTIONS—SECTION 664(G) TRANSFERS

IRC Section 664(g)—Qualified Gratuitous Transfers

IRC section 664(g) contains a special rule permitting the qualified gratuitous transfer of qualified employer securities to an ESOP provided that certain conditions are met. The qualified employer securities transferred to the ESOP must relate to securities that had previously passed from a decedent dying before 1/1/99 to a charitable remainder annuity trust or charitable remainder unitrust.

Among the requirements contained in IRC section 664(g) is that the plan must provide specific plan language pertaining to

- The qualified gratuitous transfer and
- The handling of such stock, and
- In addition, another requirement is that immediately after such transfer, the plan owns at least 60 percent of the corporation.

Refer to IRC section 664(g) for additional rules, including the allocation and suspense account requirements.

SUBCHAPTER S CORPORATION ESOps

Sub S ESOP Basics

Effective for tax years after 12/31/97, the Small Business Job Protection Act of 1996 (SBJPA) and the Taxpayer Relief Act of 1997 (TRA '97) made amendments that permitted Sub S Corporations to adopt and sponsor ESOPs. See IRC section 1361(c)(6). The ESOP *is treated as a single shareholder* for purposes of the 75-shareholder rule. In conjunction with this law change, certain special rules apply to Sub S ESOPs.

Normally, the flow-through of a Sub S Corporation's income to the ESOP would have constituted unrelated business income (UBI) and would be subject to unrelated business tax income (UBIT). TRA '97 eliminated the UBI provision, with the effect that Sub S corporate income, to the extent owned by the ESOP, is not currently taxable, nor is the income subject to UBIT.

An ESOP is required to adjust its basis in Sub S Corporation stock under IRC section 1367(a) for the ESOP's pro rata share of the corporation's item. Upon the distribution of the Sub S Corporation stock by an ESOP to a participant, the stock's net unrealized appreciation under IRC section 402(e)(4) is determined using the ESOP's adjusted basis in the stock. See, Revenue Ruling 2003-27, 2003-11 I.R.B. (March 17, 2003).

Due to the statutory limits on the number of shareholders permitted for a Sub S Corporation, IRC section 409(h) was modified to allow cash distributions in lieu of the right to demand distribution from the ESOP in the form of qualifying employer securities. See IRC section 409(h)(2)(B)(ii). An ESOP maintained by a Sub S Corporation may permit distributions of employer securities, but is not required to do so.

IRA Cannot Be a Sub S Shareholder, but an Exception Applies if Certain Requirements Are Satisfied

Although an IRA is not a permissible Sub S Corporation shareholder, a Sub S Corporation's S election will not be treated as terminated when an ESOP distributes stock of that corporation to a participant's IRA in a direct rollover provided that:

1) The terms of the ESOP require that the Sub S Corporation repurchase its stock immediately upon the ESOP's distribution of the stock to an IRA;

2) The Sub S Corporation actually repurchases the Sub S Corporation stock contemporaneously with, and effective on the same day as the distribution; and

3) No income (including tax-exempt income), loss, deduction, or credit attributable to the distributed Sub S Corporation stock under IRC section 1366 is allocated to the participant's IRA.

See Revenue Procedure 2003-23, 2003-11 I.R.B. (March 17, 2003).

Section 4975(f)

IRC section 4975(f) relates to the general prohibition involving transactions of a shareholder-employee, a member of their family or a corporation in which a shareholder-employee owns 50% or more interest with respect to the sale of qualifying employer securities. IRC 4975(f)(6) was amended to repeal this prohibited transaction with respect to the sale of qualified employer securities to an ESOP.

Several ESOP Perks Not Available for Sub S ESOPs

Even with the law change permitting the sponsorship and maintenance of an ESOP by a Sub S Corporation, several ESOP perks are not available for Sub S ESOPs. Unlike a C Corp ESOP, a Sub S ESOP is not permitted to utilize the following special ESOP provisions:

1) The IRC section 404(k) applicable dividend deduction.

2) The expanded IRC section 415(c)(6) increased limit (e.g., the $\frac{1}{3}$ HCE rule that permits certain forfeitures and interest payments to be disregarded as annual addition for purposes of the IRC section 415(c) limit).

3) The expanded IRC section 404(a)(9) deduction limit of 25% (an ESOP (stock bonus only plan) maintained by a Sub S Corp is limited to the 15% limit). However, a combination stock bonus/money purchase limit could still take advantage of the 25% limit under IRC sections 404(a)(1) and 404(j).

4) The special exception for the expanded deduction of contributions applied toward interest payments for an exempt loan in an ESOP under IRC section 404(a)(9).

5) To utilize dividends paid on the Sub S Corporation's stock to make payments on an exempt loan with respect to allocated shares. Dividends paid on allocated shares, if used to make payments on an exempt loan, will fail to satisfy the prohibited transaction exception under IRC section 4975(d)(3). See Reg. section

54.4975-7(b)-5 and PLR 199938052. However, dividends paid on unallocated shares would be treated as earnings on the collateral and therefore could be used to service the exempt loan debt (but would still not be deductible under IRC section 404(k) for a Sub S ESOP).

6) The tax deferral of gains received by a shareholder on the sale of qualified securities to an ESOP (an IRC section 1042 transfer).

See IRC section 1042(c)(1)(A), which limits the definition of qualified securities for purposes of the nonrecognition of gain treatment to C Corporations.

Several ESOP Perks Not Available for Sub S ESOPs
EGTRRA Passed Additional Legislation

EGTRRA passed additional legislation to eliminate a perceived abuse by certain closely held Sub S ESOPs, generally effective for plan years effective after 12/31/04, but effective 3/14/01 for newly established Sub S ESOPs. This will be covered later in the chapter.

Examination Steps

1) Determine the type of entity that has adopted the ESOP under examination. If adopted by an electing Sub S Corporation, apply the statutory requirements relevant to Sub S ESOPs. In addition, confirm whether a valid existing ESOP was adopted and effective on or before March 14, 2001. Refer to the next section if an S Corporation makes an "S" election after March 14, 2001 or if the ESOP is started after March 14, 2001, in which event the new anti-abuse provisions of EGTRRA will go into effect. This is covered in the next section.

2) If dividends were declared and issued for the year under audit, confirm that no deduction was taken under IRC section 404(k).

3) Review the allocations made and perform an analysis of the IRC 415(c) limits. Verify that the Sub S ESOP did not attempt to utilize the IRC section 415(c)(6) exception, relating to disregard of certain forfeitures and interest payments as annual additions.

4) Verify that the expanded IRC section 404(a)(9) deduction limit of 25% is not utilized by the S Corporation. A stock bonus ESOP should be limited to the 15% limit, for years prior to January 1, 2002.

5) If an exempt loan is utilized, verify that the expanded deduction of contributions applied toward interest payments per IRC 404(a)(9) is not utilized.

6) If an exempt loan is utilized, confirm that dividends paid on allocated shares is not used to service the exempt loan debt.

7) Verify that no IRC 1042 transfers have been made to the Sub S ESOP.

8) Carefully scrutinize any Sub S ESOP, where all, or substantially all outstanding stock of the Sub S, is owned by the ESOP. Please conduct detailed interviews with the taxpayer and/or representative. The operation of the business, business

customers and related corporations for which they perform services should be discussed. If it is determined that this Sub S entity is a organization whose principal business is performing, on a regular and continuing basis, management functions for another organization (or for 1 organization and other related organizations), additional development may be needed. It is possible that an affiliated service group may exist under IRC section 414(m)(5).

PROHIBITED ALLOCATIONS IN SUB S Esops

Introduction

On June 7, 2001, the Economic Growth and Tax Relief Reconciliation Act (EGTRRA) of 2001 amended IRC section 409 by adding subsection (p). This is a very complex anti-abuse provision. The intent of this law change was to prevent perceived abuse from closely held ESOPs with few employees that established ESOPs to provide a shelter for income generated by the Subchapter S Corporations.

Basically, the **anti-abuse provisions** are triggered if a **"disqualified person"** receives a **"prohibited allocation"** during a **"nonallocation year"** in a Sub S ESOP. There are three tax costs if the anti-abuse rules are triggered. They are:

1) The "disqualified person" will be deemed to have received the amount of allocated stock in the "prohibited allocation" and must include the value of the allocated stock in taxable income. See IRC section 409(p)(2)(A).

2) An excise tax is imposed on the S corporation equal to 50% of the amount involved in the "prohibited allocation" (subject to a special rule in the case of the first "nonallocation year"). See IRC section 4979A.

3) An excise tax is imposed on the S corporation with respect to any "synthetic equity" owned by a "disqualified person." See IRC Section 4979A.

Defining a Disqualified Person and Deemed Shareholder Group

A disqualified person is one who is either:

1) A member of a "deemed 20% shareholder group" or

2) A "deemed 10% shareholder."

A person is a member of a "deemed 20% shareholder group" if the number of "deemed-owned shares" of the person and the person's family is at least 20% of the total S corporation shares held by the ESOP.

Defining "Deemed Owned Shares"

The term "deemed-owned shares" is the sum of:

1) Stock allocated to an account of an individual by the ESOP and

2) An individual's share of unallocated stock held by the ESOP. The impact of the 2nd part of this definition is important. Essentially, for purposes of this

definition, a participant is considered owning their own proportionate share of unallocated qualified employer securities held in the leverage ESOP's suspense account. IRC section 409(p)(4)(C)(ii) provides that a person's share of unallocated S corporation stock held by such plan is the amount of the unallocated stock which would be allocated to such person if the unallocated stock were allocated to all participants in the same proportions as the most recent stock allocation under the plan.

Defining a Deemed 10% Shareholder

A person is a "deemed 10% shareholder" if the person is not a member of a "deemed 20% shareholder group" and the number of the person's "deemed owned shares" is at least 10% of the total S corporation shares held by the ESOP.

318 Attribution Rules Apply

For purposes of determining ownership, the attribution rules of IRC section 318 apply, modified with the exception that the members of an individual's family shall include members of the family described in IRC section 409(p)(4)(D). See IRC section 409(p)(3)(B). Family members will include the (i) individual's spouse, (ii) ancestors or lineal descendant of the individual or the individual's spouse, (iii) brother or sister of the individual or the individual's spouse and any lineal descendant of the brother or sister, and (iv) the spouse of any individual described in (ii) or (iii).

Defining Nonallocation Year

The definition of a "nonallocation year" is any ESOP plan year where, at any time during the year, "disqualified persons" own directly or through attribution, 50% of the number of outstanding shares of the S corporation. The attribution rules of § 318 apply in this computation except there are some modifications that will not be addressed here. See IRC section 409(p)(3)(B) for the attribution rules.

Deemed Owned Shares in ESOP Is Treated as Held by Individual

In arriving at the 50% test, the "deemed-owned shares" held in the ESOP are treated as held by the individual that is deemed to own them.

Prohibited Allocation Defined

A "prohibited allocation" is one that violates the requirement that, during a "nonallocation year," no portion of the assets of the ESOP may be accrued (or be allocated directly or indirectly under any qualified plan of the S corporation) for the benefit or any "disqualified person." According to the legislative history, a "prohibited allocation" occurs if income on S corporation stock held by an ESOP is allocated to the account of a "disqualified person."

Example A newly established ESOP is adopted by a Sub S Corporation on November 30, 2001 and is immediately subject to the new EGTRRA requirements related to the prohibited allocations under IRC section 409(p). The ESOP owns all outstanding shares of the Sub S Corporation (totaling 2100 shares). These shares were acquired through the use of an exempt loan in December 2001.

For the plan year ended December 31, 2001, only three participants were eligible to receive allocations. Participants A, B & C each received an allocation of 100 shares of stock for the plan year ended December 31, 2001. The remaining 1800 shares are maintained in the ESOP suspense account (pending subsequent years' contributions and resultant release from suspense).

For purposes of IRC section 409(p), Participants A, B and C are considered owning both the shares allocated to their accounts and their proportionate share of stock in the unallocated suspense account (i.e., treat all unallocated stock as though fully allocated in such year to eligible participants). As such, Participants A, B and C each have "deemed owned shares" of 700 shares for the plan year ended December 31, 2001.

Accordingly, all three participants are "disqualified persons" by reason of being "deemed 10% shareholders." Next, as "disqualified persons" own at least 50% of all outstanding shares, the prohibited allocation rules and restrictions of IRC sections 409(p) and 4979A apply. The 100 shares allocated to each participant are subject to inclusion as taxable income per IRC section 409(p)(2)(A).

In addition, any Sub S income that flows through to the ESOP and is attributable to such shares and allocated to such participants, is also taxable to the participants. In addition, the Sub S Corporation is liable for the 50% excise tax under IRC section 4979A.

Other Nonallocation Situations—Including Synthetic Equity

In addition, IRC section 409(p)(7)(B) states that the Secretary may, by regulation or other guidance, provide that a nonallocation year occurs in any case in which the principal purpose of the ownership structure constitutes an avoidance or evasion of the prohibited allocation rules.

Special rules also apply to "synthetic equity" as to the treatment of any person as a "disqualified person" and as to the treatment of any year as a "nonallocation year."

The term "synthetic equity" means any stock option, warrant, restricted stock, deferred issuance stock right, or similar interest or right that gives the holder the right to acquire or receive stock of the S corporation in the future. Except to the extent provided in regulations, synthetic equity also includes a stock appreciation right, phantom stock unit, or similar right to a future cash payment based on the value of such stock or appreciation in such value.

EFFECTIVE DATES FOR ESOPs HOLDING STOCK IN S CORPORATIONS

Effective Dates of IRC Sections 409(p) and 4979A

These provisions enact very strict penalties on ESOPs holding stock in closely held S corporations. Therefore the effective date is very important.

The general effective date is for ESOP years that begin after 12-31-04. This allows the current S corporation ESOP's time to restructure the stock ownership. *The special effective date is for ESOP years ending after 3-14-01.* The special effective date applies to corporation that converted to S status or established ESOP's after 3-14-01. In these situations the provisions apply to plan years ending after 3-14-01. Therefore if an S corporation makes an election after 3-14-01 or the ESOP is started after 3-14-01, the ESOP will always be subject to the new anti-abuse legislation.

Special Ruling for S Corporations Established after 3-14-01

There is an interesting ruling dealing with S corporations established after 3-14-01. In Notice 2002-2, Question 15, it was held that the S election had to be filed by 3-14-01 in order to meet the general effective date. Therefore, if a C corporation that has an ESOP elects S corporation status on 3-15-01, effective as of 1-1-01, it will not meet the requirement that it had an S election in effect on 3-14-01.

Rev. Rul. 2003-6

Refer to Revenue Ruling 2003-6, 2003-3 I.R.B. 286, January 21, 2003, which provides guidance with respect to certain arrangements involving the establishment of ESOPs holding securities in Sub S Corporations that the Service determined will not be considered timely established on or before March 14, 2001.

In effect, this ruling provides that the delayed effective date for IRC section 409(p) does not apply in certain circumstances. The facts of this revenue ruling pertain to A, a person in the business of providing advice to other companies or individuals, who arranges for the establishment of a number of S Corporations that have no substantial assets or business and the formation of ESOPs for each of these corporations on or before March 14, 2001. Employees of A are initially covered by these ESOPs, but there is no reasonable expectation that these individuals will accrue more than insubstantial benefits under these plans or more than an insubstantial share in the ownership of the S Corporation. The Sub S Corporations are then marketed to other taxpayers, along with the associated ESOPs, after March 14, 2001.

The Service's position is that for purposes of IRC section 409(p), these ESOPs are not considered established on or before March 14, 2001 and therefore, are not entitled to the delayed 2005 effective date. The Service is developing further guidance to address other abusive arrangements involving Sub S Corporations. See Revenue Ruling 2003-6.

Example 1 A Sub S Corporation does not elect Sub S status until July 1, 2001. As this date is later than the special effective date of March 14, 2001, the ESOP maintained by this Sub S Corporation is immediately subject to the new anti-abuse provisions of IRC sections 409(p) and 4979A. An analysis of stock ownership will be necessary to determine if any plan participants are "disqualified persons" subject to the prohibited allocation requirements.

Example 2 An examiner is assigned an ESOP adopted by a Sub S Corporation that was created in December 2000 and that adopted an ESOP on January 5, 2001, with an effective date of January 1, 2001. The Sub S only employs two persons, with the ESOP covering both. The company has the unusual name of "Working Woman Five." Based on this date, the ESOP appears to eligible for the general effective date for IRC sections 409(p) and 4979A for years beginning after December 31, 2004. However, based on interviews and further analysis, the examiner determined that both the Sub S Corporation and the ESOP were originally established by a pension practitioner. Subsequent to March 14, 2001, ownership of both the S Corporation (and the ESOP) was transferred to the current plan sponsor. Based on this information, the agent should apply the special effective date of March 14, 2001, with respect to the potential application of IRC sections 409(p) and 4979A, based on Revenue Ruling 2003-6.

EXAMINATION STEPS—SUB S CORPORATION

Examination Steps

1) Determine the type of entity that sponsored the ESOP under examination. If adopted by an electing Sub S Corporation, ascertain whether a valid existing ESOP was adopted and effective on or before March 14, 2001. In addition, confirm that a valid "S" election was made on or before March 14, 2001.

2) Before accepting the validity of a timely March 14, 2001 adoption, the agent should consider the potential that the scenario contained in Revenue Ruling 2003-6 applies. If based on interview(s) and/or other case development, it appears that abusive step transactions such as those covered by Revenue Ruling 2003-6 apply, then the agent should pursue the earlier effective date of plan years ending after March 14, 2001, with respect to IRC sections 409(p) and 4979A.

3) If the Sub S ESOP was timely adopted and effective on or before March 14, 2001, the general effective date of plan years beginning after December 31, 2004 will apply with respect to IRC sections 409(p) and 4979A.

4) If not timely adopted by March 14, 2001, the agent should apply IRC 409(p) and 4979A, effective for plan years ending after March 14, 2001.

5) If effective for the year under examination, the agent should analyze the ownership percentages of stock owned by the ESOP to determine if the tax sanctions of IRC section 409(p) and 4979A apply. This analysis should include a determination as to whether any participant(s) in the plan meet the definition of a "deemed 10% shareholder," a "deemed 20% shareholder group" and "disqualified person." The analysis should include consideration of the attribution rules of IRC section 318 and the definition of family member of IRC section 409(p)(4) (D). If exempt loans are involved, the agent should consider such stock as part of a participant's "deemed-owned shares."

6) If during any "nonallocation year," disqualified persons own, directly or through attribution, 50% of the outstanding shares of the S Corporation, then the agent

should apply the new anti-abuse provisions of EGTRRA under IRC sections 409(p) and 4979A. Discrepancy adjustments under IRC section 409(p) should be made to the income tax return of the individual "disqualified person," and Forms 5330 should be picked up with respect to the IRC section 4979A excise tax imposed on the S Corporation.

SUMMARY

The lesson covered various form and operational requirements of both leveraged and nonleveraged ESOPs. This lesson described the requirements that an ESOP must satisfy to qualify under IRC sections 401(a), 409 and 4975(e)(7), including the rules related to the use and handling of exempt loans. In addition, this lesson also covered certain special rules related to ESOPs, such as the special IRC section 404 deduction rules, IRC section 1042 transfers, the partial interest exclusion and Sub S ESOPs. At the conclusion of this lesson, you should have learned:

1) How to determine whether the ESOP operated in a qualified manner.

2) To verify that the ESOP is properly invested in IRC section 409(l) qualifying employer securities.

3) To verify that the appropriate distributions were made to participants and beneficiaries, both as to the form and timeliness.

4) For nonpublicly traded stock, how to ascertain that participants were given the appropriate post-distribution rights involving "put" options with respect to distributions of stock.

5) How to determine whether the stock transactions involving the ESOP properly valued the stock at fair market value.

6) How to determine the applicable deductible limits for contributions to both leveraged and nonleveraged ESOPs, including special rules related to IRC section 404(k) applicable dividends.

7) How to consider the impact of a premature sale of QES in the suspense account to pay off the exempt loan, by considering the facts and circumstances surrounding such decision.

8) To determine whether certain allocations in an ESOP sponsored by a Sub S Corporation were subject to the new prohibited allocation requirements with respect to certain disqualified persons.

Notes

Chapter 1

1. ERISA Act Sec. 3(14).
2. ERISA Act Sec. 3(16)(B).
3. ERISA Act Sec. 406.
4. IRC Sec. 4975.
5. ERISA Act Sec. 407(d)(5).
6. ERISA Act Sec. 407(d)(3).
7. ERISA Act Sec. 408(e).
8. ERISA Act Sec. 407(d)(1).
9. ERISA Act Sec.407(d)(6).
10. ERISA Act Sec. 404(a)(2)
11. ERISA Act Sec. 408(b)(3).
12. IRC Sec. 404(k).
13. IRC Sec. 512(e).
14. IRC Sec. 512(e)(3).

Chapter 3

1. Marshall Stevens Valuation Consulting, "What an ESOP Can Do for Your Clients," *www.marshall-stevens.com/esop_can_do.htm* (June 2004) (with alterations by the author of this book).
2. Gilbert, Ronald J., "The ESOP Decision," *ESOP Services, Inc., Employee Stock Owner-ship Plans, www.esopservices.com/decision.htm* (June 2004).
3. *See* note 2.
4. NCEO, "How Small Is Too Small for an ESOP?" *www.nceo.org* (June 2004).
5. *Id.*

Chapter 4

1. *Black's Law Dictionary,* 5th edition, p. 13.
2. *Reich v. Valley National Bank of Arizona,* 837 F. Supp. 1259, (SDNY 1993).
3. *Dairy Fresh Corporation v. Poole* [The "Dairy Fresh" Case], 108 F. Supp. 2d 1344 (2000).

4. "To ESOP or Not to ESOP?" *The Tax Advisor* (May 2004), p. 271.
5. *Delta Star v. Patton,* 76 F. Supp. 2d 617 (W.D. Pa. 1999).
6. Ron J. Lint, "Repurchase Liability Funding for ESOPs (The Requirements, The Choices)," unpublished manuscript (Estes Park, CO, 2003).
7. *Id.*
8. Riva T. Johnson and David R. Johanson, "Comprehensive Update on the Enron Corporation Litigation: Legal Update," *ESOP Report* (Washington, DC, May, 2004).
9. *Id.*
10. *Moench v. Robertson,* 62 F (3rd Cir. 1995).
11. John A. Kober, *Tax Management Compensation Planning Journal,* vol. 30, no. 6 (June 7, 2002), p. 161.
12. Riva T. Johnson and David R. Johanson, "Comprehensive Update on the Enron Corporation Litigation: Legal Update," *ESOP Report* (Washington, DC: May, 2004).
13. ERISA Act Sec. 404(a).

Chapter 6

1. Michael Keeling, The ESOP Association, "Responding to Enron: Resources for Employee-Ownership Companies," *Ownership Associates, Inc., Notable Quotations* (May 11, 2004), www.ownershipassociates.com/enron3.shtm.
2. Ownership Associates, *Making an ESOP Work for You* (May 2004), www.ownership-associates.com.
3. *Id.*
4. Douglas Kruse, *Testimony before the Subcommittee on Employer-Employee Relations Committee on Education and the Workforce,* U.S. House of Representatives, February 13, 2002, www.ownershipassociates.com/kruse.shtm.
5. Douglas Kruse and Joseph Blasi, "Rutgers Study, 2000," www.nceo.org.
6. Peter A. Kardas, Adria L. Scharf, and Kim Keogh, "Wealth and Income Consequences of Employee Ownership: A Comparative Study from Washington State," *Journal of Employee Ownership Law and Finance,* vol. 10, no. 4 (1998), pp. 3–52.
7. Margaret Blair, Douglas Kruse, and Joseph Blasi, "Is Employee Ownership an Unstable Form? Or a Stabilizing Force?" in Thomas Kochan and Margaret Blair, eds., *Corporation and Human Capital* (Washington, DC: The Brookings Institute, 2000).
8. Kruse and Blasi, 2000.
9. Data from Margaret M. Blair, Douglas L. Kruse, and Joseph R. Blasi, "Employee Ownership: An Unstable Form or a Stabilizing Force?" Georgetown University Law Center Working Paper No. 142146, 246.
10. Data from the General Social Survey from the National Opinion Research Center.
11. NCEO, Travel and Transport, Inc., ESOP CASE STUDY, *NCEO Employee Ownership Report,* vol. 23, no. 3 (May/June 2003), p. 6.
12. F.W. Rudmin and J. W. Berry, "Semantics of Ownership: A Free-Recall Study of Property," *The Psychological Record,* vol. 37 (1987), 257.
13. Loren Rogers, "What Do Employee Owners *Really* Think About Ownership?" *Ownership Associates, Inc.* [originally published in January 1999, by the National Center for Employee Ownership].

14. Kevin Ruble, and Juli Baldwin, The Pearl Group, LLC, "Help! Our Ownership Culture Is Broken!" *NCEO Employee Ownership Report,* vol. 22, no. 2 (March/April 2002), p. 5.

15. *Id.*

16. NCEO, "Keeping Things Sweet at Sara Lee," *NCEO Employee Ownership Report,* vol. 22, no. 3 (May/June 2003), p. 4.

Chapter 8

1. 29 C.F.R. § 2509.75-9.

2. I.R.C § 401(a)(28)(C).

3. I.R.C. § 170 (a)(1).

4. Treas. Reg. § 1.170A–13(c)(5).

5. *Capital City Excavating Co., Inc. v. Commissioner,* T.C. Memo 1984-193. For a review, see Leon E. Irish, Ronald L. Ludwig, and Ronald Rizzo, *Prentice Hall Law & Business Update 1990: Employee Stock Ownership Plans* (1990), p. 208.

6. Revenue Ruling 59-60.

Chapter 10

1. Department of Labor, Proposed Regulation 2510.3-18(b) and Proposed 29 C.F.R. 2510.3-18, "Definition of Adequate Consideration, published in the *Federal Register* on May 7, 1988 at 53 FR 17632.

2. William W. Merten and Robert S. Socol, "Using ESOPs and Stock-Based Compensation to Facilitate Liquidity, Business Succession Planning, Intergenerational Wealth Transfers, and Employee Corporate Ownership," *Insights Quarterly Journal* (June 7, 2004), *www.willametteinsights.com/99/ESOPsandstockbased compentation.html.*

Chapter 12

1. Internal Revenue Bulletin 2004-7, February 17, 2004.

2. I.R.S. § 401(a)(9) and (14).

3. I.R.S. § 409(o).

4. I.R.S. § 409(h).

5. *Lemishow v. Commissioner,* 110 T.C. No. 11, (1998).

6. "Managing Repurchase Obligations in an S Corporation ESOP," *NCEO Employee Ownership Report* (March/April 2002), p. 8.

7. *Id.*

8. *See* note 2.

9. *See* note 2.

Chapter 13

1. Proposed Regulation Relating to the Definition of Adequate Consideration, 29 CFR Part 2510.

Chapter 14

1. Shannon Pratt, *Valuing a Business: The Analysis and Appraisal of Closely Held Companies,* 2nd ed. (Homewood, IL: Dow-Jones-Irwin, 1989), p. 398.

2. Department of Labor Proposed Regulation Relating to Adequate Consideration, 29 CFR 2510, (1988).
3. Andy Fedders, U.S. Internal Revenue Service, speech delivered at the Ohio ESOP Association Meeting, Columbus, Ohio, November 19, 1993.
4. Department of Labor, Proposed Regulation 2510.3-18(b), Proposed 29 C.F.R. 2510.3-18, "Definition of Adequate Consideration, *Federal Register* 53 FR 17632 (May 7, 1988).
5. Kleinrock Publishing, Kleinrock Tax Service Section 127.5, ESOPs, (a)(3), Voting Rights, p. 3 (2004).
6. Preamble to Section 2550.404c-1, 57 FR 46927 (October 13, 1992).
7. Revenue Ruling 95-57.
8. NCEO, "The Rights of ESOP Participants" (June 2004), *www.nceo.org/library/rights.html.*
9. "Critical Numbers," *NCEO Employee Ownership Report,* vol. 22, no. 6 (November/ December 2003), p. 7.

Chapter 15

1. Steven Linder, Internal Revenue Service Notice 2002-2, A-11, p. 7.
2. *Id.*
3. Internal Revenue Service Notice 2004-39, October 1, 2004.

Chapter 16

1. *The Estate of Blount v. Commissioner,* TC Memo 2004-116.

Chapter 17

1. Christopher Z. Mercer, "Quantitative Marketability Discount Methodology," *The Journal of Business Valuation* (1995): Proceedings of the Third Joint Business Valuation Conference of the Canadian Institute of Chartered Business Valuators and the American Society of Appraisers, pp. 201–208. The conference was held November 3–4, 1994, in San Diego, California. A follow-up presentation was also given at the 14th Annual Advanced Business Valuation Conference of the American Society of Appraisers, November 2, 1995, Boston, Massachusetts.

Chapter 18

1. Steven J. Hayes, "Writing Quotes/Quotes about Writing from Basic Quotations," *Basic Quotations* (2004) in *Basics 4 Life, www.basicquotations.com/index.php?cid=319.*
2. Tax Reform Act of 1986.
3. IRM 4.72.4.2.12.2 (8-13-2001) and IRC 401(a)28(C) and IRC 170(a)(1).
4. Regs. Sec. 54-4975-11(d)(5) and IRM 4.72.8.7.1.
5. The Department proposed regulations under section 3(18)(B) on May 17, 1988 (53 Fed. Reg. 17632); no final regulation has been published to date.
6. Rev. Rul. 59-60, Section 3.01, 1959-1 C.B. 237.
7. Internal Revenue Service Business Valuation Standards, Sections 4.1.1 and 4.1.2 Reporting Guidelines, p. 8.

8. Department of Labor. PART 2510 of Chapter XXV of Title of the Code of Federal Regulations [AMENDED]. The authority for Part 2510 is revised to read as follows: Authority: Sec. 3(2), 111(c), 505, Pub. L. 93-406, 88 Stat. 852, 894, (29 USC 1002(2), 1031, 1135); Secretary of Labor's Order No. 27-74, 1-86, 1-87, and Labor Management Services Administration Order No. 2-6. Section 2510.3-18 is also issued under sec. 3(18) of the Act (29 USC 1003(18)) and Sections 8477(a)(2)(B) and (f) of FERSA (5 USC 8477).

9. Rev. Proc. 66-49, Section 2.02(4).

10. Rev. Rul. 59-60 was modified by Rev. Rul. 65-193 (1965-2 C.B. 370) regarding the valuation of tangible and intangible corporate assets. The provisions of Rev. Rul. 59-60, as modified, were extended to the valuation of corporate securities for income and other tax purposes by Rev. Rul. 68-609 (1968-2 C.B. 327). In addition, Rev. Rul. 77-287 (1977-2 C.B. 319) amplified Rev. Rul. 59-60 by indicating the ways in which the factors listed in Rev. Rul. 59-60 should be applied when valuing restricted securities.

11. Department of Labor. PART 2510 of Chapter XXV of Title of the Code of Federal Regulations [AMENDED] The authority for Part 2510 is revised to read as follows: Authority: Sec. 3(2), 111(c), 505, Pub. L. 93-406, 88 Stat. 852, 894, (29 USC 1002(2), 1031, 1135); Secretary of Labor's Order No. 27-74, 1-86, 1-87, and Labor Management Services Administration Order No. 2-6. Section 2510.3-18 is also issued under sec. 3(18) of the Act (29 USC 1003(18)) and Sections 8477(a)(2)(B) and (f) of FERSA (5 USC 8477).

12. Appraisal Standards Board, *2004 USPAP—Uniform Standards of Professional Appraisal Practice and Advisory Opinions* (The Appraisal Foundation, 2004).

13. American Society of Appraisers, "Business Valuation Standards," *BVS-VI Reaching a Conclusion of Value* 2003 (August 25, 2004), *www.bvappraisers.org/standards/bvstandards.pdf*.

14. National Center for Employee Ownership, "A Comprehensive Overview of Employee Ownership/ESOP Valuation," online posting (NCEO, August 25, 2004), *www.nceo.org*.

Index

Ownership culture, 48–51
  and disclosure of financial information,
    118
Ownership of shares by plan, 76

P

Participants, qualifying termination from
    plan
  distributions at termination, 118
  diversification requirements for retiring
    employees, 50, 102, 103
  lump-sum or installment distributions, 102
  promissory notes, use of, 100–102
  put rights. *See* Put options
  repurchase of shares, 97, 98
  rollover to IRA, 98, 99, 128, 129
  sponsoring company's repurchase
    liability, factors affecting, 99, 100
Participants, rights of. *See also* Employees
  asset diversification, 42, 50, 102, 103
  distribution rights (put option). *See* Put
    options
  vesting. *See* Vesting
  voting rights. *See* Voting rights
Party of interest, 2
Pass-through dividends, 40
Pearl Group, 51
Plan administration, trustee duties, 31, 32
Plan documents
  corporate governance, 30, 31
  essential documents, 29, 30
  information requirements for
    participants, 117, 118
  trustee's duties, 29–31
Plan operations, trustee duties, 31, 32
Plan sponsor as party of interest, 2
Plan termination, 88
  and premise of engagement, 76
Plan trustee. *See* Trustees
Pledge agreement, 31
Preliminary appraisal, 21, 22
Productivity, improvement of, 47, 48
Profit sharing plans, 2
Prohibited transactions
  and determination of adequate
    consideration, 62
  generally, 2
Promissory notes
  from company/employer to lender, 31
  lack of GAAP financial reporting
    requirement, 101
  nonrecourse, between trust and
    company/employer, 31
  to terminated participants, 100–102

Prudent investor standard, 110, 111
Prudent person standard of care, 26, 36
Psychology of ownership, 48–50
  and disclosure of financial information,
    118
Purchase price, trustee's duty to negotiate,
    28, 29
Put options, 43, 87. *See also* Repurchase
    liability
  generally, 97, 104
  leverage, impact of, 141
  liquidity as purpose of, 104
  lump-sum or installment distributions,
    102
  and marketability adjustments, 140, 141
  nonterminable, 104
  participant's rights, 117, 118
  and plan termination, 88
  promissory notes, use of, 100–102
  repurchase of shares, 98
  repurchase preference, 97, 98
  rollover of shares to IRA, 98, 99
  tax status, impact of, 141, 142
Put right, 97. *See also* Put options

Q

Qualified retirement plans
  design study considerations, 22
  ESOP as, 1
  history of, 1, 2
Qualified securities, 2, 126, 127

R

REA, 2
Recycling method, 35
Redemption of stock, 125
Reports
  adequate consideration, 110, 111, 143,
    146
  annual reports, 144, 145
  conclusion of value, 145
  contents of, 147–150
    DOL proposed regulation, 161–164,
      167, 168
  defined, 143
  fairness, 144
  formal (self-contained), 143, 147
  generally, 143, 150, 151
  objective of, 145
  presentation of, 146
  purpose of, 145
  regulation of, 145, 146
  summary (informal), 143, 146, 147